THE DIVORCE DANCE

THE
DIVORCE
DANCE

Protect Your Money, Manage Your Emotions, and Understand the Legal Issues

STAN
COREY

ISBN-13: 978-0-692-54580-5

Library of Congress Control Number: 2015917556

PRINTED IN THE USA

10 9 8 7 6 5 4 3 2 1

To my grandson, Patrick Corey. In 2004, he was severely injured in an auto accident at just five months old. He passed away on May 12, 2015. Although he never spoke a single word throughout his entire life, he touched many lives and taught us all about inner strength and humility.

And to my loving and caring wife, Jayme Juncker. Together we survived our own divorces and discovered that you can have a happy life after divorce. For the past two decades, she has been instrumental in turning my life around as my trusted adviser and my best friend.

TABLE OF CONTENTS

FOREWORD

Have you ever wished you were a fly on the wall and able to observe the beginning of the end of a marital relationship? Would you want to be able to experience the pain and emotional roller coaster of that journey from afar while at the same time learning how a divorce can change your life forever? *The Divorce Dance* takes you through that journey and more.

Through the eyes of a divorcing couple, Jim and Natalie, we experience the truth about divorce. We also learn what Jim and Natalie find out about themselves as they go through one of the most stressful experiences of their lives.

In addition to describing their emotional turmoil, *The Divorce Dance* provides a detailed step-by-step analysis of almost every aspect of divorce. There are chapters devoted to choosing the right attorney and how to negotiate a resolution of property, custody, and support. Key considerations you need to know and key questions you need to ask are covered in precise detail. The handlings of complex financial issues (loss carryforward, defined benefit plans, and net spendable income among others) are topics that even experienced divorce attorneys often overlook.

As a divorce attorney practicing for thirty-five years in multiple jurisdictions, I have never encountered a publication as helpful as *The Divorce Dance*. In the era of reality entertainment that serves to educate us, *The Divorce Dance* will change your understanding of divorce in a powerful way.

Stan Corey is uniquely qualified to bring to life this captivating story rooted in real life experiences. I have had the privilege of knowing him as a personal friend and colleague for many years. As a Certified Financial Planner, mediator, and collaborative divorce professional, he has helped hundreds of couples get through the financial crisis of their divorce. Over the last twenty-five years, he has worked cooperatively with mental health professionals and attorneys to gain a complete understanding of the intricacies of the divorce process.

What you learn from Jim and Natalie's divorce will have a profound impact on the resolution of your own divorce. *The Divorce Dance* will provide the building blocks you and your family will need to build a new life.

Who knew that being a fly on the wall could bring so much power and comfort?

Albert M. Bonin, Esquire

PREFACE

I was born into a family during the post-World War II baby boom and raised at a time when *Ozzie and Harriet* appeared on TVs across the country. My mom was a full-time homemaker, and my dad was a commercial airline pilot. His work required him to be away up to two weeks per month, which meant my mom ran the household by herself throughout most of my childhood.

My mom's parents died when she was young, so she and her six siblings were raised by her extended family, who treated all of them as if they were their own.

My dad's father was an attorney who practiced law in New York and married three times throughout his life. He and his brother were products of my grandfather's first marriage, and from his third marriage, he had two more children, both of whom are close to my own age.

While my sisters and I were growing up, my dad was convinced his father, who had amassed a significant amount of wealth, would pay for our university expenses. Unfortunately, my grandfather died of a heart attack long before my sisters and I would enroll in college. His third wife retained all his assets and disinherited my dad and his brother.

So my dad was dealt a double blow: He was devastated by his father's premature passing and heartbroken that he and his brother weren't included in his father's estate. He never completely recovered from the death and was convinced that he and his brother were collateral damage stemming from his father's divorces.

My mom and dad remained married for the rest of their lives. While they experienced rough patches, divorce was not an option—especially after what he had experienced with his own father. Regardless of the struggles they faced, my parents remained resolute in their commitment to stay the course.

I, on the other hand, seemed less concerned about the risks associated with romance and seemed to easily follow my heart. In fact, as a naïve college kid, I fell in love and married during my senior year. Although marriage at such a young age was far more frequent back then than it is today, for me, it signaled the start of my serial relationships.

That is to say, I've experienced my share of breakups accompanied by financial shocks and eventual recoveries! I've also learned a great deal about how decisions I made in the past have affected my life, my family's life, and our financial well-being over the long term.

MY ROLE IN DIVORCE MEDIATION

When I became active in divorce mediation in the 1990s, I realized most divorcing men and women were completely unprepared for the legal, financial, and emotional obstacles they faced. And their lack of preparedness made sense. After all, people usually don't divorce multiple times, so they can't rely on prior experiences to guide their future divorce decisions. Their lack of knowledge causes them to rely too heavily on their one source of expertise—family law attorneys. Without a doubt, lawyers are the best source for legal counsel. On the other hand, most aren't as qualified to address issues related to finances and mental health as they are trained to provide legal advice.

Through my work helping divorcing men and women, I also witnessed the shockingly high financial cost of divorce—particularly when couples went to court. This motivated me to explore alternative approaches that made divorce less financially and emotionally costly and gave participants more control over decisions that would affect the rest of their families' lives.

I also observed that during divorce, many secrets came to light. Often, husbands and wives had hidden their bad behavior. The falsehoods ranged in magnitude from easily forgivable to jaw-dropping. In many instances, they were made to hide income and undisclosed or undervalued assets. In particular, business income—especially for those who were self-employed—invariably and conveniently seemed to decrease during the prior year, as well as the year of the divorce itself.

In addition, divorcing husbands and wives frequently spent money on a variety of unexplained items, or marital assets disappeared or were greatly reduced during the separation period. This often turned out to be the result of extra-marital relationships.

Also, the mental stress of the divorce process typically kept working men and women from focusing on their jobs. And this distraction could put a significant dent in their earnings.

Lastly, divorcing men and women frequently found themselves charged with the following:

- ◘ Wading through their history as a married couple to figure out who was entitled to what;

- ◘ Making financial decisions that would most likely influence the rest of their lives;

- ◘ Figuring out how the breakup would impact their children.

Despite all these pitfalls and obstacles, higher-income spouses, in particular, tended to recover fairly quickly once the divorce was final.

THE COURTS SHOULD BE YOUR LAST RESORT

Unfortunately, many who have wound up in court have come away disappointed with the judge's final decision. In my opinion, I never thought asking a judge to review a person's entire personal life and financial history in a few short hours and then use that information to make a decision that would impact the rest of his or her life was the best approach.

While the courts have been modern society's means to end a marriage, I believe courtroom litigation should only be used in instances when other options aren't feasible.

For many divorcing men and woman, the following better alternatives have emerged:

- Professional negotiation between family law attorneys
- Mediation
- Collaborative divorce
- Hybrid versions that employ elements of the above

Understanding these options, including their strengths and weaknesses, and then deciding to use them can greatly enhance the outcome of your divorce settlement.

They can also allow each party to have a respectful relationship moving forward. This is especially critical when young children are involved because they can easily become pawns in a marriage breakup.

The alternative approaches often consider the psychological impact of divorce. Within several of these divorce models, mental health professionals are trained to address the emotional obstacles that wives, husbands, and their children will encounter.

For instance, in collaborative divorce, one of the roles of the mental health professional is to provide a voice for the children whose perspectives may otherwise go unnoticed. Addressing children's fears and concerns can dramatically improve family well-being over the long term.

Speaking of children, a dirty little secret in the divorce world is parents with sons and daughters spend *less than an hour* discussing the divorce with them. What's worse is many times children are left out of the divorce process altogether, which creates additional residual emotional issues for the whole family.

I have found including children in the divorce conversation significantly improves the likelihood of resolving many divorce conflicts with less animosity and emotional energy than is otherwise possible.

A CONTEMPORARY CASE STUDY

My intention for this book is to describe the tough financial issues divorcing couples face. No doubt, you'll find countless online and print publications that address divorce financial topics ranging from opening up IRAs to creating a budget. But most resources either are too complicated or oversimplify the complexities of divorce.

I've written a book that allows me to leverage my over-twenty-five years of experience in divorce financial analysis. Within these chapters, I've addressed the family and emotional issues that impact financial decisions in the divorce process. I've told a story highlighting the most salient and significant pitfalls men and women face when making one of the biggest financial decisions of their lives.

As you'll see, *The Divorce Dance* reads less like a textbook and more like a novel. Think of it as a comprehensive, fictional case study. Throughout these pages, the technical discussions are abbreviated and simplified, the figures are rounded to easy-to-handle, large numbers, and I've covered complicated but essential topics most divorcing individuals need to understand.

All the characters are a creation of my imagination. In addition, this book is not intended to give specific financial advice, legal counsel, or provide psychological therapy.

My greatest hope is *The Divorce Dance* will encourage you to seek help by assembling a team to guide you through your divorce. In doing so, you'll avoid putting your family's future financial well-being in the hands of a judge, and you'll increase the likelihood of experiencing a lasting and respectful relationship with all family members.

ACKNOWLEDGEMENTS

The following people and organizations have played an instrumental role in my understanding of divorce issues. They've also had a profound impact upon my professional career.

Frances Fite: Her powers of persuasion motivated me to engage in mediation to the point where we co-wrote and co-taught a course along with her husband, Max McCullough, for the Northern Virginia Mediation Service (NVMS) in Fairfax, Virginia, in the late 1990s. Thanks to Frances's encouragement, I also decided to become a founding member of the Virginia Collaborative Professionals organization in 2006.

Jim Pope and Jeannette Towmey: When Frances and Max retired, Jim, Jeannette, and I carried on Frances and Max's legacy and continued to teach the course Economic Issues in Divorce for another ten years. To this day, Jim and Jeannette teach the course with an associate of mine.

Northern Virginia Mediation Service (www.nvms.us): Initially,

I provided my financial expertise to this organization but wound up gaining a deep understanding of the mediation profession, which culminated in my becoming president of the non-profit organization for three years.

Virginia Collaboration Professionals: As a founding member and treasurer during the first six years, I benefitted from the many professionals involved in the collaborative process—including attorneys, financial professionals, and mental health professionals. They have had a major impact on my personal and professional career.

In particular, I thank attorneys Kathleen O'Brien and Al Bonin for encouraging me to make a difference in people's financial lives by helping divorcing couples resolve their complex and difficult financial issues during and after the divorce process. I also thank Lisa Herrick, PhD, author of *Telling the Children about the Divorce,* for her contribution to the parenting plan conversations in this book.

I am grateful to my longtime friend and legal and tax mentor, Lewis Schumann. He and I have supported each other through life's ups and downs over the past thirty-eight years—including through our own divorces. Lewis encouraged me to grow my knowledge and understanding of income and estate tax issues early in my professional career. What I've learned has helped me better serve my clients' needs.

Lastly, I thank my editor, Lawrence Ineno, for taking the time to work with me and guide me in writing this book. While I've written countless newspaper and magazine articles throughout my career, completing *The Divorce Dance* required much more time and energy than I had ever realized. I couldn't have done it without his help.

CHAPTER 1

THE DIVORCE DANCE

When I think of divorce, I'm reminded of the tango. The Argentine dance is famous the world over for its passionate movement and astonishing precision.

One moment the couple weave their bodies tightly together. The next moment they forcefully push each other away. Sometimes they seem to be barely hanging on to one another while at other times they move as one.

Like the tango, divorce is full of twists and turns, pushes and pulls between two spouses. One partner may take the lead while the other may succumb to pressures resulting in poor decision-making.

Make no mistake, no matter how contentious or amicable, at one point the divorce dance *will end*. But regardless of how exhausted or energized you are, as the saying goes, "The show must go on!" And after twenty-five years of helping divorcing men and women, I've learned it always does.

THE DANCE BEGINS

Imagine hearing or saying the following:

- I've been unhappy for a while, and we seem to be arguing all the time.
- I don't want to spend the rest of my life with you.
- I've fallen in love with someone else.
- There isn't anyone else; I just want out.
- I still care about you and will take care of you and the kids.
- You keep your retirement plan, I'll keep mine, and we'll split the rest evenly.
- Don't worry; trust me. I'll take care of the kids' educational costs.
- We just want different things now that I'm retired.

Being told any of the preceding may bring about an endless stream of questions fueled by uncertainty and fear: Is this really happening? What am I supposed to believe? Will I be okay? Whom do I seek for help?

For many of us, the thought of our spouse dropping the D-word is the equivalent of having our doctor diagnose us with the C-word (cancer). Upon hearing "I want a divorce," our bodies turn cold, we feel light-headed, and we scramble to form a coherent response. In that instant, our lives have changed forever.

A REALITY CHECK

Although I'm not proud to admit it, disclosing to my second wife the four painful words "I want a divorce" signaled that yet another marriage had failed. Considering I'd gone through it before, I believed I knew how the divorce events would unfold. In addition, this time around, I had established my career as financial planner, and my client base included a number of divorced men and women whom I had helped throughout their breakups.

As a result of my personal and professional experiences, I concluded I could easily participate in drafting the property settlement agreement (PSA), which is a document that outlines the financial and legal terms of the divorce. In fact, I was confident my thoughtfully planned strategy, based on years of providing financial advice to clients, would spare my family from unnecessary pain, suffering, and financial burden. But I soon realized that my plan was a dream and the reality was a nightmare.

Once my wife and I plunged into our divorce, I quickly became overwhelmed with the complexity of family law, my emotions, and my finances, which meant my well-intended but nonetheless misguided planning had provided only short-lived security.

In retrospect, my marriage would have ended more amicably had I understood what I know now. But after my messy breakup, rather than dwell on my mistakes and second-guess decisions, I committed to learning all I could about the financial and legal aspects of divorce, which would allow me to improve my clients' lives. My exploration led me to realize the following divorce truth:

Divorce almost always comes down to issues about money.

Notice the divorce truth doesn't mention emotions. Based on my personal experience and that of helping countless divorcing clients, I know divorce and emotion are inseparable. But when it comes to negotiating a settlement, *the numbers are all that matter.* In the following chapters, you'll learn why.

The good news is no matter how difficult the issues you encounter, *you will eventually settle.* So, if settling a case is a virtual guarantee, what else do you need to consider? I've identified the two questions, which all divorcing people should ask themselves:

TWO ESSENTIAL DIVORCE QUESTIONS

1. How much financial and emotional currency am I willing to spend?

2. Will the settlement allow me—both with my children and independent of them—to be financially secure now and in the future?

Think of divorce as a journey (albeit a trip you never wanted to take). Throughout your divorce, you'll be presented with multiple paths, and all of them may lead to the same destination. Thus, divorce is about *how* you arrive at the solution, even if the solution would be the same no matter what.

While one path may not necessarily be better than another, the journey itself may be dramatically different depending on the choices you make. The essential divorce questions are intended to help you determine the best path for you.

Unfortunately, few men and women ever ask themselves these two questions as they begin the divorce process—let alone when they're negotiating a settlement. Instead, couples (and their attorneys) focus on the quality of their side's negotiation skills, dividing assets, and determining spousal and child support using cold formulas and guidelines.

Fast-forward a year or two after the divorce is over, and these same men and women realize they may be in financial trouble, a headache they could have avoided had their decisions been guided by the essential divorce questions. For example, what if an ex-wife doesn't participate as planned under a joint custody agreement? Or what if an ex-husband doesn't meet the conditions outlined in the PSA?

As much as fulfilling the PSA is a joint responsibility, suddenly only one ex-spouse is charged to enforce it. Unfortunately, many deadbeat men and women use this to their advantage because they know the cost of collecting may outweigh any benefit their ex-spouses would experience recovering what they're owed. Also, in many instances, *the emotional cost of enforcing the PSA may outweigh the monetary benefit*, especially if the divorce is highly contentious.

In your case, your attorney may say, "You can certainly go after your ex, but I don't think it's worth pursuing." And after your lawyer shares how much going after your ex will cost in legal fees, you may likely agree.

Or maybe you recall the PSA had a provision stating that failure to pay means your ex-spouse will be liable for legal costs. So why not pursue him or her in court? Then you reflect upon the time this process will take, the emotional drain you'll experience, the possible trauma to your children, and how opening old wounds will make you feel. Is it worth it now?

In the subsequent chapters, you'll learn how to act in accordance with the divorce truth and answer the essential divorce questions. By doing so, you'll avoid financial and emotional pitfalls millions of divorcing men and women experience every year.

You'll learn about your divorce options through the eyes of a couple dealing with the four deadly words—I want a divorce!—as well as the separation and the divorce process itself.

Although I present fictional characters, their story is inspired by many divorce cases I've been involved with over the years—my own included. Their experience is intended to alert you to the various pitfalls you may succumb to in your own divorce, help you find solutions to address tough issues, and prevent problems before they arise.

THE CAST OF CHARACTERS

Natalie and **Jim** take you through their marriage breakup. They have three children: **Ben** (twenty-two years old), **Ryann** (eighteen years old), and **Rachel** (fifteen years old).

Natalie and Jim are professionals who live in the Commonwealth of Virginia. Natalie is forty-eight years old, and Jim is forty-nine years old. As their divorce progresses, they both gain knowledge, which helps them make better financial decisions.

Kathleen is Natalie's lawyer.

Al is Jim's attorney.

Patrick is Natalie's financial adviser.

Dr. Michaels is Natalie's therapist.

Courtney is the mediator.

Through Natalie and Jim's experience, you'll identify key areas you need to address. No doubt, divorce is most likely not what you intended for your life. But what you'll read in these pages will guide you in your journey and help you experience the best possible outcome.

Chapter 2
THE ANNOUNCEMENT

Natalie clicked her remote. The garage door opened, and she saw Jim's car already inside. "Jim *never* arrives home before me," she thought to herself.

She slid her car into her space on the right and cautiously opened her door—careful not to hit his BMW M3 that was uncomfortably close to her. She entered the kitchen with groceries in one hand and a bag full of essays to grade in the other.

Jim sat at the kitchen counter. His eyes and thumbs were restlessly scrolling through his smartphone's ESPN app—"electronic nail biting" was what Natalie called his nervous habit.

She walked over to him, and they kissed.

"How were the students today?" he asked.

His eyes were fixed on his device. It was a question she hadn't heard in a while. For the first couple of years of marriage, talking about work was a Monday-through-Friday routine. But that was years ago, back when they had shown interest in each other's lives.

"The same old. My new principal drives me nuts. But the kids were good. How about you—why are you home so early?" she asked.

"Finished my afternoon meeting and decided to call it day," he said.

Natalie opened the refrigerator and began loading her groceries inside.

"Natalie, we have to talk," he said. His tone was serious.

She froze, fixing her gaze on a milk carton she had just set on the shelf.

"About?" she asked.

"Us . . . I've been thinking about us for a while now."

She turned around and looked at him. "What do you mean?" she asked.

Jim wished Natalie would make the conversation easier for him, that she would acknowledge how unhappy they both were in their emotionally dry and nearly sexless marriage and that she would admit they were equally tired of trying to fix something beyond repair. At the same time, he wondered if her uncertainty was sincere—*maybe she really doesn't know what I mean*. So he clarified.

"I think we need to call it quits. . . . Well, *I'm* ready to call it quits," he said.

Natalie felt her heart pound. "Calling it quits" was something she too had thought of countless times over the past few years. But she had never considered turning her words into actions. In fact, now the kids were older she thought she and Jim would be able to focus on their relationship and iron out their problems. In her eyes, marriage was for life *no matter what*. It was a perspective instilled by her strict religious roots.

"You mean divorce?" she asked. She couldn't believe she had just said the D-word. It was something other people used—celebrities, politicians, and friends. She immediately regretted saying it, as if she had fed him an idea he didn't otherwise have.

"Yes. Divorce," he said. Jim felt relief his wife was now shoulder-ing some of the conversation. "I've packed some of my stuff already and put it in the basement. I'll move out once I have a place." He really meant *I've found somewhere already and I'm moving out.* But Jim didn't think the timing was right to disclose the brutal truth.

Natalie faced the refrigerator and stared inside its bright inte-rior. Tears pooled in her eyes. Jim heard her sniffle them back in.

"Natalie . . .?" he asked.

She closed the refrigerator door, dashed upstairs, sat on the edge of their bed, and sobbed. A series of thoughts flooded: *How can this be happening now, especially just before the Christmas hol-idays? What am I going to do? What am I going to tell the children?*

Jim let out a sigh—his relief was immediate and intense. He could now put to rest the fears he had built up over the past cou-ple of months regarding the most difficult conversation of his life. At the same time, he felt guilty because his announcement hurt her. But he immediately reminded himself, in the long run, she too would benefit from no longer being stuck in a hopeless partnership.

JIM HAD ALREADY BROKEN UP WITH NATALIE

If Jim's marriage was a car ride, for the past few years, it had been on cruise control—traveling countless miles through a dull des-ert, dotted with a few dicey detours.

While his commitment to meeting his family's needs was his number-one priority, his life felt both uninspiring and downright depressing.

Jim traveled extensively for work, which had lost its appeal after ten years on the job. And when he was at home, the te-dious pattern was wake up, go to work, come home, end the day plopped in front of the TV, sleep, repeat. The weekends inject-ed a modicum of excitement into the formula: work around the house and an occasional Saturday morning golf game. And every year, he looked forward to springtime when he would escape to the marina and attend to his sailboat, occasionally spend entire weekends on the bay, or just hang out around Annapolis, which is considered the best sailing town on the Chesapeake Bay and one of the finest on the entire East Coast.

Eventually, Jim began sating his sexual needs outside of marriage. He largely blamed his infidelity on Natalie: If his wife made more effort and showed more interest, he wouldn't need to look elsewhere. At the same time, he enjoyed the thrill of the pursuit. It fed the part of him that feared middle age had made him less of a catch. The fact other women welcomed his advances increased his resentment toward Natalie and quashed any lingering desire to be passionate with her.

Five years ago, he and Natalie had sent their son, Ben, to college, which signaled the start of the empty nest. Once Ryann, their daughter, left for college earlier this fall, Jim felt the pressure to take charge of his life while he was still healthy and motivated. As a result, he made a personal pledge that his next birthday—the big five-oh—would signal making a dramatic turnaround.

A couple of months after his forty-ninth birthday, he had convinced himself divorce was the prerequisite to reclaiming his life. As a result, he had declared his marriage over—but only to himself. Between then and now, he had spent hours researching divorce online, calculating a settlement, and even locating a temporary place to live.

The townhouse was far smaller than the 4,500-square-foot home they had built together in Reston, Virginia. But it had three bedrooms, which would accommodate his fifteen-year-old daughter, Rachel. His two other kids could use the third room on an as-needed basis—Ryann was attending Christopher Newport University only four hours away, and Ben was earning his MBA at Fordham University in New York. Jim's plan was to reach a settlement within the next few months, so he could move on with his life.

For the past fifteen years, Jim had worked as an executive at Science Systems, Inc. (SSI) overseeing a team of 150 employees.

His $350,000 per year salary far exceeded his wife's income as a middle school teacher.

Based on his countless hours of divorce research, the wide salary gap between the two would place a significant dent in his personal wealth and cash flow as a divorced bachelor. In the best-case scenario, he calculated he would forego nearly half of his assets. Despite this bad news, he realized he was still in his prime income-earning stage. No doubt, rebuilding his net worth would be difficult, and it would take years, but the freedom was a price worth paying.

A BUDDING ROMANCE

Six months ago (after deciding to call his marriage quits), Jim met Claudia at a technology conference in Atlanta. She was speaking on a panel, "Technology Challenges in Healthcare: Preventing Medical Identity Theft." Throughout the discussion, Jim was impressed by her expertise and speaking skills, that is, when he wasn't focused on her smooth neckline that led down to her loosely fitting blouse—fantasizing his way through a work event aroused far more interest than learning about stolen identities in the digital age, particularly when the object of his desire wore no wedding ring.

The session ended at noon, and Jim approached the attractive panelist. He complimented her delivery, and during their introductory chat, they exchanged business cards and realized they worked in neighboring offices in Tysons Corner, Virginia. They also discovered they lived only twenty miles apart.

Jim wanted to ask her to lunch that afternoon, but he wasn't sure how to broach the matter. He then reasoned because he was there on the company's dime, it was his duty to network. Claudia accepted his networking invitation.

As they sat together in the hotel restaurant, Jim experienced a connection that, at first, felt foreign. Before meeting Claudia, the romance-fueled excitement he experienced had been dormant to the point he'd forgotten it existed.

The sad reality was, as far as Jim and Natalie were concerned, their near non-existent love life left him feeling like a breadwinner without benefits, which led him, several years ago, to indulge in a series of affairs—most of which were one-night stands. And among those one-night stands, several were with coworkers. When it came to feeding his sexual appetite, human resources' codes of conduct regarding intra-office relations were more suggestions than rules.

This time around, however, his attraction was stronger than any he'd experienced during his previous extramarital flings. Claudia's intelligence and career accomplishments, all wrapped in an irresistible body, made for a lust-worthy combination. At the same time, he wondered if his feelings were just another notch on his belt or represented a genuine connection.

Meanwhile, the rigors of academic life and scientific research afforded Claudia little opportunity to contemplate intangibles such as sexual cravings and romance. At the same time, despite being fiercely independent, busy, and accomplished, she sometimes found herself wanting nothing more than to be wrapped in a man's embrace.

By the time Jim and Claudia finished lunch and the server brought the bill, the conference had resumed.

"Can we meet again once we're at our home offices?" Jim asked.

"Sounds like a plan. But I'll expect an executive summary when I see you next. This is work after all," Claudia said.

"Only if I'm allowed to mention sailing in it," he said.

Years leading a team of 150 employees and networking at the executive level had honed his communication skills, which taught Jim the art of skillfully injecting the non sequitur. He seized on the opportunity to introduce his passion and gauge her interest in it.

"You sail?" she asked.

"For most of my life," he said.

Jim's seafaring fascination started at age five, when his dad taught him to sail on a fourteen-foot-long Sunfish. Through his father's influence, Jim acquired an insatiable appetite to spend time in the creek nearby and explore Long Island Sound as he grew up. At ten years old, he discovered another way to enjoy the outdoors—waterskiing on his friend's parents' boat.

Once he became a teenager, Jim bought a thirteen-foot-long Boston Whaler, paid for by mowing neighborhood lawns. Around this time, he became interested in sailboat racing. Unfortunately, youth racing didn't exist at his club, so he competed against adults. One year later, he won his first club championship, the Fourth of July Club Regatta. Next, he won the Labor Day Weekend Race.

Over the next three years, he continued racing with the local sailing club and won a series of regattas. At sixteen years old, he became his club's youngest sailing instructor for kids aged five to twelve years old. The next year, he took his inaugural journey as a first mate on an ocean cruise. Over six weeks during the summer, he headed up the New England coast and traveled to Maine and back on a sixty-five-foot ketch.

In college he continued competing, winning several sailing regattas in 420 Class sailboats. After graduating and embarking on his career as a computer scientist, he chose to keep his beat-up car and allocated his transportation funds toward satisfying his seagoing cravings—he bought his first large sailboat, a twenty-nine-foot sloop.

While he and Natalie were dating, they regularly spent weekends on his boat. Sailing was a hobby Natalie grew to appreciate as their relationship evolved. But unlike Jim, she didn't have an interest that pulsed in her veins—one rooted in a childhood at sea. In fact, Natalie's enthusiasm was more from the thrill she experienced spending time with the man she loved.

After becoming a dad twenty-two years ago, Jim found it nearly impossible to make it to the marina on a regular basis and work on his boat, let alone set sail for hours. To his disappointment, his boat increasingly became a burden—the upkeep costs outweighed the benefit of a diminished seafaring schedule. Jim eventually sold his beloved boat and loosened his grip on the passion he had tightly held onto since he had been a kid.

For a few years after being boat-less, Jim fed his maritime appetite by attending annual weeklong sailing trips with his best friends. But once Jim and Natalie's third child, Rachel, was born, Natalie insisted he put an end to his yearly separate vacation—raising three young kids alone for seven days was not only unacceptable; it also became unbearable for her. After all, Natalie was never afforded the luxury of an extended holiday sans children. In reality, after she gave birth to Rachel, the couple had not taken any vacations together.

Over the next few years, Jim was feeling the weight of being a career man, breadwinner, dad, and husband stuck in a mediocre marriage, and Natalie took notice. Although she didn't know the specifics of his discontent—and he probably couldn't articulate the reasons behind his unhappiness even if she asked—she couldn't deny his overall malaise.

After Rachel's ninth birthday, Natalie suggested they buy a sailboat. She hoped the purchase would feed his hunger for the high seas, which would resuscitate their moribund marriage. Jim cashed enough stock options to cover the costs of a used thirty-five-foot sailboat—one large enough to accommodate the family for weekend cruises.

With the vessel, Jim envisioned inspiring his kids with the same seafaring zeal he had inherited from his father and was part of his DNA. Unfortunately, the gene skipped the next generation. Plus, soon after he bought the boat, Ben, Ryann, and Rachel were at an age where the thought of spending any extended time together, let alone in the middle of the Chesapeake Bay stranded in a stuffy boat, was met with a lukewarm response.

JIM AND CLAUDIA MEET AGAIN

Two weeks after the technology conference, Jim and Claudia arranged to meet for lunch at Café con Leche, a casual restaurant near their offices. Between the conference and their current lunch meeting, they had texted each other every day. He learned more about her research, which sent Claudia to conferences around the world. Claudia also shared about the stresses and isolation associated with living out of hotel rooms and computer labs. Jim found out she had grown up near the waterfront. In fact, Claudia, as a young girl, had sailed on the same waters where Jim currently moored his boat. But the responsibilities of adulthood pushed her seagoing hobby aside.

"Hi, Jim," Claudia said.

She towered above him as he was scrolling through his smartphone while seated at the restaurant. Seeing her for the second time, he thought she looked even more beautiful. He stood up and kissed her cheek.

Professional decorum trained him to look directly in her eyes, but he wanted nothing more than to lower his gaze down her neckline and stare.

The two took a seat at the table. Claudia glanced at his wedding ring, which she had noticed when they had first met. Working in a male-dominated field, she was used to being surrounded by married members of the opposite sex. Thus she had accepted his initial lunch invitation because she concluded it was strictly work related—although part of her was flattered because she found him attractive.

This time, however, his welcoming kiss and compliments about her beautiful eyes and the body that "you obviously take amazing care of" were clear signs the networking boundary had been crossed, which both aroused her suspicion and piqued her interest.

"I tried my hand at married life and a demanding job—I just couldn't pull the combo off. How's it working out for you?" she asked as she threw a pointed glance at his ring finger.

He had met his non-sequitur-interjecting match, and her question jarred the typically smooth operator. "Fine. I mean . . . you know, all relationships have their ups and downs," he bumbled. He resisted the urge to seek relief by reaching into his pocket and scrolling through his ESPN app.

"According to that metric, I guess most of mine have been more down than up," Claudia said.

Her self-deprecating humor loosened the tension her question had created. Jim seized the opportunity to reveal the current state of his marriage.

"Down is probably a good way to describe mine right now too," he said.

He then disclosed his divorce intentions. His demanding job, responsibility to provide for his wife and kids, and his dull marriage left him longing for freedom and someone with whom to share his passion for life—one that had been in hibernation for the past few years. He confessed to having a one-night stand, which implied only one rather than the truth of many times with many women.

Claudia could relate with his loneliness. The forty-two-year-old expressed how she often felt trapped in a challenging job whose responsibilities only increased over time. After her divorce, which took place when she was twenty-eight, more than a decade of dating yielded no long-term result other than cynicism based on meeting men who cheated on her.

"I've been working through the details for months because I have the kids to think about. I want to be sure they're taken care of once this is settled and we're moving on with our lives. I think I'm now ready to tell my wife," he said.

What he didn't tell Claudia was his main concern: how he would fare financially after the divorce. By focusing on the children, he thought he would earn her sympathy and respect.

In a peculiar way, Jim's having a wife comforted Claudia. As long as he had a ring around his finger, they were just friends—no commitments and no risk of broken hearts.

Regardless of her attraction to Jim, being the other woman was a role she had pledged never to play. After all, she knew what it was like to be cheated on. So Jim's married state meant what they were developing was platonic—at least that's what she told herself.

"Are you free this Saturday? I'd love to take you for a day sail," he said.

Work had been particularly intense leading up to the technology conference, and Claudia appreciated the opportunity to revel in a maritime escape with her new friend.

"I'd love that. But won't that raise a red flag with your wife?" she asked.

"We've moved beyond that stage; it's over between us," he said, knowing Natalie had no clue about his outside endeavors.

A DAY AT SEA

Friday, after work, Jim drove to the harbor and spent the night on his boat, which was his regular routine and the inspiration for christening his sailboat, *Relentless*. He woke early the next morning and readied it for his Saturday outing.

At 11:00 a.m., Claudia arrived at the dock and saw Jim in the cockpit. A Jimmy Buffet CD played in the background.

"Jim!" she said.

"You made it," he said.

He walked toward her and extended his hand. As she reached for it, she noticed he had removed his wedding ring. He then led her from the pier, over the lifeline, and onto the deck.

"Probably took it off to work on the boat," she told herself.

Jim gave her a tour of the boat and the cabin below. He was proud of how he had kept *Relentless* in pristine condition. Afterwards, they cast off for a day sail. The unusual balmy southern breeze motivated Claudia to remove her billowy blouse, which unveiled the bikini she wore beneath it. Jim imagined pulling her close to him and feeling her warm skin against his.

The two sailed gently on a beam reach across the bay as they ate the lunch Jim had prepared. Sharing a bottle of wine, Jim revealed more details about his unhappy marriage and his future plans, and Claudia opened up about her most significant breakup.

Claudia's marriage was short lived. Her work had always been intense while her husband's never was, and eventually he could no longer tolerate playing a secondary role in her life. Reaching a divorce settlement after only three years of marriage was relatively painless, in large part because their assets were easy to divide and their breakup lacked the complications that arose when kids were part of the divorce equation.

Although her split was much simpler than Jim's would be and took place years ago, her experience convinced Jim he could carry out a divorce that would be resolved amicably and with as little impact to his future financial state as possible. Armed with this optimistic outlook, he looked forward to what life post-marriage would look like, which at this point seemed even more exciting because it included a woman he had just met whose beauty matched her intellect.

Hours later, they headed back to the dock, the sun floating over the horizon behind them.

"What are your plans for the rest of the evening?" he asked, after securing the boat in his slip.

"Have to take care of Einstein," she said.

Jim recalled the name of Claudia's Glen terrier from their text messages. "Next time, I'll send over my family's dog sitter so you won't have to rush home so soon," he said.

He escorted Claudia to her car. She gave him a peck on the cheek, and the two exchanged a hug. She took pleasure in the close-up view of his blue eyes.

"Text me when you get home," he said.

As he made his way back to the sailboat, he pulled his phone from his pocket and phoned his wife.

"Hey there. Been working on my boat all day, and I think I'll just crash here tonight," he said.

"No problem," Natalie said. "Rachel and I are planning to watch a movie you'd hate anyway—a sappy romantic comedy. I'll see you in the morning."

Jim cleaned his boat and then strolled to Annapolis harbor for dinner. Afterwards, he headed to the Crow's Nest for a glass of rum. Sitting at the bar, he pulled out his phone. A text message appeared:

> Took Einstein for a long walk. Thanks for a fun day.
> Have a good night. ☺

"Jim?" the woman asked as she tapped him on the shoulder.

He turned around.

"Do you remember me? I'm Sam," she said, loud enough to be heard above the Saturday night crowd packed inside the bar. She reminded him of how they met two years ago at a bar in Oxford, another small sailing town on the eastern shore of Maryland.

"If I had a penny . . .," Jim thought to himself as he recalled the many times he'd run into women who were eager to share about their no-strings-attached night he'd long forgotten about. He feigned recollecting the dalliance.

As Sam continued to reminisce about their time together, the details added up to the point where he remembered who she was. Jim always had a weak spot for redheads—he soon recalled running his fingers through her shiny, thick hair as they lay naked on the forward berth in his boat.

For the next two hours, the two exchanged sailing stories they'd amassed over the years. He drank more rum, she downed Coronas, and then they each toasted a lemon drop to top off their night together.

Jim glanced at his smartphone. "Where'd the time go? It's getting late," he said.

"You're right. I've totally lost track of where my friends even are," Sam said.

The jukebox music and late night crowd's din filled the silence between them. She placed her empty shot glass on the bar, gently reached for his left hand, and stared at his bare ring finger.

"You still married?" Sam asked.

"Separated, working on being divorced, and you?" Jim asked.

"Never remarried," she said.

"How about I give you another tour of my boat?" he asked.

She took him up on his offer. Sam left to find her friends who were chatting by the pool table and let them know she was heading out with Jim.

The two left the Crow's Nest and held hands as they strolled on the boardwalk, their tipsy conversation infused with giggles brought on by too many Mexican beers and rum. They spent the night together on the boat continuing where they'd left off a couple of years ago.

CHAPTER 3

NATALIE GOES PUBLIC

Natalie lay on her side wrapped around her pillow. What Jim had just told her in the kitchen seemed dreamed up. She imagined walking downstairs, seeing him, and learning the entire conversation was a misunderstanding. But then she recalled his words, "I'm ready to call it quits."

Jim's declaration played over and over in her head, and it eventually led her to the bathroom where she threw up. She then returned to her bed and shut her eyes.

The buzz from her smartphone woke her up. She grabbed her glowing mobile device and read the text message:

> Hi Mom! Studying 4 bio test w Sally. B home at 7.

She squinted at the small screen to check the time: 5:00 p.m. An hour had passed since she had said the dreaded D-word.

"What am I going to tell Rachel tonight?" she thought to herself.

Natalie realized saying anything at this point was both premature and downright irresponsible. "It's not as if he's moving out, so why worry her?" she asked herself.

She texted her daughter back: Dinner would be waiting for her.

Natalie stood up and slowly descended to the kitchen. Jim had left the house.

Rachel arrived home at 7:00 p.m. Jim's absence was no surprise because he often stayed late at the office. Natalie gave her daughter a hug, reminded her dinner was ready, and then excused herself to grade papers.

That night, Natalie tossed and turned in bed for what seemed like hours until she finally fell asleep. The next morning, she awoke to Rachel knocking on her door.

Her daughter entered the bedroom. "Mom, it's already seven fifteen. Is everything okay?" Rachel asked.

Normally, when Jim was on his way out the door at 6:00 a.m., he would tap Natalie on the shoulder and give her a kiss good-bye on the check—her signal it was time to get up.

"I can't believe I overslept! I haven't even made you breakfast," Natalie said.

"Don't worry about it, Mom. I already ate. And I made you breakfast for a change—ready to eat on the road," she replied. Rachel placed the tray on the bedside table. Coffee in a thermos and fresh fruit in a plastic container were waiting for Natalie.

"Thanks, sweetie. Now we have to get you to school!" Natalie said.

Natalie quickly got ready, took breakfast to go, and hurried downstairs. The two hopped in the car. She dropped Rachel off at school and rushed to make it to work by the morning bell.

After school Natalie stopped by Fresh Pavilion to shop for the week's food.

"Are you okay?" a woman asked.

The words snapped Natalie out of her daze. She had no idea how long she'd been staring at the rows of perfectly waxed apples in the produce section. Natalie turned to her right. Jen stood beside her.

Natalie recalled Jen's third child, Will, had been on the same high school lacrosse team with Ben. Although she and Jen were never close, they were always friendly to one another.

Natalie wiped the tears from her face, abruptly abandoned her shopping cart, and swiftly exited the grocery store, unable to say a word to her friend.

Jen caught up with Natalie, sitting on a bench that rested against the front of the supermarket. Her face was buried in her palms. "What's wrong, sweetie?" Jen asked and took a seat next to her.

Natalie paused to calm herself down. She then summarized the news Jim had dropped on her last night.

"Honey, I'm so sorry," Jen said. "If it's any help, I know exactly how you feel—I was in your shoes just three years ago."

To hear Jen had gone through a divorce both relieved and saddened her. Natalie instantly felt a bond with her.

"It took over a year and a half for the damn thing to end. The entire ordeal probably shaved a decade off my life," Jen said.

Jen married Scott shortly after college graduation. Six months later, she was pregnant. When Jen quit her part-time job during her third trimester, it marked her retirement from the workplace. Over the years, she raised four kids as a stay-at-home mom while Scott ascended the corporate ladder as a human resources executive.

By the time Scott declared he wanted a divorce, he had fallen in love with Melissa, a colleague he had first met at a company holiday party. At the time, Jen and Scott's three oldest were in their early twenties, college graduates, and living on their own.

Meanwhile, Stewart, the couple's youngest child, was a college sophomore. He had attended the University of Virginia for his freshman year, but the following fall, he had to drop out and attend his hometown community college because his cash-strapped parents could no longer afford university tuition. He was currently living with his friend in a modest apartment. Out of all four children, he took the news the hardest, and his emotional state deteriorated as the divorce became increasingly hostile. Despite Jen's and Scott's best efforts to address the breakup's impact on their son (they even sent Stewart to therapy for a few months), he maintained a cool and aloof distance toward his parents.

From child custody to the chaise lounge, the couple waged war over nearly every aspect of their final settlement. The divorce wound up on the steps of the county's family law court where the judge set the terms of the property settlement agreement (PSA). Once their marriage was over, Jen and Scott had depleted nearly all their savings and most of the proceeds from selling their five-thousand-square-foot house.

Life post-marriage marked Jen's return to singlehood and the workforce. She moved into a two-bedroom condo in a complex located in the town's center and nicknamed Queen's Manor. Despite being a college graduate, two decades of full-time motherhood meant her work skills were pre-Internet. In her search for administrative assistant positions, she recognized she needed to beef up her computer literacy. With help from one of her daughters, Jen found a tutor who trained her on computing essentials. She eventually landed a job as an administrative assistant at an estate tax law firm in Fairfax, Virginia. The legal lessons from her divorce benefitted her in her new career where she continued learning about the law. Her appetite for legal knowledge even motivated her to take classes to become a paralegal.

Jen received monthly spousal support, but because Scott had failed to meet many of the settlement's financial obligations, she lived in perpetual fear that over time he'd turn into a full-fledged deadbeat.

"What keeps me up at night is fear of becoming a bag lady!" she told her attorney.

Despite Jen's worries, her lawyer advised her against using the courts to collect from her ex; her efforts would be more expensive than any amount she would ever recover.

When Natalie heard Jen's story that started with infidelity and ended with fears of homelessness, she felt nauseous.

"Do you think Jim's traded me in for a younger model?" Natalie asked.

"No way I'd know. And I hate to kick you while you're down, but the truth is you may *never* know," she said.

"That's not exactly reassuring," Natalie said.

"But listen, there's no point going there yet. Right now, you've got to focus on taking care of you. You can think about Jim later," she said.

Jen pulled out her smartphone and asked Natalie for her contact information.

"I've learned more than I ever wanted to about divorce," Jen said. "But now that I look back on that train wreck, the whole process is pretty fascinating. I know you're beyond overwhelmed now. So when you're ready, I'm happy to share anything I know. I'm texting you my number. Call me anytime."

Natalie gave Jen a hug, and the two walked back into Fresh Pavilion.

That Friday afternoon, Natalie returned to an empty house. Rachel was away earning high school community service hours at the local food bank. Natalie slumped in her master bedroom's Barcalounger and closed her eyes. The shame of an impending divorce weighed heavily on her.

"Mom and Dad are celebrating their fifty-fifth and still going strong. How could this be happening to me?" she asked herself.

Natalie was the middle of five, and so far, all her siblings' marriages were intact. She had always done everything right, so she couldn't comprehend how she had been wronged so badly. From kindergarten to college, she had received good grades and went on to earn a master's degree in special education. Natalie was a public school teacher and devoted parishioner at St. Luke's, which was where she married Jim and had their children baptized. She embraced her church's teachings that marriage was a sacrament and wanted nothing more than to carry on the legacy of lifelong commitment her parents had upheld for decades.

As Natalie reflected on her marriage, she tried to pinpoint the moment when her relationship headed to divorce. When she met Jim at a friend's spring-themed party, the young woman was instantly smitten with Jim's good looks and charm. Most of their early dates were day sails on the bay. During their time together on his sailboat, she admired the confidence and ease at which he took command of his boat—as well as his broad, sculpted chest that he revealed whenever the weather called for him to go shirtless.

Although she had grown up around brothers, overall, she was timid around the opposite sex. Her mother had always made it clear Natalie's duty as a good girl was to keep her distance from boys.

By the time they started dating, Jim had firmly established his reputation as a playboy. Experience had taught him the combination of blue eyes, a handsome face on a six-foot-two-inch frame, and a shelf full of sailing trophies would provide him with plenty of opportunity to sleep around.

When he met Natalie, he had no intention of slowing down his pursuit of women. In fact, he wanted nothing more than to add her name to his long list of conquests. He fantasized undressing her in his bedroom and staring at her naked body before a passionate night of sex. Despite her consistently conservative dress, he could clearly see full breasts that perfectly enhanced her slender figure.

But as their relationship developed, he realized she wouldn't be easily persuaded into bed. Meanwhile, every other woman he dated was ready to sleep with him right away. His respect for her grew as they continued their courtship.

Natalie was committed to faith and family, and she appreciated he didn't demand sex from her. As her trust in him increased, she grew more comfortable exploring her sexual side, which she believed was for marriage.

The night when she broke from the teachings of her church and had sex outside of marriage, she felt guilty, relieved, and thrilled all at once. Finally, the good girl, who had always done exactly what she was supposed to, slept with the man she loved. By the time they had sex, Natalie knew she had met her husband.

When the couple announced their engagement a year and a half after they met, she was surprised her mother decided to dispense sex advice to her. Her parents had never talked to her about the birds and the bees, and based on the content of their current conversation, her mom had limited personal experience herself. "Sometimes he may ask you to do things that aren't pleasant, and sometimes you won't be interested at all, but part of being a good wife is meeting his needs," she said.

After the birth of their first child, meeting Jim's needs fell to the bottom of her long and exhausting to-do list. From the start, Ben required her full attention. If she put him down for just a few seconds, he would let out an ear-piercing wail. And he refused to nap, which gave Natalie no break to refuel.

As their family grew, her commitment to her kids did as well. She assumed her role as homemaker just as she did every other responsibility she took on—with complete dedication. In addition to raising her kids, she cooked, cleaned, and shopped. In fact, Jim counted on her to cover nearly every aspect related to the kids, and she *always* came through—she planned all birthday parties and holiday celebrations, bought all presents, and the kids' Christmas gifts were purchased and wrapped by Thanksgiving. Jim's only task was to say, "You're welcome," when his children thanked him on Christmas Day.

As the years passed, Jim's gift-buying ability atrophied to the point that Natalie didn't receive any presents from him either. "You know what you want, so go ahead and buy something for yourself" was his way of saying happy birthday, anniversary, and Valentine's Day and merry Christmas.

When it came to discipline, Natalie played the role of bad cop. Meanwhile, Jim was afforded the luxury of being the good one. He was the children's friend and playmate. He also coached them throughout their youth sports years.

On the other hand, Natalie enforced rules and made sure Ben, Ryann, and Rachel never settled for mediocrity. Early on, psychologists diagnosed Ryann with a learning disability. Despite recommendations from school staff, Natalie refused to hold her back a year. Instead, she worked tirelessly to keep Ryann at grade level. The highest reward for her hard work came when Ryann received her college acceptance letter.

Natalie's commitment to parenthood left her with little time for herself. And once all her kids reached school age, any free time she could have had was spent in the classroom. She first returned to the payroll as a half-day teacher. When Ben left for college, she went back to work full-time. That was five years ago.

As far as sex was concerned, she always knew Jim wanted more of it, so she tried to give him the pleasure he sought. But she would be the first to acknowledge that one of the after-effects of motherhood was a decreased sex drive. In fact, she'd prefer watching a new Netflix series to having sex anytime. And Jim's comments about her post-baby weight gain only served to lessen her already waning desire.

Natalie's hope was Rachel's high school graduation in a couple of years would mark the moment they'd rekindle their marriage, including their romance.

Among her siblings, Barrett was Natalie's closest, her confidante. The two sisters talked about everything, including sex, specifically, the absence of it in Natalie's case and Barrett's high libido-driven activity, which more than made up for her older sister's sexless state. Thus, despite being younger, when it came to matters of the bedroom, Barrett was far more experienced—and incredulous with Natalie's lack of a sex life.

Barrett found her sister's innocence both amusing and annoying. Determined to help, Barrett introduced Natalie to *Fifty Shades of Grey*. "We've got to break you out of your shell. *Read this book!*" Barrett told her. The tale shocked and intrigued Natalie. She couldn't believe the subculture depicted in the book existed. It made Natalie question her strict views about sex, which she vowed to rethink and explore with Jim when the time was right.

To her dismay, with his abrupt holiday announcement, any hopes of experiencing her own *Fifty Shades of Grey* with Jim were dashed.

She recalled the talk she had with Jen at Fresh Pavilion. The thought of Jim's infidelity terrified her. She looked around her bedroom and feared, like Jen, she would be forced to sell the walls and everything within them that had provided her shelter for so many years and held such precious memories. And she definitely didn't want to be forced to move to Queen's Manor. She called Jim.

"I just met with a mom from Ben's old high school lacrosse team. She'd been through a divorce a few years ago. Jim, I just need to know the truth."

"About what?" he asked.

"Is there another woman?" she asked.

"No," he said.

"So this isn't about someone else?" she asked.

"No," he said. "Listen, I don't think we should have this discussion over the phone. Let's talk later."

His answer satisfied her for the moment. She already felt she had pushed the conversation as far as she could handle it and decided not to press him for more answers.

CHAPTER 4

HOLIDAY SURPRISE

With Ben and Ryann due to arrive for winter break in a week, Natalie wondered how she and Jim would hide Jim's divorce intentions. Up to this point, Jim had managed to conceal from Rachel that he was sleeping in the basement.

Two weeks after he broke the divorce news to her, Natalie felt a combination of denial and a firm belief his divorce phase would pass. "Why worry the kids about something that will be old news in a couple of months?" she told herself.

The couple agreed to keep up the appearance of life as usual so as not to spoil the holidays for their family and prematurely drag their children into their troubled marriage. They both knew how frenzied the next few weeks would be, which would be a natural distraction for everyone. So they decided to defer any divorce talk till after the New Year. They also agreed to sleep in the same room while the kids were home. But that plan abruptly ended after the first night. In the morning Natalie sidled beside Jim for an early spooning session and suggested having sex; Jim had no interest.

When Ben and Ryann returned home, Jim made sure to retire to the basement after his kids had gone to bed in their respective bedrooms or left for a night out with friends—whichever came first. He also woke up before anyone else. The plan worked for the first week.

The second week, Ben arrived home late after drinking with friends and fell asleep on the family room couch. That morning, Jim exited the basement. As he walked through the family room, his entrance woke Ben up.

"Dad?" he asked. Ben was bleary eyed and moderately hung over.

"Yeah, Ben, it's just me. Go back to sleep," Jim said.

Ben closed his eyes, about to follow orders, but the disconnection of what he'd witnessed meandered in his foggy awareness. He thought it through and then called out, "Wait! Did you come from the basement?"

"Yeah, son. I had trouble sleeping last night, so I crashed downstairs," Jim said.

Jim's explanation sounded reasonable enough—at least for someone who'd drunk too much the night before. Ben fell back asleep.

Despite the couple's best intentions to keep a united front for the kids—particularly during the holidays—the near miss with Ben made Jim realize he and Natalie needed to reevaluate their plan. That morning, the couple spoke quietly in their bedroom.

"We've got to tell them now. That way we can control the message," Jim said.

His habit of using corporate-speak outside the workplace always annoyed Natalie. It demonstrated how everything to him was a business transaction—including their marriage. His lack of expressing emotions in the language of regular humans, rather than marketing consultants, was always an issue with her.

"No way," she whispered emphatically so as not to be heard outside their bedroom.

"Natalie, they're going to start asking questions," he said.

"Then make something up . . . say you've been snoring," she said.

Ever since her kids were little, Natalie had made the holidays one of their most memorable times of the year. Thus the thought of spoiling their Christmas was unacceptable.

"So you're basically telling me to lie to them," he said.

"Yes," she said. "At least till *after* the holidays. Do it for the family."

Jim agreed to continue keeping up the current holiday masquerade.

For Natalie, the days leading up to Christmas were consumed with schoolwork, family events, and attending holiday school functions. Meanwhile, Jim experienced the intense workload that always came at year's end. Their busy schedules provided the perfect cover-up for their covert plan.

On Christmas Eve and Christmas Day, the two did their best to pull themselves together. Gifts were exchanged, dinners were quiet but relatively uneventful, and all arguments put on hold. At the same time, they wanted nothing more than to put this year's holiday behind them.

Despite parents' efforts, children often uncover what the adults would prefer kept secret. Ben had shared discovering his dad's exit from the basement with his siblings, which put the three on the alert. The day after Christmas, Ryann texted Ben regarding what she had witnessed that morning:

> *Ryann*
> Have u noticed mom's been acting weird?

> *Ben*
> Not really. Why?

Ryann

I caught her crying in the kitchen. She said she was happy 2 see us.

Ben

and what's up w/dad in the basement?

Ryann

I think something's going on.

That evening, the family gathered for dinner, except for Natalie, who remained in the kitchen preparing dessert. She had reached her emotional limits and was on the verge of melting down. The kitchen was the perfect hideout.

"Mom, join us. The food's going to get cold," Rachel said.

"I'll be right in!" she said.

Natalie took a deep breath and entered the dining room. The combination of fatigue from creating the family's holiday magic and fears this could be their last Christmas together made her cry. She used her sleeve to quickly wipe her tears from her face and took a seat.

"Mom, have you been crying?" Rachel asked.

"Not at all," she said. Her voice quivered, and she cast her gaze downward.

Natalie's impending breakdown signaled to Jim the holiday façade had cracked. Christmas was officially over. "Your mom and I have decided to get a divorce," he said.

The family sat in collective stillness.

Jim wished he could take his words back.

"Jim, how dare you!" Natalie said.

For the second time in a month, he had made an unexpected announcement. Natalie couldn't believe she used to think his alpha-male decisiveness was sexy. Now, she viewed his unilateral proclamations as a form of bullying—like announcements from the leader of a rogue nation, threats rooted in cries for attention.

Jim amended his initial statement: "I mean, your mom and I have been having some difficulties. We're considering an initial separation to see if things will work out. This has nothing to do with you. We both love you all. We just need time to sort things out."

"Is this why you've been sleeping in the basement?" Ben asked.

"Yes," Jim said.

"So it wasn't because you were snoring?"

"Ben I know this is—"

"Bullshit! You lied to me. How long have you two been hiding this from us? I'm outta here," Ben said. He slammed the door on his way out. His car roared down the street.

Rachel abruptly left the dinner table and ran upstairs to her bedroom. Meanwhile, Ryann, her body frozen, sat next to Natalie and cried. Natalie wrapped her arm around her daughter and glared at Jim.

"Is this what you call 'controlling the message'? Look what you've done," she said.

"This isn't all my fault. Remember I didn't want to lie about it. You're the one who wanted to keep up this stupid charade for so long—not me," Jim said.

Natalie hugged Ryann and escorted her upstairs to Rachel's room where the three consoled each other.

Jim sat alone in disbelief. He had wanted to say he had worked out the details and that the divorce wouldn't change anything. After the hours he had spent planning, poring through financial statements, and creating impeccable spreadsheets, he couldn't understand how the announcement could have gone so badly. He was filled with anxiety and was looking for quick relief. He texted Claudia:

> Talk was a disaster. Can I come by?

Claudia replied yes right away.

Jim then approached the staircase and peeked up to the second floor. "I'm going for a drive. I'll be back," he shouted, wondering if anyone cared.

At the start of the New Year, maternal guilt set in. Natalie had a tough time forgiving herself for ruining her kids' holiday. Jim too felt lousy, but every year she had shouldered the burden of creating Christmas magic, so she felt more responsible than he did.

Once Ben and Ryann returned to school, Jim told Natalie he had found a furnished apartment he would rent month to month. His move was another sign challenging Natalie's denial about the split. It motivated her to plunge into divorce research.

Over the next two weeks, she spent hours on her iPad and laptop reading self-help books about divorce and saving marriages, as well as bookmarking websites and blogs. Her search results produced a wide range of online content: "How to Rescue Your Marriage," "Steps to Stopping Divorce," "Do-It-Yourself Cheap Divorce," "Children and Divorce," "God and Divorce," and countless others. Unfortunately, the more she explored online, the more overwhelmed she became.

After reading so many digital divorce stories with miserable endings, Natalie wondered how she would keep her family together. She also worried about the breakup's financial impact—would retirement be a dream she'd never experience in her lifetime? Throughout their marriage, she had feared something catastrophic would happen to Jim. Now, she wondered if their divorce would leave her worse off than his death.

NATALIE SEEKS HELP

Although Natalie believed the relationship was far from over, she also recognized Jim's divorce news was, if anything, a sign their marriage was in trouble. As she grew to accept Jim's intentions, she felt a need to reach out.

When she told Barrett what had happened, her younger sister

wasn't surprised. She had known about their non-existent sex life, which was a red flag.

"Is there another woman?" Barrett asked.

Natalie told her she had specifically asked Jim about infidelity. His answer was a clear no. Barrett wasn't so easily persuaded.

"I guarantee he's lying. Just think about it, sweetie. What do you think he's doing on that boat all the time?" she asked.

She encouraged Natalie to find a lawyer. "*A ruthless one.* Then take the bastard to the cleaners for every penny he's got," she said.

When Natalie reached out to her parents, they expressed sadness—particularly for the grandchildren they adored. Although Ben's, Ryann's, and Rachel's advanced ages reassured the grandparents the children would be better able to handle the divorce than if they were little kids, they expressed disappointment that the two parents couldn't fix their marriage.

"Do you think there was anything else you could have done?" her mother asked.

Natalie knew the old-school subtext of the question was she had fallen short as a homemaker and perhaps didn't do enough to meet Jim's needs. From now on, as far as her parents were concerned, Natalie would only share the most basic details.

Next Natalie arranged to meet with her priest. She respected Father Jack. During their counseling session, he reminded her marriage, in the eyes of God, was a sacrament and bond that mustn't be broken.

"I know you're devoted to Christ's teachings, which is why I'm going to pray for you and Jim to resolve your issues and revive your marriage," he said. "If it is God's plan for you, doors will open, so don't give up."

The two prayed together for healing and that "God's will be done." The priest ended their time together by recommending marriage counseling. Father Jack provided Natalie several websites where she could find a therapist and arrange for a couple's session.

On the one hand, Natalie's sister Barrett urged Natalie to go out for blood and give her ex-to-be the comeuppance he deserved. On the other, Father Jack encouraged her to pray for reconciliation and seek marriage counseling. Listening to both positions, two ends of a relationship spectrum, at the same time would be a challenge—and downright exhausting. But she believed it was in her best interest to both protect herself and fight for her marriage.

CHAPTER 5

CONVERSATION WITH JEN

A little over a month had passed since Jen and Natalie had run into each other at Fresh Pavilion. Filled with uncertainty and despondent over Jim's recent move, she decided to reach out to Jen. They planned to meet for coffee.

After Jen ended her day at the law practice, she met Natalie at the Starbucks near her office. Jen was glad to put her miserable divorce experience to good use.

"When Scott told me he was leaving me, I was an emotional wreck. But to avoid making a bad situation even worse, I had to pull myself together to find a lawyer—what a hellish time that was. I remember how each prospective lawyer shared a ton of information with me. At the time, I could barely keep track of what day of the week it was, let alone follow an in-depth legal conversation," Jen said.

"I feel exactly the same way, and I haven't even started my search yet! I think that's why I decided to write down my concerns and questions," Natalie said. She pulled her iPad out of her bag. "If you don't mind, I want to run some of my questions by you."

"Happy to do anything to help you avoid some of the mistakes I made," Jen said.

A DIVORCE INFORMATIONAL INTERVIEW

Natalie read from her tablet. "How did your interviews with the lawyers work?"

"I was surprised by how much they varied in their approaches and temperaments. Overall, I think it's important to find a lawyer you're comfortable with and you feel will best represent your interests. In the end, I hired Pamela. She listened to me and explained things in a way I could understand. I also thought her fees were reasonable. She billed $400 an hour and requested a $7,500 **retainer**," Jen said.

"Can you tell me how a retainer works?" Natalie asked.

Jen described how it was a pre-paid fee arrangement that secured a lawyer's services. The client receives a monthly statement reflecting the current balance, including the amount spent during the billing period. Usually, once the balance drops below a certain amount, the client will add funds to the account. A retainer is similar to a prepaid debit card—you pay in advance for future use. While other types of lawyers have different ways they're compensated, billing by retainer is a fairly standard practice in family law.

"You'll also hear most divorce lawyers use the term 'family law' instead of 'divorce lawyer' to describe what they do," Jen said.

"So why did you choose Pamela?" Natalie asked.

"I wanted someone with good experience and who had working relationships with other professionals in family law," Jen said. She explained she was drawn to Pamela's ten-year family law career. In addition, Jen preferred a multi-attorney firm to a solo practitioner; she believed a team of lawyers working together would provide more talent and support staff to help her.

Jen knew solo practitioners were perfectly qualified and could properly represent her. But she felt slightly more peace of mind with a group practice.

"After everything you've learned, would you still pick Pamela today?" Natalie asked.

"Yes and no. She was a *great* listener. But my husband's attorney was such a bully, and I wished Pamela had fought back a little harder. Don't get me wrong, I'd never want an attack dog as he had. So I think I'd like a little more aggressive version of Pamela," Jen said.

"What would you do differently if you could change the outcome?" Natalie asked.

"We fought endlessly over small stuff and didn't invest enough time addressing things that would become big problems later," Jen said.

During their divorce negotiations, Jen asked Pamela to include a list of reimbursements in the final settlement for the various expenses she would incur with her kids—ones she felt should be shared expenses. Examples included medical co-pays and deductibles, tutoring, therapy, summer programs, and after-school activities, all of which wound up being a constant battle to recoup. Even with an enforcement clause in place, the issues created endless arguments between them.

A year later, Jen wondered why she had instructed her lawyer to add items to an agreement her ex would never honor. The bottom line was she clung to each support check as if it would be her last.

"Over time, it just became easier to cut my losses," Jen said.

Even if the judge ordered Scott to pay what she was owed, returning to court again and again to recover small amounts of money—and possibly incur even more lawyer fees in the process—became a very time-consuming and emotionally draining experience.

"Anything else you'd do differently?" Natalie asked.

Jen added she and Scott hadn't established a clear path to post-divorce parenting and their attorneys didn't provide any guidance in that regard. So when Scott forgot to pick the kids up or returned them hours past their scheduled time, she had no mechanism to address his carelessness.

"By the time I heard about **parenting plans**, it was too late," she said.

"What are those?" Natalie asked.

Jen explained parenting plans were joint agreements detailing how mothers and fathers could best work together for the benefit of their children. Holidays, birthdays, graduations, weddings, day-to-day interactions, and dealing with grandchildren—being parents meant their lives would be forever connected. It also meant there would be many opportunities for conflict. A well-crafted parenting plan could help a couple avoid disputes or provide a process to deal with conflicts when they arose.

Divorcing couples consult with their attorneys or mental health professionals or both who are experienced in drafting parenting plans. They address duties and obligations, including visitation and how to communicate about disagreements. They outline how to fulfill commitments to each other and their children, such as being on time to pick up or drop them off.

"What was most surprising about the divorce process?" Natalie asked.

"The cost, for sure! Next, the emotional toll on the whole family. The final bill was about $200,000, around $120,000 for him and $80,000 for me. And that doesn't include therapy, which is ongoing for the kids and me," Jen said.

"I'm really struggling to wrap my head around those numbers," Natalie said.

"No kidding. Imagine how I feel. I learned the hard way that divorce can have the biggest financial impact on your future. But I've also realized you do have options," Jen said.

"What do you mean?"

"You have many divorce choices that don't require going before a judge, and they could reduce your emotional and financial costs—sometimes significantly," Jen said.

"Do you have any recommendations?" Natalie asked.

"Because we went before a judge—which, by the way, was the scariest day of my life—I only have direct experience with courtroom litigation. But since then, I've learned there are several ways to avoid going to court, including the **traditional approach**, **mediation**, and something called **collaborative divorce**. From what I gather, with all three of these, couples can choose to work with someone who helps them reach a settlement *without* litigating in court. I *highly recommend* you do your homework. Research as much as possible before you decide which approach you'll take. I wish I'd known about other options before I went through the wringer," Jen said.

Outside of courtroom dramas she'd seen on TV, Natalie didn't know much about divorce. Thus she didn't realize alternatives besides litigation existed. Jen had piqued Natalie's interest. She typed the following into her iPad:

> Find out about traditional, mediation, and collaborative!!!

"I really appreciate your help, Jen. There's so much to figure out, especially since I'm still trying to salvage my marriage," Natalie said.

"More power to you. Be sure to explore your options. Protecting yourself is always a good idea—even if you're able to make your marriage work," Jen said.

The two left Starbucks. The conversation with Jen motivated Natalie to continue her research online once she arrived home.

CHAPTER 6

NATALIE BEGINS HER EDUCATION

When Natalie arrived home, she reviewed the notes she had taken on her iPad. One by one, she looked up the different divorce approaches Jen had mentioned during their talk. Natalie quickly became overwhelmed with the legal jargon and the massive amount of content available online. She decided she needed to organize her research.

She opened her laptop and propped up her iPad—on her tablet's screen, divorce websites, and on her laptop, her word processor and spreadsheet. She spent the rest of the evening organizing divorce facts.

Natalie arranged her divorce notes based on five criteria: cast of professionals, self-determination, transparency, understanding the property settlement agreement (PSA), and cost.

FIVE ELEMENTS OF DIVORCE

1. CAST OF PROFESSIONALS

These are the professionals who will play a role in the divorce process. Depending on the type of divorce, they include attorneys, financial professionals (such as CFPs [Certified Financial Planners] and CPAs [Certified Public Accountants]), mental health experts (such as licensed clinical psychologists, LCSWs [Licensed Clinical Social Workers], MDs, and PhDs), judges, and child advocates (legal and mental health).

2. SELF-DETERMINATION: *LOW, MEDIUM, OR HIGH*

Self-determination refers to the extent to which you're involved in the ongoing divorce process, including the division of property, support, childcare, college expenses, preparing for your long-term financial stability, and the negotiations related to these matters.

A *low level* of self-determination means the spouses depend upon the cast of professionals to drive the divorce process during negotiations. This does not mean the spouses relinquish any involvement. Rather, it means they defer to their attorneys to argue on their behalf and consult with other professionals before they make any decisions.

A *high level* of self-determination means the spouses are actively involved in the divorce process and are encouraged to work jointly with the cast of professionals to make decisions. In addition, negotiations involve all parties working together to find the best solutions.

A *medium level* of self-determination falls somewhere between the two extremes and reflects aspects of both *low* and *high*.

Think about this in terms of driving a car. Two people sitting in the back seat of a driverless car are like the couple with a very low level of self-determination. They place full confidence in and depend fully upon the car taking them to their destination.

If the couple are in the front seat, one person behind the wheel and the other checking the map and giving directions, they are in a very high level of self-determination. They decide where to go, based on the information they have.

If, instead, the couple in the front seat are listening to their GPS navigator, they are in a medium level of self-determination. They consider the advice they receive and may or may not follow it; they hold the wheel so have the final say in where they go.

3. TRANSPARENCY: *LOW, MEDIUM, OR HIGH*

This refers to how much of the process is open to all participants. Do the clients and their cast of professionals have an understanding that the other side will disclose what they are thinking or planning? Do they expect to jointly reach solutions or negotiate all aspects of the divorce? Is all relevant information shared?

A *low level* of transparency means neither spouse is kept informed of the other spouse's intent or strategy. The negotiation is primarily left to the attorneys; the spouses become bystanders to the negotiations and are asked to make the final decisions. The clients provide the requested data, but the attorneys drive the overall process. In this instance, the attorneys work to obtain the best result for their clients. And seeking the best result for their clients oftentimes does not consider how a particular decision will impact the other side. In the end, however, both parties reach an agreement based upon guidance from their respective attorneys.

While attorneys will negotiate on your behalf and you're responsible for making final decisions about the property division and related issues, if you're unable to reach an agreement through negotiations, then a judge will make the decisions for you in court.

Although full disclosure is a requirement of all divorce proceedings, full disclosure pertains to the data and *not* to other important matters such as alternative strategies to resolve disputes, emotions, the long-term effects of the decisions, and the continuing relationships when children are involved. Keep in mind, the goal of the attorney is to reach an agreement, after which he or she will move on to the next case. Once the case is settled, attorneys will not follow up with their clients unless retained to enforce a broken agreement.

A *high level* of transparency means clients and the cast of professionals are kept fully informed throughout the proceedings. During meetings, all participants discuss the process and issues openly, and they work jointly on reaching a solution. The proceedings may also include input from outside professionals, such as mental health professionals who represent the children's concerns and perspectives as well as any emotional issues that may arise in the children during the divorce process. Divorcing moms and dads sometimes need to be reminded about how their breakup will impact their children and the long-term effects their decisions will have on their children's lives.

A *medium level* of transparency reflects aspects of both *high* and *low*.

4. UNDERSTANDING THE PROPERTY SETTLEMENT AGREEMENT (PSA)

The PSA outlines custody, spousal and child support, property division, and legal terms of the divorce. The problem is many divorcing men and women are emotionally incapacitated and unable to make good decisions during the development of the PSA as part of the divorce process.

If the divorce negotiation's main focus is reaching an agreement concerning the division of marital assets, custody, and child and spousal support, and the divorcing spouses rely on their lawyers to perform most of the related tasks on their behalf, then ex-husbands and ex-wives may not fully understand the real-life consequences of the PSA until the divorce is final and they are living under the PSA's terms and provisions.

This explains why you may have heard someone who had gone through a divorce say, "My ex wore me down, so I just gave up, gave in, and signed," "I didn't really understand what I was agreeing to at the time," "My ex practically held the kids hostage in order to get what he [or she] wanted," or "I was going broke, so I did whatever was necessary to stop the out-of-control costs."

As a result, it may take a year or more before divorcing couples wake up to the harsh, real-world implications of their agreement.

Remember, once you've signed the PSA, you can't revise the property portion later. In other words, *while your marriage may have not lasted forever, your PSA will!*

Natalie typed the following:

> Do not sign PSA without understanding what it means to me over the long term.

5. COST

This refers to a range of expenses, from start to finish, of the process itself.

Costs can vary widely depending on your geographical location, the complexity of your case, the type of divorce process you use, and the speed at which you and your spouse reach an agreement. Costs don't include the psychological costs and lasting emotional damage, both of which you and, sadly, your children may never fully recover from.

The itemized costs from an attorney's office may be startling at first—even if you were well aware of his or her hourly rate. But you'll most likely incur other expenses too, such as professional staff time, administrative costs, phone, fax, photocopies, emails, and scanning. In addition, you'll quickly learn that each billable hour is counted from five- to fifteen-minute intervals. For example, you could be charged five minutes for a one-minute call to your lawyer. *Buyer beware: The amount of time a lawyer spends on the phone or reading emails can quickly mount up!*

The following are questions to ask yourself as you assess cost:

- How much money do I have access to at this time?

- How much of it am I willing to spend?

- How much money will be left after the settlement?

- Will I be able to maintain my current lifestyle?

- Will the kids be able to go to college?

- When will I be able to retire?

- What changes will be necessary, including selling my house, buying a car, and moving to a new area?

- Lastly, how much emotional currency am I willing to spend?

Natalie used these five criteria to organize the following list of the types of divorce.

FOUR TYPES OF DIVORCE

Natalie learned there are four main types of divorce: the traditional approach, which may involve litigation; mediation; collaborative divorce; and a hybrid combination.

1. TRADITIONAL APPROACH AND LITIGATION

Traditional Approach
In a negotiated divorce settlement, the lawyers representing each party will negotiate on behalf of their clients and help them reach

an agreement. The attorneys also help negotiate spousal support and then use the statutory guidelines to determine child support, if any is applicable. In a traditional approach, the divorcing couple will not have their case heard in a courtroom in front of a judge; instead the parties will come to an agreement based upon negotiations between their attorneys.

Once the agreement is completed, the PSA is submitted to the court for a judge to review. Upon approval, the judge then issues the Decree of Divorce, which makes the divorce final. Note that until the Decree of Divorce is issued, you are considered married under the state laws and for income tax purposes.

Litigation

A divorce that winds up in court often results from a negotiations impasse between the spouses. Sometimes, however, a divorce will go straight to court without negotiation. In either case, your lawyer will present your case in front of a judge, who will make a final decision.

Five Elements of Divorce

1. Cast of professionals

- ◘ One or more lawyers for each spouse
- ◘ Optional: financial professionals, mental health professionals, and other experts
- ◘ Judge

If you're unable to reach a negotiated settlement, then you'll have your day in court and a judge will determine your settlement for you. He or she will listen to the parties, and their respective lawyers will present their cases. In addition, expert witnesses and other witnesses may participate in the process. The court proceedings may take as little as a day, or they can last more than a week under more complicated circumstances.

Keep in mind that in most cases who is at fault is not an issue. Thus going to court to air out your dirty laundry may not be in your best interest. Most states are considered **no fault**, which means divorce does not have to be based upon a particular event, such as adultery.

2. Self-determination: *Low to medium*

3. Transparency: *Low*

4. Understanding the Property Settlement Agreement (PSA): *Medium*

5. Cost: *Varies widely, depending upon many factors*
As a general rule, the simpler and more amicable the split-up, the lower the costs will likely be. For example, if a couple uses the traditional approach, has few conflicts regarding assets, has no children (or if they have children, the squabbles over them are minimal), and reach an agreement through negotiations (in other words, no courtroom appearances in front of a judge are necessary), the divorce may cost under $25,000—and even less depending on how quickly and easily they're able to divide their marital assets. If, on the other hand, a couple ends up in court with a judge deciding most of the issues, the cost could typically run $100,000 or more depending upon the complexity of the case—the sky can be the limit.

As a general rule, the more complicated or the more adversarial the situation between a couple, the more likely the financial cost will increase dramatically.

Misconceptions
Unlike TV divorces, the traditional approach doesn't mean you'll inevitably wind up in front of a judge in court. In fact, over 90 percent of cases are settled without a trial. Only when negotiations break down is setting a court date the sole remaining option.

Examples of breakdowns include the following:

- Spouses reach an impasse over money or things.

- A spouse refuses to negotiate in good faith.

- A spouse's anger is so high he or she loses any ability to negotiate.

- A spouse is seeking revenge.

- A spouse is determined to win without regard to cost.

- Other extenuating circumstances are present, such as drug, emotional, or physical abuse.

In other cases, negotiation breakdowns may be a result of disagreements regarding child custody, caring for special needs children, or which party is responsible for certain debts.

If you're among the 10 percent who wind up in court, during the court session, a judge will review evidence after hearing from the parties, which include the witnesses (if applicable). After careful review of all the relevant facts, the judge will make a ruling that will influence the rest of your life.

Husbands and wives often believe they'll have their "day in court" where the judge will listen to their side of what went wrong and rule in their favor.

To the contrary, what usually takes place is spouses leave the courthouse unhappy with the results after a judge makes his or her ruling—neither spouse receives what he or she expected. In rare instances, both participants leave the courthouse with a smile. The more likely scenario is both exit the courtroom, return to their cars alone, slump in the driver's seat, and break down in tears asking themselves, "What happened?" followed by "Now what?"

Advantages

✓ Allows independent representation, true advocacy.

✓ Threat of going to court may force settlement.

✓ May be the best option when abuse is involved: physical, emotional, child, or drug.

✓ May be the best option if you're unable to communicate with your spouse.

✓ May be the best option if the couple's assets are substantial and complications exist requiring a number of specialists to resolve them.

Disadvantages

✖ Limited to low self-determination.

✖ Can be very expensive.

✖ May take a long time to reach a settlement.

✖ Difficult to predict outcomes.

✖ May be emotionally draining.

✖ Emphasis on short term (reaching an agreement) may come at the expense of long term (the financial and emotional impact the divorce will have on the spouses and their children).

✖ Buyer's remorse—for example, an ex-spouse wishes he or she could revise the PSA once its property provisions play out in real life.

✖ Complicated cases may require hiring a number of outside consultants.

Summary

The traditional approach is the type of divorce most people are familiar with. It is having your lawyers represent your interests in the negotiation process or in court or both.

The statutory guidelines are almost always used when calculating the amount of child support; the amount is always subject to review and modification. In other words, if a significant increase or decrease in income for either party occurs post-divorce, the support amount may be adjusted.

Spousal support may be fixed, modifiable, non-modifiable, or deferred; it all depends upon the final negotiations. There are no statutory guidelines for permanent spousal support, but they do exist for temporary spousal support.

2. MEDIATION

Five Elements of Divorce

1. Cast of professionals

- ◻ Mediator: a **neutral** professional who facilities negotiations between parties in conflict.

- ◻ One or more lawyers for each spouse. Having a lawyer is not a requirement but is strongly encouraged. Attorneys serve as outside consultants to each party and may be involved from the start of mediation or brought into the process as the mediation progresses.

- ◻ Optional: Financial and mental health professionals who serve as outside consultants.

Neutral means the mediator can only offer mediation services. He or she may not provide legal or financial advice to either spouse individually or jointly. Many mediators are lawyers, but if they're playing the role of mediator, they are prohibited from providing legal advice throughout the mediation process. The mediator assists the couple to reach an understanding on issues that may be blocking them from reaching a final PSA. Through this understanding, the couple may be able to reach an agreement together.

Mediators may also help develop the final agreement. One of their roles is as scrivener (or scribe) who writes the agreement using straightforward (common) language. They play this role when they produce a **memorandum of understanding** (MOU), which is frequently used as the basis for the PSA. An MOU is a summary of what the parties have agreed to as a result of the mediation process. Both the MOU and the PSA are legally binding.

2. Self-determination: *High*

3. Transparency: *Medium*

4. Understanding the Property Settlement Agreement (PSA): *Medium to high*

5. Cost: *Typically significantly less expensive than the traditional approach*
The more complicated the case, however, the higher the cost will most likely be. Before signing a mediated settlement, each spouse should obtain legal and financial counsel.

Misconceptions
Often couples seek mediation as a cost-saving option. They think, "We don't need an attorney." Or they seek mediation because few assets are involved, or the couple believe they can make the decisions themselves and only want someone to help them finalize the divorce.

First, mediation can work well, even if significant assets are involved. In addition, attorneys are usually involved to finalize the agreement or at least provide a review of the MOU before the agreement is completed. In fact, lawyers often play an important role in many mediated divorces, and many are trained in mediation. Because mediation is often misunderstood, it is underused in family law.

Also, in many cases, mediation can be a subset of the traditional approach. In other words, if an impasse occurs during negotiations, a mediator may be employed to resolve the specific issue.

Advantages

✓ Compared to the traditional approach, mediation is less contentious.

✓ Decisions are made jointly.

✓ May be a cost-effective process.

✓ Clients drive the process.

✓ Generally faster than the traditional approach.

Disadvantages

✖ May not work well in an imbalanced relationship, for example, when one spouse maintains emotional control or when one spouse possesses the financial knowledge and the other spouse is not well-informed about financial matters and does not have outside support.

✖ Lack of guidance—as a neutral participant, the mediator cannot provide legal or financial advice or guidance.

✖ Couples may still need to hire professional help, such as financial advisers, appraisers, attorneys, therapists, and accountants.

✖ Requires joint participation from both spouses.

✖ May not be suitable for highly complicated cases unless the mediator has an understanding or experience in dealing with the issues presented.

Summary

Alternative dispute resolution (ADR) is the technical name for a series of approaches that aim to aid individuals to reach an agreement based upon a commitment to find common ground and avoid litigation. Mediation is one of the most common forms of ADR and is used in all types of legal disputes, not just divorce. For instance, collective bargaining by unions is one example of ADR. Companies regularly use ADR to resolve lawsuits against other companies in order to avoid costly courtroom battles.

Mediation uses a third-party, neutral mediator to help divorcing spouses reach a settlement. The mediator doesn't represent the husband or wife. Rather, the mediator's role is to help couples reach a mutual understanding of the issues, which will enable them to make decisions. Although husbands and wives may have retained their own lawyers, they may or may not be directly part of the mediation process.

If the spouses are struggling emotionally during the divorce, then they should seek the support of mental health professionals—this recommendation applies to all divorce approaches.

3. COLLABORATIVE DIVORCE

Five Elements of Divorce
1. Cast of professionals

- ◘ One or more collaborative lawyers for each spouse.

- ◘ One or two coaches (mental health or mediator) for the team who manage and keep the team on track throughout the collaborative process. The coach oversees all communications and may provide insights into emotional issues as they relate to the divorce. A mental health coach may also be working with both parties to aid in understanding the emotional issues that are causing an impasse or to identify the real concerns of one party or the other in regards to reaching a decision.

- ◘ Optional: One neutral financial professional for the team.

- ◘ Optional: One mental health professional for a spouse and a child specialist who may also be a mental health professional for children.

- ◘ Optional: Non-neutral financial professionals as external advisers to either party individually.

- ◘ Optional: Professionals such as accountants or appraisers.

2. Self-determination: *High*

3. Transparency: *High*

A high level of self-determination and transparency are the hallmarks of a successful collaborative divorce process. The team and clients openly discuss the issues and work together to find solutions that will work well for the divorcing couple.

The professionals assist the couple, and in many cases, the team is able to develop custom and unique solutions that would not have been addressed under other divorce approaches. This is where having a team approach can really pay off. Overall, clients drive the process, and they play an integral role in developing solutions. As a result, couples often experience fewer post-divorce issues or problems.

4. Understanding the Property Settlement Agreement (PSA): *High*

5. Cost
In general, collaborative divorce is typically less expensive than the traditional approach and somewhat more expensive than mediation. Key cost savings usually come from being able to reach a resolution in much less time than in the traditional approach and

not having court as a solution to fall back upon (you'll learn more about this aspect in the summary).

Misconceptions

When divorcing couples learn about collaborative divorce, many of them believe it will be the most expensive option, or at least a significantly costly one, because it requires hiring a team of professionals.

But what people frequently fail to realize is the collaborative divorce team is working closely together and is specifically trained to find the best possible outcome. As a result, the overall cost can be much lower than the traditional approach. And because collaborative divorce has inherent processes that are designed to prevent future disputes—or at least provide a means to resolve them amicably—the long-term emotional and financial costs can be significantly lower when compared to other divorce approaches.

Advantages

✓ Compared to the traditional approach, less contentious.

✓ Decisions are made jointly and with increased awareness of outcomes.

✓ May be a cost-effective process.

✓ Cannot use the court as a last resort without terminating the process.

✓ Clients drive the process.

✓ Efficient use of professional time and effort—the team works together to develop solutions.

✓ Neutral financial professional participation.

✓ Mental health professional may represent children's emotional interests.

✓ Parties often have a higher likelihood of complying with agreements when compared to orders entered by a judge.

✓ Parenting plans may be part of the outcome in the process.

Disadvantages

✖ May not work well in an imbalanced relationship, which may result in one spouse's inability to participate, for example, in instances when one spouse is emotionally or financially dominant or an imbalance of power or knowledge may impede the process.

✖ Need to hire professional help, such as one's own financial or mental health professional.

✖ Cannot use litigation as a default.

✖ Spouses' lawyers must withdraw from the case if the spouses decide to litigate.

✖ Requires joint participation from both spouses.

✖ Process can slow down due to difficulties scheduling collaborative divorce meetings.

✖ Hiring cast of professionals for all meetings may be expensive.

✖ Spouses cannot keep secrets or develop competing strategies.

✖ May not be suitable for highly complicated cases or where abuse is involved.

Summary

Collaborative divorce is another type of ADR. The following are the distinct features of collaborative divorce:

- ◘ In collaborative divorce, each spouse has a lawyer that plays a role in all collaborative divorce meetings.

- ◘ The attorneys agree they will not go to court if the collaborative process breaks down. In the event the collaborative process breaks down, the couple may need to pursue the traditional approach as a way to reach a settlement, which will require hiring *new* attorneys and other professionals. Avoiding this arduous scenario creates an incentive for couples to reach an agreement under the collaborative process.

- ◘ Once the process is over, the collaborative agreement prohibits participating professionals from continuing representation of the parties. This is the case regardless of whether or not the couple reaches an agreement through the collaborative process.

- ◘ All team members are trained in the collaborative divorce process and are required to maintain their certification via continuing education.

- ◘ The mental health professional often acts as the team coach, whose role is to keep the process on track and address the various emotional issues that arise between the couple. Also, children may have mental health professionals or other child specialists throughout the process.

- ◘ The optional neutral financial professional is trained in the collaborative process and often plays an invaluable role. He or she doesn't represent either spouse. Thus the financial professional does not make recommendations. Instead, the financial professional advises the team on the couple's financial issues. His or her role is to provide financial information in order to help the parties make informed decisions.

◼ The financial professional also evaluates the consequences of all financial decisions and assists in developing alternative solutions. The neutral financial professional generates his or her financial analysis based on the team's decisions. This analysis allows the team to identify financial outcomes of the divorce.

4. HYBRID DIVORCE

Couples sometimes use both the traditional approach and ADR. For instance, a case initially starting under the traditional approach may add a mediator to address specific issues that cannot be resolved through negotiations between the lawyers. Rather than going to court to reach a settlement, the couple may choose to hire an independent mediator to resolve a particular impasse. Once the issue is resolved, they return to their attorneys to complete the negotiations.

Other times, a divorce may begin in mediation, but the spouses eventually realize they have too many legal obstacles, which make them unable to come to an agreement through this process. As a result, the clients go through negotiations with their attorneys and use mediation solely to address specific issues.

An experienced financial professional may also work with both parties to develop the framework for the division of the assets. The financial professional will help his or her clients reach an understanding of the financial issues involved in the divorce. Unlike in collaborative divorce, the financial professional may have a continuing relationship with his or her client. This is the case with mediated divorces as well.

Attorneys may also recommend their clients meet separately with a financial professional to help them understand the financial matters in the divorce process. This is especially the case for family law attorneys who realize their client may not be well-informed about financial matters. Thus they want their client to have a financial advocate working with them as part of the divorce team. In this instance, the financial professional is representing the interests of one particular spouse.

The financial professional's role also relieves the attorney from having to act as both attorney and financial adviser. The financial professional helps his or her client determine how best to deal with financial issues.

Within each model itself, couples may use some aspects of each one but not others. For example, in collaborative divorce, a financial professional may not be necessary. Or one spouse may decide he or she doesn't need a mental health professional.

Just as every marriage is distinct, every divorce is different as well. With many options today, divorcing spouses can create a custom approach to meet their particular needs, which means a hybrid divorce can appear in many different ways.

NATALIE PREPARES TO FIND LAWYERS ONLINE

Natalie created the following chart to summarize what she learned about different divorce strategies:

Divorce Type	Self-Determination*	Transparency*	PSA Client Understanding*	Cost
Traditional Approach	L	L	M	$$$$
Mediation	H	M	M	$$
Collaborative	H	H	H	$$$
Hybrid	M	H	H	$$$

*High (H), medium (M), low (L)

Compiling this information provided Natalie the background she needed for her next step: meet with lawyers. Although she believed it was premature to retain one—after all, keeping her marriage together was her first priority—she knew worst-case scenario planning was in her best interest.

Natalie now had basic divorce information, but she still lacked real-world knowledge of the legal aspects of divorce. She knew there was no substitute for a face-to-face meeting with an experienced family law attorney.

Based on her research, she concluded some form of ADR would serve her and her family's interests best. Although her kids were no longer little children, she still feared the breakup would hurt them. Furthermore, she had no interest in litigating her divorce in a courtroom in front of a judge. At the same time, she knew Barrett would disagree. In her sister's eyes, litigation was the only means to protect her interests, receive what she was entitled to, and give Jim his comeuppance.

Although collaborative divorce sounded like the kinder, gentler approach, Natalie was concerned about its costs and whether she needed to hire so many experts. She looked forward to having in-person meetings with lawyers in order to explore her options and receive expert advice.

CHAPTER 7

FINDING AN ATTORNEY

The next day, Natalie resumed her Internet research.
She discovered several online attorney directories. On one site, she found nearly three hundred family law attorneys near her home. Although the number overwhelmed her, she knew what she was looking for—her prior preparation gave her the information she needed to narrow her search.

As she pored through each attorney's profile, she looked for the following:

- At least ten years of family law experience

- Neither a solo practitioner nor a partner in a large law firm, which she defined as an office with more than ten partners

- ADR and specifically collaboratively trained a plus

- Experience with cases similar to the issues of her size and scope

From the hundreds of lawyers, she was able to narrow her search to ten. She then created a spreadsheet in order to streamline her findings.

Natalie explored each attorney's individual website. Some sites were nothing more than online business cards: contact information, headshot, and background. A few were content-rich sites with YouTube clips and divorce articles. Based on her latest round of research, she was able to reduce her search from ten lawyers to three, which she put in her spreadsheet:

Name	Experience (Years)	Firm Size (Partners)	EXPERTISE: Traditional Approach (TA) Mediation (M) Collaboration (C)
Frank	25	4	TA
Lewis	20	12	TA, M, C
Kathleen	30	3	TA, M, C

To her disappointment, no matter where she looked, she couldn't find information regarding a particular lawyer's fees. She recalled Jen's sticker shock, which prepared her for the possibility any or all of the attorneys on her list might bill up to five hundred dollars or more per hour. But she knew the only way to find out was to contact each firm.

The next day, Natalie began phoning prospective lawyers. Unfortunately, all three lawyers' calendars were booked for some time, and the first available appointment would be in three weeks. She planned to take the time between now and then to develop a list of questions to ask each one.

Natalie drew from her discussion with Jen and visited various divorce websites in order to create the following questionnaire.

ATTORNEY QUESTIONNAIRE

1. What is your practice's breakdown in terms of litigation, mediation, and collaborative divorce?

2. What is your hourly rate and retainer?

3. What is your typical client's financial situation?

4. How long does the divorce process typically take?

5. How much should I expect to pay in total costs to reach a settlement?

6. If we end up going to court, will you be representing me or will it be someone else in the practice?

7. Do you work with other professionals, such as financial planners and mental health professionals?

In particular, Natalie was eager to find out how each attorney addressed the different divorce approaches.

COMMON QUESTIONS ATTORNEYS ASK CLIENTS

Through her research, Natalie also learned lawyers would ask her questions as well. All their inquiries were variations on the following theme:

Tell me about your situation.

Some questions would help the attorney identify the biggest obstacles in Natalie's case. Other questions would allow the lawyer to determine the complexity of her case and assess the likelihood it would settle without going to court.

In her iPad, she jotted down questions she found on multiple websites that reflected what attorneys might ask her. She also prepared her answers. Her questions and answers appeared as follows:

1. **Has either party *premeditated* the divorce? (This means it has been planned ahead of time.)**
   Yes, although I don't know for how long before, I know Jim had been planning the announcement.

2. **What was your date of marriage?**
   October 20, 1990.

3. **Do you have an understanding of financial issues?**
   My husband took care of nearly all financial matters, so not really, which really concerns me.

4. **Do you have children? If so, how many and what are their ages?**
   Yes, three: Ben 22, Ryann 18, and Rachel 15.

5. **Have you agreed to anything with your spouse, such as whether you'll sell your primary residence and where each of you will live?**
   No. But I prefer to remain in the house—until at least Rachel graduates from high school but ideally until she graduates from college.

6. **Are there particular areas of major conflict where both of you have significant disagreements?**
   I have a long list of concerns about the future. But no major areas of conflict between us—at least so far.

7. **What do you and your spouse do for a living, and how much income does each of you generate?**

   I'm a middle school teacher. My income is $47,000. My husband is a corporate exec. And I think he makes around $300,000.

8. **Can you describe your ideal outcome for this divorce?**

   That I won't be a bag lady in retirement. And I'll be able to support myself and help my daughters through college as we have done for our son, Ben.

NATALIE'S FIRST APPOINTMENT

When she met with Frank, Natalie was immediately impressed with his demeanor and stunning office—both of which demonstrated success. The two sat in his Alexandria, Virginia, high-rise suite that had a stunning view of the Potomac River. Frank was in his late fifties, had been practicing for thirty years, and had the bravado of a seasoned power broker.

"I won't waste your time with a dog-and-pony show. Divorce is tough on all aspects of your life—I've been through two myself. The bottom line is I'm great at what I do, and I have the track record to prove it," Frank said.

Frank immediately described his fee schedule: $500 per hour with a $15,000 retainer. Although his no-nonsense communication jarred Natalie, she appreciated his honesty and candor.

"I read on your website you have experience with mediation, but it doesn't indicate whether you actually practice it," she said.

"My three partners and I practice 100 percent litigation. When a couple hits a roadblock—for instance, if they can't decide how to divide the home—I'll recommend they hire a mediator. So my mediation experience is on an as-needed basis," Frank said.

Frank described his comfort with the mediation process but added he wasn't a mediator himself.

"What are your strengths?" Natalie asked.

"As far as my lawyering style is concerned, I characterize myself as a bulldog rather than an attack dog: When a client wants something, I stand my ground, and I do my best to resolve things outside of court through the negotiation process," he said.

Natalie continued through her list of questions.

After their meeting, Natalie was convinced Frank was a top family law attorney and would advocate aggressively on her behalf. He would have been exactly the type of lawyer Jen would have wanted in her breakup. At the same time, she noticed Frank hadn't asked about or described the role of Natalie's children in her divorce. While she appreciated his overall objective perspective and straightforward communication style, it seemed too dispassionate and lacked empathy.

"Does he have the interest and patience to help me understand the challenges my kids and I will face throughout the divorce and my future?" she asked herself.

NATALIE'S SECOND APPOINTMENT

Lewis was in his mid-forties and practiced with twelve partners in his family law firm. Although the number of partners exceeded her ten-partner cap, his superb credentials motivated her to make an exception to her rule.

"What is your experience with ADR?" Natalie asked during their introductory consultation.

"I'm impressed. Most people who walk into this door have never heard of ADR," Lewis said. "For me, mediation is the only way to go. In fact, my litigation career only lasted a couple of years—once I learned about ADR, I embraced it 100 percent. About five years ago, I also trained in collaborative divorce. Do you know what this is?"

"Yes," Natalie said.

"Good. But just in case, allow me to explain the process," he said.

Although she knew his intention was to educate her, she didn't require rudimentary explanations. After all, she had spent hours researching her options and doing her divorce homework. Besides, she was already convinced ADR, in one form or another, was the approach she wanted to take. So she didn't need to be sold on it.

During what seemed like a lecture on ADR fundamentals, he covered points she had already learned on her own: the differences between standard mediation and collaborative divorce and how collaborative divorce uses a team. He also launched into the history of ADR: how it had roots tracing back centuries ago, when ancient civilizations attempted to resolve disputes with other nations, and how its use in the United States had steadily grown in recent decades.

Throughout his presentation, Natalie noticed he hadn't asked her many questions. In fact, she was convinced, had she walked out of the meeting, he would have carried on with his monologue sitting by himself.

This rankled her nerves because it reminded her of how Jim would sometimes explain matters she was unfamiliar with as if she were a child. Rather than spend most of their time together discussing the ADR process, she would have preferred Lewis had addressed her questions and concerns about her particular case.

Once Lewis had finished his description, which took about half an hour, Natalie asked him the questions that appeared on her iPad's screen.

Toward the end of their appointment, Lewis finally asked her a few questions about her case. Most of his inquiries focused on the assets she and Jim had, when they acquired them, and where they were invested. Natalie was able to respond but only in broad strokes because she had not yet collected all the financial information she needed.

NATALIE'S THIRD APPOINTMENT

Kathleen was in her sixties, which meant she was the oldest attorney among the three on Natalie's list. They sat together in Kathleen's conference room. Natalie expressed interest in ADR, and Kathleen shared about her experience.

"I entered family law over thirty years ago. At that time, attorneys basically had one divorce option: litigation. But after years of going to court, I saw how it was emotionally draining for my clients and me, and I grew tired of the fighting," she said.

Kathleen described how, starting twenty years ago, she was looking for better ways to help her clients. She researched ADR and believed its strengths addressed litigation's weaknesses, so she began training in it. As she took on more mediation cases, she saw how it improved her clients' divorce outcomes and allowed them to avoid the stress and expense of appearing in front of a judge.

She eventually concentrated her practice on mediation and was proud of the reputation she earned helping divorcing couples who sought to avoid litigation. While she represented clients using the traditional approach occasionally, it comprised a small percentage of her overall practice. In the rare instances when the traditional approach or mediation failed, she referred her clients to an attorney in her practice who specialized in litigation.

Kathleen's belief in mediation eventually led her to collaborative divorce. She appreciated how it was comprehensive and addressed the shortcomings she encountered in mediated cases. Ten years ago, she became trained in collaborative divorce and began taking on collaborative divorce cases.

"Are you familiar with collaborative divorce? If so, are you leaning toward traditional mediation or collaborative?" asked Kathleen.

"The more I learn about collaborative, the more it appeals to me," said Natalie.

"Do you have any children?" Kathleen asked.

"I have three; the youngest is in high school," Natalie said.

"Surprisingly, divorce can be as tough on older kids as it is on younger ones—I'd say even tougher sometimes. When couples agree to ADR—and go the collaborative route, in particular—I've seen how it often decreases the divorce's impact on the kids," she said.

"The mental health component is one of the reasons collaborative appealed to me," said Natalie.

"Speaking of mental health professionals, are you or the kids seeing a therapist currently regarding the divorce?" asked Kathleen.

"No, none of us is right now," said Natalie. She still held on to hopes for reconciliation, which made hiring a therapist both premature and a declaration her marriage was over. At the same time, if divorce were inevitable, its effect on Ben, Ryann, and Rachel weighed heavily on her. Thus she appreciated Kathleen's consideration of her children. While children were often an afterthought in divorce, Natalie wanted to make sure her decisions had their best interest at heart.

"If you need a therapist referral, I'd be happy to provide one. Also, regardless of the divorce route you take, I recommend you consider including a parenting plan," said Kathleen.

"My friend Jen told me she wished she had had one of those after her breakup," Natalie said.

Kathleen explained that parenting plans were one of collaborative divorce's strengths. She added they were optional in mediation and the traditional approach as well. In Natalie's case, the parenting plan would focus on Rachel because she was the only minor involved in the divorce, but the parenting plan would also be a guide for how best to deal with all her children.

Kathleen asked Natalie about the couple's income and major assets, such as their home. Natalie provided details to the best of her knowledge. Overall, however, Natalie acknowledged she knew very little about her financial state. She also noted that Jim took care of their financial matters.

After hearing this information, Kathleen knew the couple would most likely have to address several complicated financial issues. As a result, she suggested Natalie consider working with a financial adviser whose background included helping divorcing men and women. Kathleen had a referral source if Natalie needed one.

If the couple opted for a collaborative divorce, Kathleen recommended that a neutral financial professional be part of the team itself. She also suggested Natalie consider hiring her own financial adviser to explain the various financial matters to her and to give her guidance the neutral adviser could not.

"If we go the collaborative route and include a financial adviser on our team, how is he or she compensated?" Natalie asked.

"When it comes to collaborative divorce, financial advisers typically have their own independent collaborative agreements. Or in some cases, the financial adviser's compensation is part of an agreement that covers the entire collaborative team. One thing to keep in mind is if a financial adviser is part of a collaborative team, he or she cannot provide guidance post-divorce nor can the adviser provide financial products to either participant—this rule is embedded within the collaborative agreement in order to avoid conflicts of interest," Kathleen said.

"Since we're discussing fees, can you help me understand how attorney fees work in mediation or collaborative?" asked Natalie.

"Every case is different, so providing an accurate estimate is impossible. If you're mediating and it's non-contentious, my fees as an outside counsel may be less than $25,000 and my retainer is $7,500. This lower cost is largely because I'm playing a supportive role by acting as a legal adviser and am not directly involved in the mediations themselves. The price will increase significantly if the divorce is highly contentious because it will require much more time on my part. If you go the collaborative route, your cost may include a financial adviser and a mental health professional. So the overall cost is not that much different from the other approaches. Based on what you've told me, I would expect legal costs for a collaborative divorce in your case to be below $50,000. However, if you and your husband agree to use mediation, then your cost may be only about $15,000 to $25,000," said Kathleen.

Prior to researching divorce costs, Natalie would have been shocked to hear legal fees of $25,000 being in the lower cost category. And given what she knew now, the $15,000 figure was a downright bargain.

"So considering what I've shared about my case, what type of divorce would you recommend, mediation or collaborative divorce?" Natalie asked.

Based on Kathleen's preliminary assessment, she thought the couple should consider collaborative divorce for the following reasons:

- Natalie indicated she and Jim wanted to work together.

- Because they did not appear to have any volatile issues, they should be able to avoid litigation and instead use ADR, which would save them time and money.

- Collaborative divorce would be able to address the potential imbalance between Natalie's and Jim's experiences in dealing with financial matters.

- They both cared deeply for their kids.

Kathleen explained the perceived cost of hiring a team of experts sometimes turned divorcing husbands and wives off of collaborative divorce. The assumption that collaborative divorce was an expensive approach was a misconception she frequently had to dispel.

Kathleen then described that in the event one spouse preferred mediation while the other wanted collaborative divorce and they couldn't agree on one method, a **hybrid divorce** might be the best alternative.

She explained that in Natalie's case, this strategy could combine mediation with certain aspects of collaborative divorce. For instance, one spouse could hire his or her own team of experts to work on his or her behalf. This team might include a lawyer and financial adviser that prepared their client for the mediations but would most likely not attend them. Meanwhile, the other spouse, for various reasons, might forfeit forming any team at all, or his or her team might comprise only an attorney.

If Jim accepted mediation but rejected collaborative divorce, Natalie was relieved to know Kathleen could act as her attorney. Given how Jim handled the couple's finances, she was far less knowledgeable than he was, so she knew she needed the support of a financial expert.

After she wrapped up her meeting with Kathleen, Natalie returned home and updated her spreadsheet, which included the following information:

Name	Billable Hour	Retainer	PRACTICE RATIO: Traditional Approach (TA) Mediation (M) Collaboration (C)
Frank	$500	$15,000	100% TA
Lewis	$350	$5,000	80% M, 20% C
Kathleen	$400	$7,500	50% M, 40% C, 10% TA

Each attorney had his or her own strengths. Overall, Natalie felt most confident about Kathleen's ability to represent her interests for these reasons:

- ◘ Her fees were reasonable.

- ◘ She invested most of her time working with clients who sought to avoid litigation.

- ◘ Her mediation experience was extensive.

- ◘ She was concerned about the divorce's impact on Natalie's children.

- ◘ She was experienced working under the collaborative team approach.

- ◘ If Natalie went the hybrid route, Kathleen would be an important part of her team.

In the event divorce was inevitable and Jim agreed to collaboration or mediation, Natalie believed her lawyer search had ended. But she was still far from declaring her marriage over.

CHAPTER 8

MOMENT OF WEAKNESS

After committing hours to divorce research, Natalie was relieved she had shed light on a process that had been both unfamiliar and scary. Filled with new knowledge, she experienced peace of mind. Her heart, on the other hand, felt no such comfort. She imagined herself teetering on a wall—on one side was divorce, and on the other was reconciliation. She had no certainty on which side she would fall.

Natalie scrolled through the extensive divorce notes she had taken on her iPad. She sat in her bedroom and reflected on the month that had passed since Jim had moved out. She missed him deeply and longed to have him by her side. She still believed his divorce intentions were a phase—a bump on the marriage road common to many couples who commit "till death do us part." Maybe it was a midlife crisis. If so, she wondered if the red convertible was next. She anticipated the moment he would snap out of it.

A text message from Jim appeared on her tablet's screen:

> Can we meet this week after work? I'd like to run some financial information by you.

As she read his words, she could feel her heartbeat. Was this a conciliatory gesture, the one she had been waiting for, or did he really just want to talk finances?

"How's Fri?" she nervously typed.

"I'll grab a quick bite to eat and b there at 6:00 if that works," he replied.

On Friday afternoon, Natalie set out a bottle of wine and a simple cheese plate. She changed from her work clothes into a casual yet chic dress signaling she had made a modest effort but nothing that would appear intentional.

At 6:00 p.m., she sat at the kitchen counter and began checking emails on her smartphone. She heard the garage door open. Jim entered the kitchen. His loosened tie rested on an unbuttoned shirt that exposed the top of his chest. A messenger bag hung on his shoulder. Natalie wanted to wrap her arms around him but showed restraint instead.

"Was traffic okay?" she asked.

"Not bad for a Friday," he said.

"I've opened a bottle of wine. Interested?" she asked.

"Sure. But first . . . I hate to ask. Do you have anything to eat? I was rushing out of the office and couldn't stop to grab a bite," he said.

Jim frequently skipped meals when he was stressed and busy—a habit that typically annoyed her. At the moment, however, she relished the opportunity to feed her husband.

"I have some leftovers from dinner last night. I made Rachel's favorite," she said.

"Taco salad?" he asked.

Natalie smiled. She walked to the refrigerator and took out a series of glass containers and prepared a plate of the dinner-time staple. He sat at the kitchen counter, pulled out his laptop, and opened spreadsheets and documents he had prepared prior to moving out. On his screen was a list he wanted to review with his wife:

- What are Natalie's financial needs right now?
- How should we go about covering expenses?
- Are there ways we can save money?
- Next steps regarding our divorce: Discuss mediation and why I think it's the best approach.
- Share the division of assets plan/spreadsheet I created.

Natalie handed Jim the taco salad. After weeks of eating out and foraging in his poorly stocked kitchen, his wife's homemade meal was welcome comfort. Meanwhile, Natalie was thrilled to spend an evening alone with her husband. Although she felt resentment and anger regarding his poorly timed holiday divorce announcement, she was prepared to put the past behind her and work on their marriage.

"Where's Rachel tonight?" he asked.

"Rachel's volunteering at the parish fundraising car wash tomorrow morning, so she's sleeping over at Megan's house—they'll drive to the event together in the morning," Natalie said.

With each sip of wine, the couple's conversation grew lighter and friendlier. They eventually made their way to the great room couch. Meanwhile, Jim's laptop remained on the kitchen counter. It had gone to sleep long ago and, with it, the financial talking points on its screen.

Throughout their relationship, Natalie nearly always waited for Jim to initiate sexual intimacy. But that was before Jim expressed his divorce intentions and moved out. As the evening progressed,

Natalie felt increased pressure to prove their marriage still had a chance. She craned her neck toward him and gave him a kiss.

"What are you doing?" Jim asked.

"Just feeling a little playful," she said.

"Oh, I see," he said aloud and then to himself, "Don't indulge in this. You're divorcing her." But as he gazed at how her light dress outlined her beautifully shaped breasts, he thought about how Rachel was gone for the night. With another glass of wine in his system, his resistance softened, and his desire increased. They walked upstairs to their master bedroom.

Natalie placed her head on Jim's strong chest. She could hear his heartbeat. Her arm rested across his broad and lean torso. Tonight's love making was an undeniable sign of their affection for one another. At the moment, her hopes had reached their peak since his divorce declaration last December. She looked up at him.

"I still love you. Can we work on rebuilding our marriage?" she asked.

Jim slowly sat up. Natalie separated her body from his. He was sitting at the side of their bed, and he stared at his feet that were firmly planted on the floor. "Natalie, I love our family, the kids, and I love you. But . . .," he said.

"But?" she asked.

"I'm not *in love* with you," he answered, staring downward.

Although this was the first time she had heard him say he wasn't in love with her, she could tell he had reached this conclusion long ago. Tears welled in her eyes.

Jim broke the silence between them. "I've got this taken care of," he said. "I've spent hours figuring everything out. I've made spreadsheets calculating our assets and debts. They're on my laptop downstairs, and I was going to show them to you tonight. I've already decided mediation is the way to do this as quickly and painlessly as possible. Don't worry. It'll be easy. I promise."

"Oh, you've got this all taken care of, do you? You've even decided we should mediate rather than litigate. How cavalier. . . . Should I be thanking you? What if I want to go straight in front of a judge and tell *her* what a jackass you've been?" Natalie asked as she wiped the tears from her cheek.

Natalie's sharp and forceful response surprised Jim. At that moment, he realized Natalie might know a lot more about the divorce process than he had suspected.

"I'm so stupid. How could I have thought it was a good idea to have sex with you tonight?" Natalie asked.

"Natalie, why don't you take a moment to calm down? Let's talk this through," he said.

She stood up from the bed and covered herself with her robe.

"Get out!" she said.

"I know you're really upset now—"

"*Get out!*" she repeated even louder this time.

Jim quickly dressed. He scurried downstairs to the kitchen. His laptop was open, the agenda items still asleep inside. He grabbed his belongings and left.

Natalie returned to her bed, clutched her pillow, and sobbed. For the rest of the night, she thought about what she could have done differently during the past months and years. She didn't want to believe it was over, but his words, "I'm not in love with you," pointed to the inevitability of their divorce. As much as she felt Jim's decision was beyond her control, she found comfort in the time she'd spent researching divorce.

When Natalie woke up, she grabbed her phone. Its screen read 10:00 a.m. The last time she had slept that late was before her kids were born. She called her mom.

"Can I come over?" Natalie asked. Her voice quivered as tears welled in her eyes.

"What's the matter, sweetie? Of course, we're here all day," her mom said.

Once Natalie arrived at her childhood home, her mom and dad greeted her at the door. Seeing their faces provided immediate relief, and she fell into her father's arms. The three made their way to the kitchen, and Natalie described the previous night's conversation.

"I know you both disapprove of divorce. I promise, I did my best to make it work. But Jim made it absolutely clear that it's over," Natalie said.

"You know we're here for you. What do you need from us?" her father asked.

She described her divorce research and how she had narrowed her search to Kathleen. Although she had acted as if she weren't interested in mediation during her argument with Jim, Natalie was relieved Jim had disclosed his mediation preference. This further validated her decision to hire Kathleen. One question still remained unanswered, however: Would Jim consider a collaborative divorce?

Natalie told her parents about Kathleen's retainer requirement. The amount came as no surprise to Natalie's father—a retired project manager used to developing budgets and reviewing lawyer fees.

"We'll write you a check before you leave. Don't worry about paying us back," her father said.

"Thank you. I don't want Jim to know I'm hiring a lawyer right now—so I can't express how much your help means to me," Natalie said.

After visiting her parents, Natalie picked up Rachel from the church car wash. The two saw a movie together in the evening and attended mass the next day. Throughout the service, Natalie prayed for Jim to realize the mistake he was making. At the same time, she realized she needed to take charge of her divorce.

CHAPTER 9

FINDING A FINANCIAL ADVISER

Natalie contacted Kathleen's office the following Monday morning and spoke with Kelli, her paralegal.

"I'd like to start working with Kathleen right away," said Natalie.

Kathleen was in court all day, but Kelli was familiar with Natalie's case because her boss had reviewed it with her after the two had had their introductory meeting. Kelli suggested Natalie sign the retainer agreement and submit a $7,500 check. Then Kelli would schedule an appointment for Natalie and Kathleen to meet.

After school let out that afternoon, Natalie rushed to Kathleen's office with her check. Once there, Kelli informed her Kathleen recommended she make an appointment with Patrick Skinner, a financial adviser trained in mediation.

"He has a stellar track record. Although you're under no obligation to work with him, if you do decide to, he'll be your financial go-to person throughout the divorce process. Kathleen and

Patrick will also work closely together. They make an amazing team," Kelli said.

Kelli added that if Natalie planned to work with any financial adviser, Kathleen recommended Natalie meet with that person *before* her next appointment with Kathleen. The adviser's initial assessment would help Kathleen develop her strategy.

"Isn't meeting with a financial adviser right now premature considering Jim hasn't agreed to go the collaborative route yet?" Natalie asked.

"No. Regardless of how you divorce, you'll benefit from having a firm grasp of what's at stake financially. At the same time, you and Jim should start figuring out which divorce approach you'll take," Kelli said.

That night, Natalie sat at her computer checking emails. She received a message from Jim:

> I know this is difficult for you, and I'm sorry it has to end this way.
>
> I really do care about you and the kids and don't want you to worry about your future. I know we'll all be just fine.
>
> Attached is a spreadsheet I made listing all our property. I think the simplest approach is we just divide it equally, which I've already done. I also made a note about providing for you and the kids. I don't want my relationship with the kids to change and do want to continue being with them as often as possible.
>
> Please look this over, and we can discuss whenever you'd like. I think it's fairly straightforward, and that's why I don't think we need to complicate the matter with a bunch of dueling lawyers running their billing meters. Let's keep it simple and get through this as best we can.
>
> Jim

Natalie read the message, opened the attachment, and took a quick glance. It included a division of their property and monthly spousal and child support. Seeing this detailed information stunned and upset her.

"We haven't even begun the process, and he's already figured out how this will end. If he thinks I'm going to blindly accept his division of the property, he's in for a big surprise," Natalie told herself.

She didn't bother sending a reply.

NATALIE RESEARCHES FINANCIAL ADVISERS

That evening, Natalie researched Patrick Skinner. She found his website and LinkedIn profile. Patrick had twenty-five years of experience as a financial adviser. He was a CFP (Certified Financial Planner) professional and a CPWA (Certified Private Wealth Advisor) designee. In addition, she saw that he regularly spoke at women's conferences on the issue of divorce and surviving its aftermath. She then wanted to find out more about his certifications.

Natalie learned the CFP certification meant Patrick had successfully completed the CFP Board's requirements: He had taken coursework, had passed exams, had career experience serving clients, and had upheld the board's ethical conduct standards. She read that being a CFP meant Patrick upheld the fiduciary standard, which is a professional pledge financial advisers take to act in the utmost good faith and in a manner that places their client's interest ahead of their own.

Next, she found out the CPWA certificate was developed by IMCA (Investment Management Consultants Association) with the University of Chicago Booth School of Business. Financial advisers who hold a CPWA certificate have enrolled in a yearlong course concluding with a week at the Booth School of Business and passing a daylong exam. The program's focus is on meeting the needs of high net-worth individuals.

CFP and CPWA titles require certificate holders to uphold the standards established by the CFP Board and IMCA, respectively. Also, members of both organizations must complete continuing education in order to maintain certification.

On the CFP Board's website, www.cfp.net, Natalie was able to enter Patrick's name into the organization's database and research his background. She verified his employment, active CFP certification status, CFP Board disciplinary records, and bankruptcy disclosure. His record was free and clear of any red flags.

In addition, FINRA (Financial Industry Regulatory Authority), a major independent regulator within the financial services industry, had Broker Check at www.finra.org. This feature provided financial adviser background information. Here too, Natalie entered Patrick's name into the database and reviewed his employment history, securities exams he had passed, disclosures regarding disciplinary action or customer disputes, and the outcomes of any investigations. Again, his record was clean.

On Patrick's website, he described the following qualifications:

- Trained in ADR and collaborative divorce
- Participated as an expert witness in divorce court
- Member of mediation and financial industry boards and professional associations (www.fpanet.org)

Natalie's research provided her peace of mind regarding Patrick's ability to give her expert guidance. In addition, she believed Patrick was trained to address the long-term financial impact of her divorce. After work the next day, Natalie contacted Patrick's office.

"Kathleen let us know you might be calling. We're glad to hear from you," said Sandy, Patrick's administrative assistant.

Her warm greeting put Natalie at ease. She scheduled a meeting with Patrick for the following Tuesday afternoon.

"Is there a fee for the first meeting?" Natalie asked.

"The initial consultation will take about an hour, and it's complimentary," Sandy said.

"My husband sent me a spreadsheet regarding our assets, I think. To be frank, I haven't even looked at it. Should I send this to Patrick?" Natalie asked.

"Hold onto it for now. When you meet Patrick, he'll tell you what he needs," Sandy said.

NATALIE EMAILS JIM

Next, Natalie knew that in order for her team to develop their strategy, she and Jim needed to start discussing the divorce approach they'd take. After their last conversation, however, she was in no mood to speak with him, which tempted her to procrastinate. But she realized it was in her best interest to take care of the matter as quickly as possible, so she decided to reply to his email.

> Thanks for the spreadsheet. I'll take a look at it soon. Next, I remember you brought up mediation. I did my homework, and I like what I've learned about it.
>
> Have you heard of collaborative divorce? It's another alternative to litigation. Here's a link to a great site, www.CollaborativePractice.com.
>
> In addition to its many benefits, I like how it's an inclusive process that will address Ben's, Rachel's, and Ryann's needs more than just mediation would.
>
> Let me know what you think.
>
> Natalie

Jim read the email. He was wrought with guilt after their last encounter and worried when Natalie didn't respond right away to his last email. He was relieved to hear from her and interpreted her reply as an acceptance of his overall plan—a wishful assessment he would soon learn couldn't have been farther from reality.

NATALIE MEETS WITH PATRICK

Monday afternoon, Natalie arrived at Patrick's office, which was located in a downtown high-rise. She approached his suite and saw big, clear glass doors in front of his office. They signaled transparency, which contrasted with her view that financial matters were shrouded in secrecy.

When Natalie entered, Sandy warmly greeted her and offered her a bottle of water. Moments later, the financial adviser entered the waiting area and introduced himself. She also met Patrick's associate planner, Cullen, who would be writing down notes during the meeting. This would allow Patrick to focus on their conversation. The three walked to Patrick's office.

The financial adviser invited her to take a seat on the sofa. Above it was a framed photo of the Lincoln Memorial. He noticed Natalie looking at it.

"Honest Abe," Patrick said. "He's my inspiration. Aren't we lucky we can visit the real thing anytime we want?"

"I remember taking school field trips to the National Mall as a kid," said Natalie.

The cozy setting of Patrick's office was the opposite of what she had expected. She had imagined they would meet in a big, sterile conference room.

"Divorce is *never* easy. How are you feeling overall?" Patrick asked.

"Nervous and sad. I never thought my marriage would reach this point. To be honest, I dreaded this meeting because financial matters have always scared me. My husband handled all the money and did his own investing. He was confident he could perform the necessary research to make his own decisions. As far as I know, he's done a good job. But in all honesty, I've never really paid much attention. I was fine being in the dark for all these years. But not anymore," she said.

"I guarantee after this meeting you'll feel less anxiety than you felt when you arrived. So let's begin, shall we? What are your biggest concerns moving forward with your divorce?" he asked.

Natalie described her worry for her kids and her trepidation of being left with minimal savings. She also feared she would have to work forever.

"I've seen Wal-Mart greeters, some in their seventies. Is that my future?" she asked.

"My job is to help you understand how your divorce will affect your long-term financial well-being. Rest assured, we'll work together to make sure you won't be a bag lady, and I'm confident we can develop a solution that will allow you and your family to be financially secure," he said.

Tears trickled down Natalie's cheeks after she heard his encouraging and hopeful words. Patrick passed her a box of Kleenex he always kept conveniently close by—tearful expressions of sadness or joy were frequent occurrences in his office. He managed his clients' entire financial lives, which included marriages, births of children and grandchildren, divorces, deaths, and other significant events. Patrick joked how often his clients cried when they met him.

"I researched your credentials, and I learned so much about different financial advising certifications. Are there any others that are important?" she asked.

Patrick shared he was also a Certified Divorce Financial Analyst (CDFA). But earning CFP and CPWA certifications required much more coursework and challenging exams, as well as significant continuing education requirements. He added that other professionals, such as CPAs, had training in ADR and, in some cases, collaborative divorce too.

"At the same time, most financial advisers, even the ones with industry certifications in widely recognized financial services, don't know about divorce laws and related issues. It's just not part of their basic training. That's where divorce expertise is really important, in particular, local knowledge, since divorce rules vary from state to state. You want to find a financial adviser who focuses his practice in the state in which your divorce is taking place. Some financial advisers, like me, serve multiple areas because we're within miles of neighboring states. In my case, I work with clients in Virginia, Washington, DC, and Maryland. But this scenario is *not* the case for most," Patrick said.

The two then had a discussion regarding the events leading up to the divorce, which included details about her relationship with Jim, as well as how they spent and saved money.

ESSENTIAL DIVORCE QUESTIONS

"I'll start this part of the meeting by providing you two questions to ask yourself," Patrick said.

1. How much financial and emotional currency am I willing to spend?

2. Will the settlement allow me—both with my children and independent of them—to be financially secure now and in the future?

He continued, "I don't expect you to answer these now. But as we progress through the divorce process, I recommend you regularly reflect on the essential divorce questions in order to gauge how you're feeling. Also, the questions will help you determine if resolving a particular impasse with Jim is worth the cost and how addressing it will impact your long-term financial well-being. If we keep the essential divorce questions in our minds over the days, weeks, and months ahead, I've found they can ease the decision-making process," he said.

Patrick knew money and emotions were intertwined, and he sought to have a solid understanding of how Natalie and Jim had addressed financial decisions throughout their marriage and what money meant to each of them. Patrick would use this information to help determine possible financial opportunities and pitfalls Natalie might encounter. He would also collect financial information from Natalie in order to figure out the **assets** and **liabilities** they had as a family. From there, he would then begin to identify **marital** and **non-marital assets**.

"Let's begin by reviewing the broad categories of financial issues we'll need to address," said Patrick.

He started with an explanation of assets and liabilities. He explained assets are items accumulated during a person's lifetime that have an identifiable value. Several different types of assets exist:

- **Real property**, which includes real estate

- **Personal property**, which includes cars, boats, airplanes, collectibles, jewelry, furniture, and clothing

- **Paper assets**, which includes investment accounts, retirement plans, and insurance

Liabilities are usually debts associated with a particular asset. They are either **secured** or **unsecured**. Secured liabilities include home mortgages and loans on cars. Unsecured liabilities include credit cards and lines of credit.

Both assets and liabilities can be classified as marital or non-marital (non-marital is also called separate property).

"One of the issues we have to take care of is to properly identify the types of assets and liabilities you have in order to correctly divide them when that time comes," Patrick said.

"I had no idea assets and liabilities have so many subcategories. Next, you mentioned **non-marital** and **marital assets**. Can you tell me more about those?" Natalie asked.

Patrick described non-marital assets (separate property) as those acquired prior to the marriage or received by inheritance, gift, or bequest from someone other than the spouse. Meanwhile, marital assets are all other assets acquired during the marriage.

In states such as Virginia, non-marital assets also include assets accumulated post-date of separation. Other states, such as Maryland, define the non-marital assets as ones acquired prior to marriage and after the actual date of divorce.

For every rule, an exception invariably arises. Laws regarding marital and non-marital assets vary from state to state. Thus one should always consult with a family law attorney in one's local jurisdiction.

Because Virginia uses the dates of marriage and separation to determine marital assets, these dates might have a significant impact on valuing Natalie's assets. Examples include contributory accounts, such as a 401(k), or systematic savings accounts.

Patrick pointed to an issue that might come up in Natalie's case. After separation, one spouse might spend down the marital assets and retain post-separation non-marital assets. He or she might use marital assets to cover ongoing expenses, such as the mortgage and other recurring living expenses. By doing so, this spouse is able to save his or her earned income. And the longer the separation period, the more likely divorcing spouses will *accumulate* additional separate assets and *reduce* marital assets.

"How do we divide the assets?" Natalie asked.

"That's the million-dollar question," said Patrick.

He provided the following general steps:

1. Identify assets and liabilities.

2. Figure out which assets and liabilities are marital and non-marital (separate property).

3. Determine the values of assets and liabilities in a way that is reasonable under the current circumstances.

4. Determine how to divide all marital assets.

5. Draft the property settlement agreement (PSA), which documents the division of marital property.

Patrick then asked Natalie a series of basic questions in order to assess her current circumstances. Cullen noted her answers:

◻ **Who's paying the bills?**
Jim is—she hasn't experienced any problems so far with this arrangement.

◻ **What are your biggest concerns?**
If she has to move, where is she going to live? And what will her family's environment look like? For example, she is concerned about a new neighborhood, nearby public schools, and her proximity to extended family members.

◻ **Are you familiar with your income tax returns?**
Since marriage, she signed off on tax returns without reviewing them. As a result, she doesn't know much about their taxes.

◻ **Did you keep track of your savings and investments?**
No. Jim always reviewed bank and other financial statements. Meanwhile, with the exception of her quarterly investment statement she held in her own name, she didn't.

◻ **Do you know what the balance is on your home mortgage and what the monthly payments are and your interest rate?**
She doesn't know about their mortgage balance, and she asked Patrick where she could find this along with the monthly payment and interest rate.

◻ **Did you and Jim ever talk about retirement or about his company benefits?**
She admitted she is pretty clueless when it comes to their finances. Jim took charge of nearly everything related to money, and she never questioned what he did.

Patrick then explained his role in the divorce process. He would put together an outline based on Natalie's financial information and other relevant data. He and Kathleen would work as a team and develop a cohesive strategy: Kathleen would provide legal counsel, and he would offer financial recommendations through-out the divorce process.

"Before our next meeting, here's what I'll need from you," Patrick said and handed her the following:

DIVORCE PLANNING CHECKLIST

Please bring copies of contracts, insurance policies, and any brochures or literature pertaining to retirement plans and benefit programs. I'll also need all account statements from the date of separation to the most recent, as well as information on additions and withdrawals from any investment accounts. If you acquired assets prior to marriage, please provide statements of those accounts around your marriage date.

◘ **Family Information:** date of birth, Social Security numbers, marital status, and addresses of family members (including children).

◘ **Professional Information:** Attorney, CPA, stockbroker, and insurance agent contact information including names, physical and electronic addresses, and phone numbers.

◘ **Benefit Plans:** Group and personally owned insurance, including life, health, disability, liability, and long-term care insurance. Also, identify beneficiaries of each.

◘ **Retirement Plans:** 401(k)s, IRAs, pensions, and deferred compensation plans, along with their most recent statements. Also, identify beneficiaries of each.

◘ **Non-qualified Investments:** Individual, joint, or trust-held investments with most recent statements including stock options.

- **Bank Accounts:** Statements of all accounts and the safe deposit box location, if applicable.

- **Income Tax Returns:** Last year's complete federal and state returns, including copies of W-2s.

- **List of All Liabilities:** Present debt, payments, and interest rates charged.

- **List of All Annual Expenditures:** Food, clothing, utilities, medical, education, loan repayment, insurance premiums, entertainment, vacation, charity, retirement plans (such as pension, Keogh, and IRA), auto payments (such as repairs and operation), savings and investments, support of others, and any other miscellaneous costs. We will provide a separate expense statement that attorneys will use once we obtain the information about your living expenses.

- **List of All Assets:** Include how they are owned (for example joint, individually, or in a trust), current market value, when they were acquired, cost basis, and income generated.

- **Marital Residence:** HUD-1 settlement documents from time of purchase and any refinance documents, current mortgage statement, and a copy of the homeowners' policy. Identify source of down payment. If a second home is owned, provide the same information.

- **Investment Real Estate:** Acquisition data, ownership interest, and income and expense statement.

- **Business Interest:** Ownership structure, assets and liabilities, agreements, profit and loss statement (P & L) for past two years, and current balance sheet.

◻ **Latest Pay Stubs:** Gross pay and deductions for taxes and benefits.

◻ **Estate Documents:** Current wills, trusts, and any other relevant documents.

◻ **Dates:** Marriage and separation.

Natalie's eyes grew big as she briefly scanned each item on the long list.

Patrick then went through the checklist with her. He explained that once she compiled as much information as possible, he would identify what additional data was needed.

Natalie had no idea how she'd get her hands on the mountain of paperwork Patrick needed. And the fact she was charged to do so concerned her, especially considering she didn't even recognize many of the terms and abbreviations, such as HUD-1 and P & L.

"How long do you think compiling this information will take me?" she asked.

"I know it may seem daunting. But rest assured, I'll help you organize this information, understand the financial issues, and figure out how best to work with the assets you'll keep. In the end, you may not be able to locate every single item, or the items may not be relevant to your situation. That's okay. Just do your best and call my office anytime a question comes up," Patrick said.

"Jim emailed me a spreadsheet he prepared that lists our property. He said he just wanted to divide it equally. I haven't really looked it over carefully. Should I email it to you? I can do it right now," said Natalie.

"Yes, that would be a good starting place and a guide for you to locate associated statements and documents we'll need later on," Patrick said.

Natalie took out her phone and searched for Jim's email. She forwarded Patrick the spreadsheet attachment.

"Do you know where Jim keeps your financial data in the house?" asked Patrick

"Yes, he has an office area in our sitting room where he pays the bills. There are several file drawers with old tax returns and other important papers. He left it all behind after he moved out. Do you think I should go through them?" said Natalie.

"Absolutely! Get as much of the recent data you can and make copies of any financial statements and last year's tax return," Patrick said.

"I'll try. But I've never looked in the files before. I guess it's about time I did," said Natalie.

Patrick then explained his fee structure. He required a $3,000 retainer. Similar to how Kathleen worked, he would provide a monthly statement. If the retainer dropped below $500, a request for additional funds would be sent.

"Are there any other questions you have?" Patrick asked.

"If I have to go through a divorce, I would really prefer the collaborative process, but I'm not sure if Jim will agree to it. Do I have to tell Jim I'm working with you and Kathleen yet?" she asked.

"At this stage, I don't think it's necessary. In fact, by telling him too early, he may hesitate to help you compile the items on the checklist, and from what I gather, you may need his help. As long as Jim doesn't feel threatened, I think he'll cooperate. You want to do your best to make sure *he thinks* he's in control and that you're going along with his plans. Of course, run your question by Kathleen too because she may have different advice, although I'm pretty sure she and I are on the same page about this," Patrick said.

PATRICK'S PAINFUL INQUIRY

"Now I have a question for you," Patrick said. "Going through the divorce process is very emotional. There are many twists and turns, and you'll have to answer many tough questions. I need to ask you one of these tough questions now. Are you aware of a third party that may have a role in your divorce?" he asked.

When Natalie heard "third party," she thought of Patrick, Kathleen, and Jen. "I'm not sure what you mean," she said.

"Are you aware of Jim having a relationship that may be a catalyst in the divorce?"

Tears welled up in her eyes again—but this time, they weren't a result of feeling relived or comforted. "I've actually thought he might be having an affair. It seems as if everyone else thinks so! I even asked him directly, and he said no. So I thought the divorce was part of some mid-life crisis he'd snap out of any second. Why do you ask? Will an affair change the divorce process?" she asked.

Patrick explained in divorce, adultery is all too often the reason behind it. Despite the emotional harm infidelity does to the family and the spouse who's been cheated on, judges typically rely on the financial facts when they evaluate a case. In other words, infidelity may not necessarily influence the divorce settlement. In Virginia, however, it may have an impact on potential support issues if the **dependent spouse**—in other words, the one receiving the benefits—is the person having the affair. This may be the court's attempt to avoid rewarding bad behavior. As far as other states are concerned, each has its own rules regarding support.

"But I'm no lawyer. Kathleen is your best source when it comes to answering your adultery question. I only brought it up to protect you from a financial perspective. I've worked with many clients who, upon going through the checklist and collecting financial data, found their spouses were using marital assets to fund their affairs—finding out that way is definitely not ideal. Many times, I've had to be the bearer of bad news after reviewing the financial data and uncovering unusual account activity," he said.

"This is all so shocking to hear. Maybe an affair explains why he rejected my suggestion we go to marriage counseling," she said.

"I certainly don't want to plant an idea that doesn't exist. I just want you to be aware of the possibility and how it may impact your decisions as we go through the ups and downs of the divorce process," Patrick said.

With Patrick being the third person to ask her about infidelity, Natalie questioned if Jim had told her the truth. "If I don't trust him, how can I possibly prove it?" she asked.

"If you can believe it, I've actually had clients hire private investigators," Patrick said.

Although the thought of hiring a PI made Natalie's stomach sink, actually receiving hard evidence confirming her fears made her want to throw up.

"Do I need to do this?" she asked.

Patrick said he didn't think it was necessary at this point. Infidelity was often revealed during the early stages of the mediation or divorce process.

Having to wait that long to find out made Natalie feel even worse.

"Regardless of whether or not Jim cheated, my concern is your future financial well-being. Although adultery is an emotional nightmare, as far as your divorce agreement is concerned, its impact will be minimal. Here's my advice: Rather than think about something that may or may not have happened, focus right now on what's necessary to improve your understanding of your current financial situation—don't worry about external issues until they become known," he said.

He told Natalie an old saying:

A judge is more concerned about reviewing an accurate financial statement than seeing a picture of a husband leaving a hotel with another woman!

The silly saying lightened Natalie's mood, and she giggled after hearing it.

Patrick reassured her that he had her best interest in mind and they would work together to address whatever surprises came their way.

Natalie, Patrick, and Cullen concluded their meeting and scheduled their next appointment for the week following her appointment with Kathleen. In the interim, Patrick asked Natalie to send him as much of the data on the Divorce Planning Checklist as she could find. He would use this information to prepare Kathleen an initial summary before Natalie met with her. That way, Kathleen wouldn't rely solely upon what Jim had provided.

As Natalie drove home from her first meeting with Patrick, she felt confident the financial adviser was truly on her side and he would help her untangle the financial mess she found herself in. She now knew she would have to ask her dad for more money in order to cover Patrick's retainer. To her dismay, she also questioned whether Jim had told her the truth when she had asked about his infidelity.

Once Natalie arrived home, she phoned her dad and reviewed the financial discussion she had had with Patrick. To her surprise, her dad knew the financial adviser. They were both members of the local Rotary Club in Reston. He was relieved his daughter was receiving the help she needed from a trusted source and offered to cover Patrick's retainer.

After Natalie ended her call with her dad, she checked her email and saw a message from Jim:

> Thanks for the link. I'm familiar with collaborative, and I understand your point about its strengths. At the same time, I'm reluctant to hire so many professionals because doing so will incur unnecessary expenses—and we'll both benefit from saving as much money as possible! Plus, we both love our kids, and they're getting older so I don't foresee us going to battle over them.
>
> Mediation, I think, is the easiest and most cost-effective approach. Collaborative just seems like overkill. I'm open to talk about it more. But overall, I think mediation will take care of our needs just fine. In fact, I've started the

research already. Here is a list of mediators. I'll send you links to their websites in a separate email:

Megan Johnson

James Perkins

Courtney Fitzgerald

Frank Manning

In addition, attached are a few statements you asked about for the retirement plans and the investment accounts.

Jim

His message wasn't what Natalie wanted to hear. At the same time, she was overwhelmed with the information Patrick had shared during their meeting, and her distracted state softened the blow that came from Jim's resistance to collaborative divorce.

CHAPTER 10

NATALIE CONSULTS WITH KATHLEEN

After Natalie and Patrick's introductory meeting, he reviewed Jim's spreadsheet she had emailed him. Several days later, the financial adviser then sent Kathleen the following summary:

I met with Natalie. We had a good meeting, but I know she was overwhelmed with all the information we discussed. I sent her home with the Divorce Planning Checklist. Once I receive her information, I'll prepare an initial financial summary. I hope to have this completed in time for your next meeting with Natalie.

However, Natalie gave me a spreadsheet listing their assets and liabilities that her husband had prepared. Her husband also sent an email to Natalie with several attached statements for their retirement plans and investment accounts. She has forwarded them to me as well.

Upon a cursory review of the spreadsheet, it appears that he has listed all assets without identifying ownership and told her that he just wanted to divide everything equally. Not sure that will work in this case as there appears to be a number of items that will need to be offset depending upon who retains what. I've prepared a summary based upon the data from her husband's spreadsheet and the statements she provided to me.

Please note the division of property being shown is based upon Jim's comments and it's not what I'm recommending.

I wanted you to see what he proposed so we would know where we have to go as we move forward with changes that will be needed. After your meeting with Natalie, we can have a conversation about the marital and non-marital assets, and I'll prepare a new spreadsheet for your review.

Lastly, Natalie said her Schwab account was from an inheritance, and it was included in his list of their assets. She also indicated that she used some of her inherited money for the down payment on the residence. There may also be other assets yet to be uncovered as I think his company has several executive benefit plans not shown on his spreadsheet.

The bottom line is I think this will be a bit more complicated than her husband imagined it would be!

Patrick then provided the following strengths and weaknesses:

Strengths

- Natalie is motivated to educate herself and figure out the financial issues involved.

- She realizes the need to understand her finances so she can make good decisions.

- She's an intelligent person who, with proper guidance, should be able to quickly assimilate the financial information.

Weaknesses

- Natalie is uninformed about her family's overall finances.

- She has little knowledge of how monies have been spent.

- She does not understand investments or taxes.

Lastly, Patrick provided Kathleen his suggested next steps.

I believe Natalie will have a short list of questions to go over with you when you meet. These may be at the top of her list, and I've also added topics to possibly discuss with her:

1. Review the legal framework of the divorce process.

2. Discuss spousal and child support and how it is determined, along with possible terms of the support.

3. Husband's possible adultery involved, not yet proven.

4. Inquire about their residence. I suspect it may be a *hybrid property* because Natalie had mentioned something about using some of her inheritance for the down payment and to make improvements. I don't think she knows what a hybrid property is, so if

> it comes up during your meeting, please introduce the concept to her.
>
> 5. From reviewing the spreadsheet her husband pre-pared, it appears they should have sufficient assets to both be okay post-divorce. I do, however, have concerns about a number of his spreadsheet entries that appear to be in error, especially concerning his support assumptions.

When Natalie arrived at Kathleen's office, the lawyer's administrative assistant greeted her and then escorted her to the conference room. A few minutes later, Kathleen and Kelli, her paralegal, joined her.

"I've reviewed Patrick's preliminary summary. As always, he did a great job describing your case. I'm glad you're working with him," Kathleen said.

"No kidding. I've learned more about finances in one meeting with him than I have my entire life!" Natalie said.

"Before I cover some legal basics with you, do you have any questions?" Kathleen asked.

"Actually, I have a few," Natalie said. The night before, Natalie had prepared ten questions and input them into her iPad. Her list glowed on the screen she held in her hands.

Question 1. Collaborative Divorce

"My question mainly has to do with Jim's argument *against* collaborative: Does hiring a team of experts make collaborative divorce more expensive than regular mediation or even litigation? Jim also thinks we're going to act in our children's best interest, no matter what. In this case, does collaborative divorce offer any benefit compared to mediation?" asked Natalie.

Kathleen explained Jim's misunderstanding of the collaborative process. Mediation isn't always the easiest or cheapest way to go. And a collaborative divorce can be the most cost-effective method because spouses and a team of professionals are all working together toward a solution. Many times, having the team approach can allow for the development of solutions more quickly and allow the process to conclude sooner.

Question 2. Infidelity

"Although I can't confirm this, if Jim has cheated on me during our marriage, does this have any implications regarding the divorce?" Natalie asked.

"Lust can cause smart people to make poor choices!" Kathleen said.

She described that infidelity rules varied from state to state. For example, in Virginia, where Natalie and Jim lived, separated or not, having an affair during the marriage is a crime. In certain instances, if a spouse who would otherwise receive spousal support cheats, then he or she may be unable to receive support unless it would cause unreasonable financial duress.

Thus adultery may play a role in a litigated divorce case if the spouse who was cheated on is able to provide proof. Examples of evidence include the following:

- Meeting time and date between the spouse and the other individual

- Marital assets spent to support the affair, including dates expenses were incurred and their amounts and purchases made

- The name of the individual with whom the spouse engaged in extramarital relations

- Witnesses who can corroborate the facts

Spouses who suspect infidelity often hire private detectives to obtain the necessary data. But this may not be necessary if the affair is undeniable and the cheating spouse confesses his or her infidelity.

"Divorcing couples deal with infidelity in different ways. For instance, if a cheating husband spent marital assets supporting his affair and the wife proves it, this might impact the division of marital assets. In addition, the infidelity often has strong emotional ramifications for all parties involved. These emotions may adversely influence the ability for both husbands and wives to make good decisions about their finances, which may negatively impact their long-term financial well-being," said Kathleen.

The lawyer added that the cheating, in and of itself, might not have a significant bearing on the outcome of the division of assets or amount of support. But if other contributing factors, such as domestic violence or illegal activities were involved, the courts might impose penalties in favor of the innocent spouse. Examples of penalties are a disproportionate amount of assets to the cheated-on spouse or enhanced support.

If, on the other hand, they negotiate or mediate their settlement, Natalie may be able to leverage the infidelity to her benefit. This is because cheating spouses often feel guilty, which motivates them to make favorable concessions.

"In my research, I've heard many parts of the country have **no-fault divorce** that allows couples to split up for no other reason than *irreconcilable differences*. Can you help me understand this more?" Natalie asked.

Kathleen explained that years ago, a husband or wife needed to have specific grounds in order for the court to issue a divorce decree. Examples of reasons included infidelity, desertion, illegal activities resulting in jail or prison, or financial issues such as bankruptcy.

No-fault allowed couples to divorce without requiring a particular reason. Today, most states, including Virginia, have a no-fault option, which means no blame is necessary for a husband or wife to obtain a divorce—irreconcilable differences are sufficient grounds for a legally recognized split-up.

Question 3. Assets

"Patrick has explained to me the basics of marital vs. non-marital assets. But how do we actually divide them?" Natalie asked.

"Great question! In the divorce process, once assets are identified, clarified, and then valued, the simplest method is to split marital assets in half. But it's rarely that easy because most of the time, one person wants to keep a particular asset while the other doesn't want to give it up. So they wind up *trading* assets in order to create a reasonable balance. This is where Patrick will play a major role because it's *very important* to understand differences between assets," Kathleen said.

She added that some assets have a specific way they're taxed, which makes trading them for other assets much more complicated. Trading assets, like these, without considering their tax implications can create significant and unintended imbalances later on.

"I'm very concerned about keeping my inheritance," Natalie said. "I also paid for some home improvements and made the down payment on our house out of my inheritance. Do I get that money back?"

"If you made *separate* contributions to the equity in the home, it would be considered a **hybrid property.** This hybrid concept also applies to other assets you have purchased using your inherited money. A hybrid property is when one spouse has contributed his or her separate assets toward the down payment, principal payments, renovations, or any combination of the three that have improved the home's value.

"There are methods for calculating your separate interest in the house that can enable you to receive your separate contribution. If your house is a hybrid property, we'll need to obtain the

HUD-1 statements from original purchase and any refinancing that took place so that Patrick and I can figure out the amount of separate interest in the house," Kathleen said.

"I saw 'HUD-1' on a checklist Patrick gave me. What is that?" Natalie asked.

"HUD-1 statements document when you originally purchased the home and any refinancing that took place since. We'll need these in order to calculate accurately the marital and separate equity in the residence. Also, refinancing may have involved withdrawing funds, reducing the balance, rolling the refinancing cost into the new note, or any combination of the three. The HUD-1 statement would identify this information," said Kathleen.

Kathleen then explained that under a hybrid property arrangement, figuring out the non-marital and separate interest in the property required using different methods. For example, the couple could simply determine the separate contribution first and then divide the balance as marital property. In most cases, however, the spouse making the separate contribution seeks both credit for the amount of the separate contribution plus some portion of the property's appreciation if the appreciation relates to his or her separate contribution.

In general, any hybrid asset can be a thorny and controversial area in the division of assets. Furthermore, states treat the issue differently. For instance, in Colorado, no hybrid rule exists—all accumulated equity on marital and separate property is deemed a marital asset. Because rules vary widely from state to state, divorcing individuals should always consult with a lawyer in their jurisdiction in order to understand the allocation of marital and separate property.

Question 4. Division of Assets

"Which is better to fight for: home equity, investment assets, or retirement assets?" Natalie asked.

"It depends. You have to factor multiple variables, such as cost of ownership, which occurs with a home, and income taxes. Here's where Patrick will provide you the expert advice you need," Kathleen said.

"I really want to keep the house. But do you think I'll have to sell it?"

"At this point, it's hard to say. Patrick and I will work closely together to make sure our recommendations serve your long-term interests," Kathleen said.

Question 5. Child Custody

"How will we determine child custody when we have one child age fifteen, another age eighteen, and my oldest twenty-two and about to start his career?" Natalie said.

Kathleen explained that custody, which is the time a parent actually spends with the child or children, determines child support. Parents can have **physical custody**, which is parenting time, and **legal custody**, which is the right to make decisions on behalf of the child. Both of these can be solely or jointly held.

Also, each state has its own particular definition regarding when a child has reached **emancipation,** which is when he or she is no longer considered under the custody of a parent.

For instance, in **Virginia**, custody is defined as a dependent child who has not reached emancipation, which is age eighteen. In this instance, Natalie's two older children would not be considered in any child custody matter; only Rachel would be involved.

In **California**, children over fourteen years old may be considered emancipated if they are living separately from their parents. In **Illinois** and **New York**, emancipation is anyone over sixteen years old.

Problems arise when one spouse seeks joint custody as a means to reduce his or her child support payments. Once the parent is granted custody, he or she may fail to fulfill the agreed-upon childcare time. Divorcing couples typically resolve conflicts, such as these, through mediation. As with many aspects of a divorce, courtroom litigation is the last and least desirable method to resolve the dispute.

Conversely, there are instances where parents aren't able to see their children for the amount of time they've been granted. In fact, some moms and dads will intentionally schedule activities that interfere with the visitation rights of the other parent. This violates the law, and courts will enforce parental visitation rights over child activities.

The bottom line is *child custody is negotiated*. In addition, sometimes a husband or wife uses it as a weapon or a tool to obtain other benefits. For example, a husband or wife may give in to his or her spouse's custody demand in order to receive more favorable spousal support payments or in order to offset certain assets.

Most times, a couple needs to address custody *prior to* the property division and certainly before determining any support amounts. The challenge is to figure out if one parent has primary physical custody and if the other has visitation rights, or if they both agree to a form of joint custody where each parent shares in the parenting of the children.

In many cases, the number of days (twenty-four hours) or half days (twelve hours) a parent is with a child is the determining factor for child support. For example, in Virginia, a parent must have custody of his or her child a minimum of ninety days (comprising twenty-four-hour periods) per calendar year to qualify for a reduced level of child support. Once a couple agrees on custody terms, divorcing spouses will then defer to the statutory guidelines to determine child support amounts.

Question 6. Spousal and Child Support

"How do couples usually figure out spousal and child support?" Natalie asked.

Kathleen explained spousal and child support is one of the last issues to resolve. This is because support is based on earned and investment income, as well as income from other sources. Thus a couple needs to first divide assets *and* determine all income amounts including those from separate assets such as inherited assets. In regards to income, each state has different guidelines regarding how to define it.

The order of resolving spousal and child support is as follows:

1. Divide marital assets.

2. Determine each spouse's total income from all sources.

3. Determine spousal support, if any, based upon the total amount of income for each spouse.

4. Calculate child support using the statutory guidelines.

First, a couple will use the division of assets to determine if any income is generated from them.

Second, all earned income such as paychecks and unearned income such as investments, rental income, and retirement benefits may be part of determining the amount of each party's total income.

Third, the information from steps 1 and 2 are used to calculate spousal support.

Lastly, once the couple has determined spousal support, they're able to calculate child support based upon the statutory guidelines.

Temporary Support

When the lower-income spouse requires support during the divorce process (also called the separation period), the courts may order a temporary support amount to be paid. This is called *pendente lite*, which is Latin for "pending the litigation."

Virginia has a standardized formula to determine *pendente lite*. Note that unlike child support, permanent spousal support has no statutory guidelines; it is a negotiated amount. On a temporary basis, however, some courts do use the spousal support guidelines. But the temporary support calculation is often used as a negotiation starting point in order to determine the final divorce agreement's permanent spousal support amount. Keep in mind other states have their own temporary and permanent spousal support methodologies.

As far as calculating temporary spousal and child support is concerned, two formulas exist. Which one applies to a couple's particular circumstances depends on whether or not the dependent spouse will be receiving child support during the separation.

"Once I receive the necessary financial information, I'll go over these formulas with you," Kathleen said.

Spousal Support Length or Term

"Based on my online research, I think Jim owes me lifetime spousal support because we've been married so long," Natalie said.

"Unless a couple has extenuating circumstances, such as one spouse that cannot work, this usually isn't the case," Kathleen said.

As she explained, Virginia is an **equitable distribution state**, which means the division of marital assets doesn't necessarily end up being a fifty-fifty split and spousal support isn't mandated at all. Other states may be community property states or use other methods for determining the division of property.

"My goodness," Natalie said. "Rules really vary. I'm finding that so much of the information I've researched online doesn't apply to me."

"Agreed. Divorce happens in every state, but the rules are different in each, which is why you need to have an attorney who works in your own jurisdiction," said Kathleen.

Kathleen added that in some states, such as **Texas**, spousal support is rarely paid for longer than five years—even in long-term marriages. Exceptions that would result in extending support include extenuating circumstances, such as when a spouse is unable to work due to a disability or has no other financial resources.

In **California**, if a marriage has lasted less than ten years, spousal support is often paid for no more than half the period of the marriage. But beyond a ten-year marriage, the support amount and its duration are negotiated after the settlement of all property issues.

Meanwhile, in other states the length of spousal support can be based entirely upon the facts and circumstances of the individual divorce case. In other words, the support amount and term of support can vary from couple to couple, even if the financial circumstances of any two given couples are identical.

Child Support Length

In Virginia, child support typically terminates when a child graduates from high school or turns eighteen years old, whichever occurs later. But child support does not extend past a child's nineteenth birthday, even if he or she *has not* graduated from high school.

In Rachel's case, she would turn eighteen years old on December 7, which is six months after her high school graduation. This means Jim would continue paying child support until then.

The definition of a child's emancipation and termination of child support varies from state to state. The following are examples:

- In California, emancipation can be as early as age fourteen if living independently, and child support terminates upon age eighteen, or age nineteen if still in high school.

- In Illinois, emancipation can be as early as age sixteen, but child support ends at age eighteen, or age nineteen if the child is still in high school.

- In New York, emancipation can be as early as age sixteen, but child support may last until a child is age twenty-one.

To identify the amount of spousal and child support Natalie would receive, she and Jim would first need to agree upon the financial division of assets and determine the amount of income each received from his or her separate investments, as well as from his or her work.

Once a couple agreed on the division of assets and determined the amount of support, they would be ready to draft the PSA.

Question 7. Tax Exemptions

"Who receives the tax exemption for the dependent children?" Natalie asked.

"That's a great question because tax exemptions impact your income tax liability. Thus they are subject to negotiation," said Kathleen.

"In your case, it appears Jim has income that exceeds the limitations for retaining the dependent deduction on his tax return and therefore he would not gain from the exemption. As a result, it would only benefit you. Another area you will need to address is the tax difference between filing as a single person versus as a head of a household. Again, Patrick will be able to assist you with understanding the differences and determining what is most favorable for you.

Question 8. Mediation

"Is the outcome of mediation more successful than other divorce approaches?" Natalie asked.

"There's no clear-cut answer because what defines success is so subjective. Success to one person may mean dissolving the marriage with as little conflict as possible. Meanwhile, success for another person may mean receiving as much money as he or she can. In general, I would say mediation results in fewer conflicts than the traditional approach because mediation involves both parties using a process that requires more self-determination," Kathleen said.

Question 9. Residence Equity

"How do I keep my home if Jim wants to get his share of the equity out of it?" Natalie asked.

"You have a few options: You can refinance the property, use capital from other investments, trade, or offset between investments when you divide your marital property," Kathleen said.

She added that Natalie should consider ownership costs associated with a home versus an investment with no ongoing expense.

If the house is sold, then a couple simply divides the proceeds and allocates the marital amount between the two of them. But because the couple's house appears to be a hybrid property, they will have to calculate the amount of marital and non-marital equity when determining the division of the equity. Figuring this out can become a very challenging issue and often leads to conflicts that may need to be addressed in mediation.

If either Jim or Natalie decided to retain the house, then the negotiations would deal with how to buy out the other party and figure out the timing of the transaction. In addition, if one party retains the residence, the cost of sale is not included in the equity calculation.

Question 10. Rental Property

"Is the rental property worth fighting for, or should I just let Jim have it?" Natalie asked.

"This depends on multiple variables, such as cost basis, maintenance, and growth potential. For instance, if your rental property is generating tax-free cash flow, it's worth evaluating your options. Patrick would be your best resource regarding this matter," Kathleen said.

Question 11. Collaborative Divorce and Time

"From what I've researched, one criticism about collaborative is the meetings can be long, arduous, and numerous. Is all this time worth the headache compared to regular mediation and litigation?" Natalie asked. As a public school teacher, Natalie was also concerned that collaborative divorce's multiple meetings could be prohibitive because she would have to miss teaching.

Kathleen explained that Natalie might indeed need to take half days or possibly even entire days off for collaborative divorce meetings. But, from a meeting perspective, mediation could be equally as time-consuming. Both usually require a significant time commitment. To reap the rewards of high self-determination, husbands and wives must be more involved in the process than if they employed the traditional approach.

She had previous clients who were public servants and educators. They often used the paid time off they had accrued to attend meetings and miss school. Kathleen recalled one client, a high school teacher, who intentionally postponed the collaborative divorce meetings till summer vacation.

But not every meeting would require Natalie to take time off from work. For instance, when it came to two-way meetings (Natalie and Patrick or Natalie and Kathleen) and three-way meetings (Natalie, Patrick, and Kathleen), Natalie could schedule most of those after school let out.

Although Natalie was reluctant to use the time off she had been saving for years, she recognized that her and her children's financial futures were at stake, which quickly put to rest any hesitation.

"The more I learn about divorce, the more I realize how so many aspects of it are gray areas where a one-size-fits-all answer would be completely inadequate," said Natalie.

"I agree. Many facets of divorce are clear-cut. For example, most states have standard guidelines that must be used to determine child support, and others have specific formulas for spousal support. Meanwhile, other aspects require the attention of a trained professional to provide custom recommendations based on your particular circumstances. In the end, the time you've invested in your search for your team will definitely be worthwhile," Kathleen said.

"I'm eager to take the collaborative approach, which I know is your strength. Based on Jim's arguments against it and his bias toward mediation, how can I convince him?" Natalie asked.

Kathleen reiterated that leveraging the expertise of legal, financial, mediation, and mental health professionals trained in the collaborative process might result in a better overall outcome when compared to the traditional approach, litigation, or mediation alone. But if Natalie couldn't convince Jim to agree to the collaborative divorce, a hybrid approach might be the best alternative because Natalie would still benefit from the guidance and support of a team.

The two concluded their meeting, and Natalie was now charged with convincing Jim to agree to the collaborative approach.

JIM AND NATALIE DISCUSS THEIR OPTIONS

Natalie emailed Jim and set up a call to finally settle on the strategy they would follow. Prior to their conversation, she prepared a bulleted list of counterarguments to address what he'd most likely bring up. At their scheduled time, Thursday evening, she phoned Jim. They started their conversation by exchanging polite greetings.

"So we have a few options to consider," Natalie said. "I've done my homework, and I think the collaborative approach will have the least negative impact on the kids."

"I've looked into collaborative divorce too," Jim said. "I really don't think we need two lawyers and financials and a shrink. Others may need that, but our divorce won't be complicated. Hiring all those people will only waste our money."

"We're not the richest people in the world, but you make a good living, and we own two homes. So I think our situation isn't as simple as you think it is," said Natalie.

Jim maintained his position: He had already figured out their divorce, it wouldn't be complicated, and they loved their kids, which meant they would both act in their children's best interest.

Natalie was frustrated and wanted Jim to know it. At the same time, she knew it wouldn't help her case to get angry.

"Jim, you realize you've had months to work on this while I've been in the dark the entire time. Relying on your spreadsheet, regardless of how accurate you think it is, isn't in my best interest. How am I supposed to know if what's on there is everything we have and that it's 100 percent fair?" Natalie asked.

Throughout their marriage Natalie had expressed complete disinterest in managing their finances. Thus Jim hadn't expected Natalie to take issue with his spreadsheet. Her doubts made him nervous—he wondered why she was suddenly questioning his credibility.

"Of course it's accurate. Have I *ever* been unfair to you about money? In fact, I'd argue I've always been upfront and honest. Listen, our finances really aren't that complicated—cranking out the spreadsheet only took a couple of hours. I've even generated a new one with more data. And based on what I've seen, coming to an agreement will be easy. The bottom line is I won't budge about collaborative divorce. Not only is having two teams—one for you and one for me—going overboard, it's also just too expensive, and we can't afford it," Jim said.

"We can afford it! You just don't want to spend the money. I need help understanding the financial issues in order to make good decisions, and I can't rely on you going forward," Natalie said.

"Why can't you rely on me? I'll explain whatever questions you have and provide all supporting documents. Here's what I propose. If you take collaboration off the table, I'll defer the mediator choice to you. I already sent you a list of mediators. Pick one of them or one of your own, and I'll go along with your decision," Jim said.

Natalie knew once Jim set his mind on (or against) something, convincing him to do otherwise was nearly impossible. Thus she consoled herself with Plan B, a hybrid divorce—a choice she felt comfortable with. But she had no intention of letting Jim know about the team she had formed.

She agreed to Jim's proposal and would contact the mediators on Jim's list. She would also see if more mediators needed to be added to her search.

Jim was relieved Natalie dropped her collaborative divorce intentions. He thanked her for going along with the approach he proposed. He reassured her it would benefit both of them in the long run and she wouldn't regret her decision. Completing the process as quickly as possible would allow them to move on with their lives.

"What's the big rush?" Natalie asked.

"No rush. I just think the faster we reach a decision, the more time and money we'll save," Jim said.

"You're only thinking about the money—not the family. I need to go. We'll talk later," said Natalie.

They concluded their phone call. Natalie then sat at her computer and opened the spreadsheet Jim had emailed her earlier. Giving it more than the cursory glance she had done when he had first sent it, this time around she took a more careful look at what he proposed.

She reviewed the spreadsheet, which motivated her to begin gathering financial documents. She went upstairs to Jim's office. Although he had already moved out, he had left all his financial files intact. Using Jim's spreadsheet and Patrick's Divorce Planning Checklist as her guides, Natalie spent the next several hours poring through file cabinets and boxes filled with paperwork and gathering the documents.

In her research, she found copies of their previous year's tax returns and a benefits statement from Jim's employer. When she factored in his benefits, she calculated he earned $400,000, rather than the $350,000 amount she had seen on Jim's spreadsheet.

Natalie checked each item she found on Patrick's Divorce Planning Checklist. As hard as she tried, she couldn't find any real estate closing information. Then she recalled Jim also stored financial documents in their attic.

Natalie disliked clutter and remembered regularly complaining to Jim about his habit of refusing to throw away paperwork. Now she was grateful for his hoarding tendencies. She found the real estate closing documents, including the HUD-1s, for both homes they owned, bank records from years ago, tax returns tracing back to their first anniversary, and even ones from when Jim was single.

As she went through file folders and boxes and collected relevant information, she labeled sticky notes and used them as bookmarks in order to remember their original location. She scanned the statements and other data she gathered and returned the documents to their proper place so as not to arouse Jim's suspicions.

NATALIE PHONES KATHLEEN

After school let out the following Monday, Natalie had a call scheduled with her lawyer. The hours she spent gathering supporting paperwork, checking off items from the Divorce Planning Checklist, and scanning documents gave her a sense of control of her divorce. Natalie began her talk with Kathleen by updating her about her conversation with Jim.

"Jim's as stubborn as an ox and wouldn't budge from his mediation stance. I knew I had hybrid as backup, so I wasn't too worried about giving in," said Natalie.

"I think it was a good move because Jim will still think he's in control," said Kathleen.

"That's my hope—he won't suspect a thing until it's too late," Natalie said.

"Have you hired a mediator yet?" Kathleen asked.

"Jim provided me a list of them. His consolation prize for going along with mediation was I could pick the mediator—*what a saint*," Natalie said.

While on the phone with Kathleen, Natalie named the mediators on Jim's list. Natalie was worried because she didn't know how to narrow her search down.

"I have a great solution for you. You're clearly a pro at following checklists, so I have one that will help you conduct your own mediator research, and I'll email it after this call," Kathleen said.

After their phone conversation, Kathleen emailed Natalie the following six-question checklist:

MEDIATOR INTERVIEW CHECKLIST

1. **How long has he or she been a mediator and involved in family law matters?**
   You want to know the number of years your prospective mediator has been working in the field. The mediator should be able to clearly articulate his or her expertise.

2. **What is the mediator's professional background?**
   You want a mediator who has experience working with cases similar to yours. Mediators come from a wide range of backgrounds. Some are Licensed Clinical Social Workers (LCSWs) or other mental health professionals, lawyers, and retired executives, and judges. Retired judges, in particular, often belong to mediation groups that handle complicated cases.

   Any of these professionals can be skilled mediators. Also, find out about his or her educational background including undergraduate degrees, post baccalaureate degrees (if any), and credentials and certifications relevant to mediation.

3. **What is the average net worth of the clients he or she has worked with over the past five years?**

   The higher your net worth and assets, the more complicated dividing your marital estate will be. Thus make sure the mediator has worked with cases of similar net worth to yours. He or she will be able to address the intricacies and nuances of your divorce.

4. **Does the mediator believe in holding individual caucuses (separate meetings) with clients?**

   Out of all the questions, this is the least critical. At the same time, receive the mediator's input about this. A yes answer is preferable.

5. **On average, how many meetings are required to reach a PSA?**

   Each divorcing couple is different; thus every mediation is different as well. With that said, a skilled mediator can leverage his or her extensive experience handling cases similar to yours in order to develop a timeline.

6. **What are expected costs?**

   Mediators bill by the hour, so first ask what his or her hourly rate is. Next, similar to the answer to the above question, a skilled mediator can help you estimate costs based on the particulars of your case.

"I've worked with several mediators on your list," said Kathleen. "If you're feeling overwhelmed with your search and would like a recommendation from your list, I'd suggest Courtney. I've teamed with her on a number of cases. She's a top mediator. As far as the checklist is concerned, she fulfills all criteria relevant to your case. She's also a lawyer with a solid reputation within the family law community."

Kathleen then described their next steps:

1. Natalie and Jim would need to agree upon a mediator.

2. Kathleen would provide Patrick a summary of today's meeting.

3. Kathleen and Patrick would develop a preliminary strategy using the information they'd collected so far.

4. Natalie, Kathleen, and Patrick would schedule a three-way meeting prior to Natalie and Jim's first mediation. The two experts would share their strategy with Natalie and prepare her for the first mediation.

After their phone call, Natalie made a video conferencing appointment with Courtney for Wednesday after school. When they spoke, Natalie went over each item under Kathleen's mediation checklist. As Kathleen had described, Courtney had the experience, expertise, and professionalism Natalie sought.

Courtney was her top choice, and Natalie texted Jim about her decision. As he had promised, Jim went along with Natalie's recommendation, and the two hired Courtney. In the meantime, Kathleen and Patrick began developing their client's strategy.

The next week, on the day before her next appointment with Patrick, Natalie received a call. She glanced at her phone's screen and recognized it was a friend she hadn't spoken to in years.

"Samantha Brennan, is that you?" Natalie asked.

Samantha was married to Brian—Jim's college fraternity brother.

"Yes, it's me! It's probably been five years since we last spoke," Samantha said. "We were just at Tom Healy's wedding. Remember him?"

"You mean Tom, from Jim's fraternity? I thought he'd never get married. How was the wedding?" Natalie asked.

"Really nice. Hey, we saw Jim there, and I wanted to tell you, I'm so sorry about the divorce," Samantha said.

"Oh? . . . Did Jim mention it to you?" she asked. Natalie was disappointed her husband had not told her about the wedding, let alone not asked her to be his date. She was heartbroken he was already publically declaring their separation a divorce.

"Actually, we didn't get a chance to talk to him. You know how overwhelming big weddings can be. Besides, we felt a little awkward because we had no idea about you two. So was that his girlfriend or his wife with him?" Samantha asked.

Natalie's stomach tensed. She felt weak and did her best to keep the phone in her grip.

"Are you there?" Samantha asked.

"Sorry, my phone signal is terrible. Yes . . . yes, that's his girl-friend," Natalie said clueless about who Jim's date was, pretty certain it wasn't a new wife, and feeling humiliated hearing about it this way. "Samantha, I have to run. My daughter's right here waiting for me," Natalie said.

"Of course. Listen, let's get together sometime and catch up, okay?" Samantha asked.

"Sure. Sounds great," Natalie said.

With no daughter at home to worry about, she put her phone down, sat on the floor, and sobbed.

CHAPTER 11

NATALIE'S SECOND APPOINTMENT WITH PATRICK

After Natalie and Kathleen's phone call, her lawyer reviewed her notes and prepared a summary of their conversation. The following email appeared in Patrick's inbox:

During our first substantive meeting, Natalie was well prepared and had several questions regarding the legal aspects of her divorce. Next, she asked about mediators, and I recommended Courtney Fitzgerald.

As you know, Natalie definitely needs you to coach her through her finances.

In the meantime, I'm working on spousal and child support issues. Most likely they'll share custody. At the same time, Natalie has stated she prefers to have sole physical custody and agrees to joint legal custody. As a result, they may require a separate mediation on this topic before we go down the support path.

I agree with you that Natalie has a hybrid property issue with the residence and her investment account. Her inherited property will need to be clearly identified, and then we can work on the hybrid aspects of the marital assets.

Once you review the recommended next steps, please send any comments or questions my way.

Best regards,
Kathleen

Next, Kathleen provided the following concerns:

- Natalie has made a big change—the way Jim had dictated how their assets would be divided energized her, and she's unwilling to accept his proposal unquestioned.

- She fears the divorce's long-term financial implications and being on her own.

- Dating scares her. "Just another divorced women in a used-car lot looking for the best used one," is how she put it.

- She's afraid of the divorce's possible negative impact on her children.

Lastly, Kathleen provided Patrick her suggested next steps:

- Review the differences between retirement accounts and the personal accounts so she has a clearer understanding of the tax implications.

- Help her feel confident about her long-term financial well-being, which will go a long way to improving her decision-making ability.

- ◘ Discuss marital and non-marital issues with her to reinforce information she's received up to this point.

- ◘ The division of the marital residence equity is an open item.

Three weeks after their first appointment, Natalie arrived at Patrick's office. Cullen sat with them ready to take notes. Between their first meeting and now, she had emailed to Patrick's office the following documents she had previously scanned:

- ◘ A company benefits statement

- ◘ Last year's tax return

- ◘ Bank statements

- ◘ Brokerage accounts

- ◘ HUD-1 statements from their purchase and refinancings

She also provided her date of marriage, separation date, and family history. With this information and Jim's original spreadsheet, Patrick was able to prepare an initial summary of assets and liabilities.

"Before we begin, how are you feeling about this process?" Patrick asked.

Natalie described the phone call she had received from Samantha.

"I'm really sorry you had to find out that way. Have you told Kathleen about it yet?" he asked.

"I just found out yesterday, so I thought I'd bring it up to you first since our meeting is today," she said.

"We previously talked about private investigators. Maybe now's the time to hire one. But why don't you ask Kathleen first?" Patrick said.

Natalie planned to follow Patrick's advice and call her lawyer afterwards. For now, the two proceeded with the meeting agenda.

"I was so glad I was able to collect all the items on your checklist. When I first received it, I had no idea how I'd be able to pull it off. And as much as I was tempted to, I didn't want to reach out to Jim for help. Otherwise, he might have gotten suspicious and wondered if I was getting outside help. By taking charge of my finances for the first time in my life, I've learned so much," Natalie said.

"Based on what you've learned so far, I have no doubt you'll gain mastery over your financial life. To be frank, the conversation we'll have today will cover pretty sophisticated financial topics. My goal is to bring up the main issues I've seen regarding your divorce settlement, help you make the best decisions possible, and start pouring the foundation for your mediation strategy," he said.

Patrick set Jim's spreadsheet on the table. "You'll recognize Jim's spreadsheet. I have it here in its original form. I've already found areas where Jim clearly demonstrated he didn't understand property division and the difference between marital and non-marital assets," Patrick said.

He added that his goal was to point out areas he believed would make the biggest difference to Natalie and her future financial well-being.

Division of Property: Jim's Original Spreadsheet

Account	Value 12-31	Jim	Natalie	
ASSETS				
Joint Wells Fargo Bank (WFB)	$25,000	$5,000	$20,000	
Jim's WFB	$10,000	$10,000		
Residence	$900,000	$285,500	$285,500	to be sold, $571,000 net proceeds divided
Rental Property	$550,000	$167,000		Net value if sold, $167,000
Natalie's Schwab	$125,000		$125,000	
Jim's E*Trade	$225,000	$181,500	$43,500	

Account	Value 12-31	Jim	Natalie	
ASSETS (continued)				
Household	$200,000	$25,000	$175,000	
Subaru	$15,000		$15,000	
BMW	$35,000	$35,000		
Sailboat	$30,000	$30,000		
Jim's IRA	$150,000	$75,000	$75,000	
Jim's 401(k)	$375,000	$187,500	$187,500	
SSI Stock Options	$224,000	$112,000	$112,000	
Natalie's 403(b)	$85,000		$85,000	
Total Assets	**$2,949,000**	**$1,113,500**	**$1,123,500**	

LIABILITIES				
Residence Mortgage	$275,000	$0		Payment PITI, $2000/month
Rental Mortgage	$350,000	$0		Payment PITI, $2750/month; rental income $3000/month
BMW	$15,000	$15,000		Payment $575/month
Credit Cards	$25,000	$0	$25,000	Natalie's charges since beginning of December
Total Liabilities	**$665,000**	**$15,000**	**$25,000**	

Net Balances	**$2,284,000**	**$1,098,500**	**$1,098,500**	

SUPPORT				
Spousal		n/a	$5,000	Per month
Child		n/a	$1,000	Per month

JIM'S SPREADSHEET EVALUATED

"Let's start with Jim's spreadsheet. I'll share what jumped off the page for me, and then we can review your tax return afterwards.

"In my work, I've noticed even divorcing spouses who no longer trust their exes still manage to trust their husbands or wives when it comes to disclosing accurate financial information. But because trust has been broken through his adultery, I recommend you refuse to accept any financial data without supporting documentation," Patrick said.

Overall, Patrick's biggest concern with Jim's spreadsheet was he created it without anyone else's input. He questioned Jim's ability to maintain objectivity when his financial future hinged on his calculations.

The process of dividing assets required an accurate accounting of each asset's value. Thus every item on Jim's spreadsheet needed to be cross-referenced with documents such as financial statements. In addition, the more documents Natalie collected on her own, the more information Patrick would have to develop an alternative spreadsheet, which he and Kathleen would use to negotiate a better position on her client's behalf.

Patrick then went through each item on Jim's spreadsheet that concerned him:

Primary Residence

Jim	Natalie
$285,500	$285,500

"According to the spreadsheet, the primary residence will be sold," Patrick said.

"That's news to me. How did you figure that out?" Natalie asked.

"Because Jim has estimated the cost of sale and used that figure to calculate the net equity," said Patrick.

"I did *not* agree to sell it—so typical of him to make these unilateral decisions. Considering Rachel's in high school, I don't want to move out. The divorce will be tough enough on her as it is—let alone if she has to move too. My biggest hope is I can keep it until at least Rachel graduates from high school and maybe even college. Will this be possible?" Natalie asked.

"Let me work on it. On the next spreadsheet I prepare, I'll show you'll keep the house for some period of time," Patrick said.

Patrick added that keeping the house was a major financial decision that could have a significant impact on her long-term financial well-being. She didn't have to make a decision right away, and he reassured her they would continue to explore the benefits and risks associated with whatever decision she made.

Rental Property

Jim	Natalie
$167,000	$0

Their rental property generated income and was a tax shelter. Patrick was uncertain why Jim put the entire amount in his column. He had also calculated the value as if it was sold, and he included the cost of sale. But if Jim kept it, there would be *no* cost of sale. According to Patrick's assessment, the amount of equity should be $200,000, not the $167,000 shown on Jim's spreadsheet.

Natalie's Schwab Account (Inheritance)

Jim	Natalie
$0	$125,000

Jim allocated Natalie's Schwab account to her side of the ledger, even though it came from her inheritance, which meant it was non-marital property. According to Jim's spreadsheet, including the inheritance meant Natalie had $125,000 *less* of the marital assets allocated to her.

Jim's decision to input the Schwab account on the spreadsheet was fine, but it wasn't relevant to any discussion of dividing marital assets because it was *non-marital* and thus *not* subject to division.

Jim's E*Trade Account

Jim	Natalie
$181,500	$43,500

Jim was retaining the majority of the E*Trade, which was a brokerage account. It had better tax advantages than the retirement accounts because the E*Trade benefitted from long-term capital gains while the retirement accounts were subject to ordinary taxation. Patrick believed Natalie would be better off retaining either a larger portion of the E*Trade account or a cash equivalent.

Personal Property

Jim	Natalie
$25,000	$175,000

Jim allocated the majority of the personal property to Natalie. These items included household furnishings, artwork, rugs, and her personal items. Unfortunately for her, none of them were **financial**, which meant they did not generate any income or have growth opportunities. As a result, Natalie would have less marital assets that could benefit her in the future. At the same time, some of the household items, such as art or antiques, could have value and be sold and converted to cash. For now, Patrick valued them at $1, which indicated they would not be included in the financial division of marital assets. The $1 also served as a placeholder until the couple decided upon the personal property division at a later date.

Total Liabilities

Jim	Natalie
$0	$25,000

Jim allocated the $25,000 credit card balance to Natalie.

"Is this okay with you?" asked Patrick

"I didn't realize Jim put all our debt in my column. Can that be right?" Natalie asked.

"I'll need you to identify where the charges came from and if they were incurred before or after the separation," said Patrick.

Natalie input Patrick's request in her iPad.

Monthly Spousal and Child Support

Spousal Support	Child Support
$5,000	$1,000

"Do you know how Jim determined these amounts?" Patrick asked.

"No. And I wanted your input about this. The $6,000 doesn't seem like enough to cover my expenses," Natalie said.

"That's what I'm here for: I'll provide the information and guidance you need to make the best possible decisions. When it comes to his proposed support amounts, he's really jumped the gun here. First and foremost, both of you must agree on the division of assets, and you must also factor in both of your incomes. The spreadsheet says nothing about the income of either of you, so it's clear his support amounts are based on incomplete information. Determining spousal or child support or both are also legal matters, so he should be consulting with a lawyer before drawing any conclusions," Patrick said.

"So what do I do about this?"

"His numbers are meaningless, so you don't need to take any action. Kathleen and I will work together to determine amounts that comply with the law and give you what you're entitled to," said Patrick.

A SUMMARY OF JIM'S SPREADSHEET

"My biggest concern right now is your side of the spreadsheet has most of the personal non-investment assets plus your Schwab account, which was your inheritance. Remember, non-investment assets don't generate income. You also wound up with all the credit card debt. Jim would also keep the income-generating rental property and most of the non-qualified investment assets," said Patrick.

"I've heard that term but I don't know what it is. What are non-qualified investments, and how are they different from qualified ones?" Natalie asked.

Patrick described **qualified investment assets** as those that have been accumulated in pre-tax accounts such as IRAs, 401(k)s, pensions, and other retirement vehicles. They are subject to possible withdrawal penalties as well as ordinary income taxes when withdrawn or liquidated.

Non-qualified investment assets are those in which taxes have already been paid. As a result, they can usually be liquidated with preferential tax consequences.

"I'll add that the calculations Jim used to determine spousal and child support were based upon inaccurate data, and he did not use the statutory guidelines for the child support. He seemed to arbitrarily create numbers," Patrick said.

"Based on what you've uncovered so far," Natalie said, "Jim clearly doesn't know what he's doing. Even worse, he's throwing me under the bus and setting himself up to benefit the most. I can't believe he insisted I trust him on this! Now, the question is how am I going to convince my know-it-all husband his outline is totally unfair?"

Patrick explained the question wasn't necessarily about unfairness or fairness. Natalie and her team would need to focus on the law and understand the differences between marital and non-marital assets as well as the financial implications of the division of the assets.

TAX RETURN

The next discussion topic was the couple's tax return. Patrick projected an image of it on the conference room wall. He started by explaining how Natalie would be filing taxes once they were divorced. In order to do so, she needed to understand tax fundamentals because they would significantly impact her net income after the divorce was final.

The tax return was a critical document because it frequently provided details that might not appear on a list of assets and liabilities, such as the spreadsheet Jim created. Patrick started with the first page of the 1040 federal return and then went page by page reviewing the individual tax schedules to verify the accuracy of the information and determine if there were any other matters they needed to address. He explained the **tax schedule** was a government form that was part of the IRS income tax return.

There are several schedules that hold a great deal of information about income and investment activities. Examples include **Schedule A:** Itemized Deductions, **Schedule B:** Interest and Ordinary Dividends, **Schedule C:** Profit or Loss from Business, **Schedule D:** Capital Gains and Losses, and **Schedule E:** Supplemental Income and Loss from real estate, trust, partnership and S-corporation. In addition to the tax schedules, associated forms are identified by numbers. These provide supplemental information or calculations for other tax liabilities.

Form **1040**	Department of the Treasury—Internal Revenue Service (99) **U.S. Individual Income Tax Return**		OMB No. 1545-0074	IRS Use Only—Do not write or staple in this space.

For the year Jan. 1–Dec. 31, ____ or other tax year beginning ____, 20__, ending ____, 20 ____   See separate instructions.

Your first name and initial	Last name	Your social security number
James R	Smith	123-44-5678
If a joint return, spouse's first name and initial	Last name	Spouse's social security number
Natalie C	Smith	234-56-7890

Home address (number and street). If you have a P.O. box, see instructions.   Apt. no.
1503 Cross Hair Street

▲ Make sure the SSN(s) above and on line 6c are correct.

City, town or post office, state, and ZIP code. If you have a foreign address, also complete spaces below (see instructions).
Reston VA 20194

Presidential Election Campaign
Check here if you, or your spouse if filing jointly, want $3 to go to this fund. Checking a box below will not change your tax or refund.   ☐ You ☐ Spouse

Foreign country name | Foreign province/state/county | Foreign postal code

Filing Status
Check only one box.

1. ☐ Single
2. ☒ Married filing jointly (even if only one had income)
3. ☐ Married filing separately. Enter spouse's SSN above and full name here. ▶
4. ☐ Head of household (with qualifying person). (See instructions.) If the qualifying person is a child but not your dependent, enter this child's name here. ▶
5. ☐ Qualifying widow(er) with dependent child

Exemptions

6a ☒ **Yourself.** If someone can claim you as a dependent, **do not** check box 6a . . . . .
 b ☒ **Spouse** . . . .

Boxes checked on 6a and 6b   **2**

c Dependents:		(2) Dependent's social security number	(3) Dependent's relationship to you	(4) ✓ if child under age 17 qualifying for child tax credit (see instructions)
(1) First name	Last name			
Ben	Smith	234-98-7456	Son	☐
Ryann	Smith	213-44-6589	Daughter	☐
Rachel	Smith	213-45-8970	Daughter	☒
				☐

No. of children on 6c who:
• lived with you   **3**
• did not live with you due to divorce or separation (see instructions) ____
Dependents on 6c not entered above ____

If more than four dependents, see instructions and check here ▶ ☐

d   Total number of exemptions claimed . . . .

Add numbers on lines above ▶   **5**

Income

Attach Form(s) W-2 here. Also attach Forms W-2G and 1099-R if tax was withheld.

If you did not get a W-2, see instructions.

7	Wages, salaries, tips, etc. Attach Form(s) W-2	7	402,000.
8a	Taxable interest. Attach Schedule B if required	8a	50.
b	Tax-exempt interest. **Do not** include on line 8a . .	8b		
9a	Ordinary dividends. Attach Schedule B if required	9a	3,700.
b	Qualified dividends	9b	3,050.	
10	Taxable refunds, credits, or offsets of state and local income taxes	10	
11	Alimony received	11	
12	Business income or (loss). Attach Schedule C or C-EZ	12	
13	Capital gain or (loss). Attach Schedule D if required. If not required, check here ▶ ☐	13	-3,000.
14	Other gains or (losses). Attach Form 4797	14	
15a	IRA distributions . 15a	b Taxable amount . . .	15b	
16a	Pensions and annuities 16a	b Taxable amount . . .	16b	
17	Rental real estate, royalties, partnerships, S corporations, trusts, etc. Attach Schedule E	17	134.
18	Farm income or (loss). Attach Schedule F	18	
19	Unemployment compensation	19	
20a	Social security benefits 20a	b Taxable amount . . .	20b	
21	Other income. List type and amount	21	
22	Combine the amounts in the far right column for lines 7 through 21. This is your **total income** ▶	22	402,884.

Adjusted Gross Income

23	Educator expenses	23		
24	Certain business expenses of reservists, performing artists, and fee-basis government officials. Attach Form 2106 or 2106-EZ	24		
25	Health savings account deduction. Attach Form 8889 .	25		
26	Moving expenses. Attach Form 3903	26		
27	Deductible part of self-employment tax. Attach Schedule SE .	27		
28	Self-employed SEP, SIMPLE, and qualified plans . .	28		
29	Self-employed health insurance deduction	29		
30	Penalty on early withdrawal of savings	30		
31a	Alimony paid b Recipient's SSN ▶	31a		
32	IRA deduction	32		
33	Student loan interest deduction	33		
34	Tuition and fees. Attach Form 8917	34		
35	Domestic production activities deduction. Attach Form 8903	35		
36	Add lines 23 through 35		36	
37	Subtract line 36 from line 22. This is your **adjusted gross income** . . . . . ▶		37	402,884.

For Disclosure, Privacy Act, and Paperwork Reduction Act Notice, see separate instructions.   Form **1040**

Form 1040 (Page **2**)

Tax and Credits	38	Amount from line 37 (adjusted gross income)	38	402,884.
	39a	Check if: ☐ **You** were born before January 2, 1950, ☐ Blind. ☐ **Spouse** was born before January 2, 1950, ☐ Blind. **Total boxes checked** ▶ 39a		
	b	If your spouse itemizes on a separate return or you were a dual-status alien, check here ▶ 39b☐		
Standard Deduction for— • People who check any box on line 39a or 39b or who can be claimed as a dependent, see instructions. • All others: Single or Married filing separately, $6,200 Married filing jointly or Qualifying widow(er), $12,400 Head of household, $9,100	40	**Itemized deductions** (from Schedule A) **or** your **standard deduction** (see left margin)	40	47,416.
	41	Subtract line 40 from line 38	41	355,468.
	42	**Exemptions.** If line 38 is $152,525 or less, multiply $3,950 by the number on line 6d. Otherwise, see instructions	42	3,950.
	43	**Taxable income.** Subtract line 42 from line 41. If line 42 is more than line 41, enter -0-	43	351,518.
	44	**Tax** (see instructions). Check if any from: **a** ☐ Form(s) 8814 **b** ☐ Form 4972 **c** ☐ ____	44	91,357.
	45	**Alternative minimum tax** (see instructions). Attach Form 6251	45	5,932.
	46	Excess advance premium tax credit repayment. Attach Form 8962	46	
	47	Add lines 44, 45, and 46 ▶	47	97,289.
	48	Foreign tax credit. Attach Form 1116 if required — 48		
	49	Credit for child and dependent care expenses. Attach Form 2441 — 49		
	50	Education credits from Form 8863, line 19 — 50		
	51	Retirement savings contributions credit. Attach Form 8880 — 51		
	52	Child tax credit. Attach Schedule 8812, if required — 52		
	53	Residential energy credits. Attach Form 5695 — 53		
	54	Other credits from Form: **a** ☐ 3800 **b** ☐ 8801 **c** ☐ — 54		
	55	Add lines 48 through 54. These are your **total credits**	55	
	56	Subtract line 55 from line 47. If line 55 is more than line 47, enter -0- ▶	56	97,289.
Other Taxes	57	Self-employment tax. Attach Schedule SE	57	
	58	Unreported social security and Medicare tax from Form: **a** ☐ 4137 **b** ☐ 8919	58	
	59	Additional tax on IRAs, other qualified retirement plans, etc. Attach Form 5329 if required	59	
	60a	Household employment taxes from Schedule H	60a	
	b	First-time homebuyer credit repayment. Attach Form 5405 if required	60b	
	61	Health care: individual responsibility (see instructions) Full-year coverage ☒	61	
	62	Taxes from: **a** ☒ Form 8959 **b** ☒ Form 8960 **c** ☐ Instructions; enter code(s)	62	1,598.
	63	Add lines 56 through 62. This is your **total tax** ▶	63	98,887.
Payments If you have a qualifying child, attach Schedule EIC.	64	Federal income tax withheld from Forms W-2 and 1099 — 64 — 106,840.		
	65	2014 estimated tax payments and amount applied from 2013 return — 65		
	66a	**Earned income credit (EIC)** — 66a		
	b	Nontaxable combat pay election — 66b		
	67	Additional child tax credit. Attach Schedule 8812 — 67		
	68	American opportunity credit from Form 8863, line 8 — 68		
	69	Net premium tax credit. Attach Form 8962 — 69		
	70	Amount paid with request for extension to file — 70		
	71	Excess social security and tier 1 RRTA tax withheld — 71		
	72	Credit for federal tax on fuels. Attach Form 4136 — 72		
	73	Credits from Form: **a** ☐ 2439 **b** ☐ Reserved **c** ☐ Reserved **d** ☐ — 73		
	74	Add lines 64, 65, 66a, and 67 through 73. These are your **total payments** ▶	74	106,840.
Refund Direct deposit? See instructions.	75	If line 74 is more than line 63, subtract line 63 from line 74. This is the amount you **overpaid**	75	7,953.
	76a	Amount of line 75 you want **refunded to you.** If Form 8888 is attached, check here ▶☐	76a	7,953.
	b	Routing number ☒☒☒☒☒☒☒☒☒ ▶c Type: ☐ Checking ☐ Savings		
	d	Account number ☒☒☒☒☒☒☒☒☒☒☒☒☒☒☒☒☒		
	77	Amount of line 75 you want **applied to your 2015 estimated tax** ▶ — 77		
Amount You Owe	78	**Amount you owe.** Subtract line 74 from line 63. For details on how to pay, see instructions ▶	78	
	79	Estimated tax penalty (see instructions) — 79		

Third Party Designee
Do you want to allow another person to discuss this return with the IRS (see instructions)? ☐ **Yes.** Complete below. ☒ **No**
Designee's name ▶ ___ Phone no. ▶ ___ Personal identification number (PIN) ▶ ___

Sign Here
Joint return? See instructions. Keep a copy for your records.
Under penalties of perjury, I declare that I have examined this return and accompanying schedules and statements, and to the best of my knowledge and belief, they are true, correct, and complete. Declaration of preparer (other than taxpayer) is based on all information of which preparer has any knowledge.
Your signature | Date | Your occupation: Executive | Daytime phone number (703)734-0413
Spouse's signature. If a joint return, **both** must sign. | Date | Spouse's occupation: Teacher | If the IRS sent you an Identity Protection PIN, enter it here (see inst.)

Paid Preparer Use Only
Print/Type preparer's name | Preparer's signature | Date | Check ☐ if self-employed | PTIN
Firm's name ▶ Self-Prepared | | | Firm's EIN ▶
Firm's address ▶ | | | Phone no.

www.irs.gov/form1040

Form **1040**

"Let's start with the first page of the 1040 you filed last tax year. Since you also provided a copy of your return from two years ago, I was able to see Jim had a higher income that year. Do you know why?" asked Patrick.

"I'm not sure. I think it had something to do with Jim getting a larger bonus and selling some stock," Natalie said.

"Got it. Now, let's review last year's form, so we get a better understanding of your income and taxes," said Patrick.

Patrick then highlighted lines on the 1040 that Natalie needed to pay attention to.

Line 7, $402,000, represented the wages as shown on a W-2 from an employer. It does not necessarily indicate the actual gross income of an employee—contributions to retirement plans and pretax contributions to other benefit plans would not be included on this line, which is why Patrick recommended that Natalie obtain a copy of the actual W-2 and benefit plans.

Line 8a, $50, was interest earned from investments and bank accounts. These were reported on form 1099-INT.

Line 9, $3,700, represented ordinary and qualified **dividends**. United States corporations generate qualified dividends, and they receive favorable tax treatment. They are reported on a 1099-DIV.

Patrick described that dividends are how a company distributes earnings to its shareholders. The distributions are generally taxable to the recipient, but they may have a lower tax rate if they are from a domestic corporation. As far as mutual funds are concerned, the dividends received from various companies are generally reinvested to build up the investment. If you own a company's individual stock, the company may distribute the dividend as cash or reinvest in the company's stock.

Line 13 showed $3,000 of investment losses, which also indicates more likely losses that were being carried forward to future years. These losses can be used to offset future gains. They will appear on page 2 of Schedule D.

Line 17, $134, indicated rental property income as well as any partnership or trust income. The total shown is the rental property's amount of taxable net income after expenses. A review of Schedule E would allow Natalie to determine the amount of actual net cash flow the property was generating. Many times the cash flow is sheltered by the depreciation deduction, which is not a cash flow item. If the property was generating losses, the losses would not appear on the return because the couple's total gross income as shown on line 37 exceeded the amount that would allow a current deduction.

Line 37 was their **adjusted gross income** (AGI), which is the total of all taxable income before any adjustments for itemized deductions, tax credits, or personal exemptions. AGI is important because it is the basis for limits on a number of other tax issues, such as medical **deductions** and overall itemized deductions. "Look at all the entries above to see just how you arrive at the AGI," Patrick said.

He added that deductions included medical, taxes, interest, charitable, and other miscellaneous items that, in total, reduced the amount of taxable income. Deductions are listed on **Schedule A:** Itemized Deductions.

Patrick also noted that Jim's salary and bonus comprised the vast majority of the $402,000 that appeared on line 7. The amount would also include stock options that had vested and had been sold and would be included on Jim's W-2. The amount of taxes withheld (line 64) exceeded the amount of the actual tax liability (line 63). Therefore, the couple was due a tax refund of $7,953 as shown on line 76a.

REVIEWING JIM'S W-2

a Employee's social security number	1 Wages, tips, other comp.	2 Federal income tax withheld
123-44-5678	358000.00	100240.00
	3 Social security wages	4 Social security tax withheld
b Employer ID number (EIN)	117000.00	7254.00
56-1234567	5 Medicare wages and tips	6 Medicare tax withheld
	375000.00	5437.00

OMB No. 1545-0008 **Form W-2 Wage and Tax Statement 2014**

c Employer's name, address, and ZIP code

SCIENCE SYSTEMS INC

2501 HIGH TECH BLVD
MC LEAN VA 22010

d Control number

e Employee's name, address, and ZIP code

JAMES SMITH
1503 CROSS HAIR STREET
RESTON VA 20194

7 Social security tips	8 Allocated tips	9
10 Dependent care benefits	11 Nonqualified plans 25000.00	12a See instructions for box 12 D 17000.00
12b	12c	12d
13 Statutory employee ☐	Retirement plan ☒	Third-party sick pay ☐
14 Other		

VA	358000.00	17900.00
15 State Employer's state I.D. #	16 State wages, tips, etc.	17 State income tax
18 Local wages, tips, etc.	19 Local income tax	20 Locality name

"Jim has a good salary, and according to his W-2, it appears he exercised some stock options because the amount of income is much higher than his base salary plus his bonus. Do you know if the proceeds were used for a particular item or expense?" Patrick asked.

"I remember Jim mentioning something about stock options. I think that's how we covered college tuition for our daughter, Ryann. Could you tell me more about stock options and vesting?" Natalie asked.

Patrick explained that **stock options** were when companies offered their employees the option to purchase a certain amount of the company's stock for a fixed price after a set period of time. The objective is when the employee is eligible to buy the stock at the set price, the market price of the stock will have risen. In other words, in an ideal scenario, the employee is able to purchase the stock for less than the market value at the time of vesting. Employees are not guaranteed their stock options will make them money, but this investment strategy has worked for many individuals.

"According to Jim's year-end pay stub, the proceeds from the stock sales appear to be about $50,000, which is included in line 7's amount: wages, salaries, tips, other comp. Does the $50,000 figure ring a bell?" Patrick asked.

Natalie didn't recall the amount, but she did know tuition was less than $50,000. At the same time, the couple had additional medical expenses to treat Ryann's attention deficit disorder. If there was anything left, Natalie didn't know what Jim did with it.

STOCK OPTIONS

Based on Patrick's research, Jim's options from SSI were **non-qualified stock options (NSO)**, which meant they were granted to him at a specified price—usually the current stock price. Part of the NSO agreement required him to hold them for a specified period of time, called a vesting period.

Once his NSOs vested, he then had a window in which to buy and sell the stock. If the stock price had risen from the time of the grant, he would benefit from that growth and only pay tax on the stock's appreciation. But if the stock price fell below the grant price, then it would be considered *out of the money* (also called *under water*), which meant it had no net value.

In addition, stock options are *granted* (given) to employees. In Jim's case, he was granted annual stock options a number of years ago. He was now at a stage where he needed to exercise certain options each year. Otherwise, he would lose the accumulated value.

"What is **exercising options**?" Natalie asked.

"It is requesting the sale of a stock option, after which a person receives the net value of the appreciation," Jim said.

The net values of these sales were reflected on Jim's W-2 as *additional compensation*. Patrick created a spreadsheet showing Jim's current options and made a calculation to determine the number of marital shares and the number Jim would retain as his separate shares. Currently, he was receiving about $25,000 per year in additional income as a result of exercising the options granted to him more than five years ago. Patrick also noted the actual value of the options was higher than what Jim had indicated on his spreadsheet —he hadn't included any marital portion of the unvested options.

"So you're saying SSI gave him stock he can't sell right now. But a few years after the stocks have vested, he can sell them," Natalie said.

"Precisely. Also, Jim will probably want to retain the options if he feels their value will continue to increase. This will also benefit you because this will be additional income for him that we'll use in calculating your support," said Patrick.

Because there were multiple types of stock options and each had different tax consequences, Patrick had to identify the options Jim had in order to determine their actual value.

"This discussion about Jim's work at SSI made me think of something," Natalie said. "He worked for another company for a little while early in our marriage. Will this factor into your calculations?" Natalie asked.

"Before I answer, how long did he work there?" Patrick asked.

"I know he was there a few years before we got married. And he continued there for about five years after we married. So maybe ten years total," Natalie said.

"If he had a pension with his prior employer, it may be worth exploring. Do you know about any pension?" Patrick asked.

"No, but I can ask him about it," Natalie said.

"If he did, then there may be a benefit from that employment that would be partially a marital asset, which means you could receive an additional benefit," Patrick said.

Based on his assessment, Patrick suggested Natalie let Jim have the stock options. In exchange, Natalie would request more of the E*Trade account.

Patrick's reasoning was Jim would exercise stock options each year, which would generate income for him. Meanwhile, the E*Trade would not be producing as much income for Natalie compared to what the stock options would generate for Jim. Thus Jim's income would be higher and Natalie's would be lower in relative terms. This discrepancy could be grounds for Natalie increasing her proposed spousal support amount.

"What's in it for Jim to go along with an arrangement that would increase his income, which would subject him to paying more spousal support?" Natalie asked.

"We have to determine what's more important to Jim: keeping the E*Trade and having a lower income as a result or keeping his stock options and dealing with the consequences of a higher income. We can also play to his ego with this one: Jim may view keeping the stock options as a win because he may perceive them as more valuable," Patrick said.

Patrick also considered what would happen if Natalie requested the E*Trade amount in cash instead of the actual stocks. As a result, Jim could retain the E*Trade account using a margin line of credit to pay Natalie's share without having to sell all the investments held in the account.

"What is a **margin line of credit**?" Natalie asked.

Patrick explained it is a type of loan that uses a person's investment portfolio as collateral. Basically, individuals borrow money from themselves. This concept is similar to a homeowner who withdraws money from his or her home equity line of credit. Retirement accounts, such as IRAs and 401(k)s, aren't eligible to be used for margin lines of credit.

Individuals can establish a margin anytime for a taxable portfolio simply by making a request from the brokerage firm and signing forms. *But the loan balance cannot exceed a certain percentage of the portfolio's value, which is usually 50 percent.*

Many times individuals use margin lines of credit to buy even more investments, which can increase one's net worth during a positive market period. But if the market declines, this type of loan can create problems. This is because the person would have to sell some of his or her investments to repay a portion of the loan in order to keep it within the maximum allowable percentage relative to the investment portfolio's value.

"Jim may go for that because he's definitely okay with risk. But I'm not, which bothered him to no end," Natalie said.

DEFERRED COMPENSATION

"There's also a $25,000 item on line 11, non-qualified plans, which is additional money that can be contributed to a retirement account that exceeds 401(k) contribution limits. This is usually reserved for management-level employees or executives of a company and is referred to as **non-qualified deferred compensation**. It's both non-qualified *and* a retirement account. Broadly speaking, it's another type of retirement plan," Patrick said.

He added that from an IRS perspective, *non-qualified* means the account doesn't qualify to be treated as a normal retirement account. This is one example of the many exceptions the IRS loves to create. The money in a deferred compensation plan is deferred income from a person's earnings (Jim's in this instance). It is taxed upon distribution.

Jim and SSI have a contractual legal agreement that addresses when and how he will gain access to it upon his retirement. They agree the monies are payable in the future but aren't guaranteed. The contributions to the plan are pre-tax. Thus they made his W-2 earnings appear lower than they actually were. Patrick needed to add the amount to Jim's compensation in order to determine his actual total real compensation from SSI.

"So looking at Jim's W-2, his gross wages were $358,000. But note that the amount of Medicare wages and tips on line 5 is $375,000," said Patrick.

He explained that because Jim contributed $17,000 to his 401(k), which is noted on line 12a, this reduced his income. But it did not decrease line 5, Medicare wages and tips. Thus the total income from Jim's employment was as follows:

$375,000 (Medicare wages and tips)
+ $25,000 (deferred compensation)
$400,000

"So $400,000 is the amount we're going to use for Jim's earned income for last year to calculate support," Patrick said.

Patrick then reviewed the tax return's **Schedule A: Itemized Deductions**. He found no unusual activity.

CAPITAL GAINS AND LOSSES

They next examined **Schedule D: Capital Gains and Losses**.

According to Schedule D, Jim used his E*Trade account to trade stocks fairly often in the previous year, which is reflected by the amount of proceeds generated from transactions.

Patrick noted lines 1b ($8,190) and 8b (-$14,690) reflected the couple had net losses last year and the transactions produced large amounts of **proceeds**. These are generated whenever an investment is sold, which is also called a transaction; it is not the total value of the account. For example, if you have $100,000 in investments but you hold the positions rather than trading (buying and selling), you will not show any proceeds. If, however, you were to trade frequently, you could have $200,000 of proceeds from transactions but still only have $100,000 of value in the account.

Then Patrick explained how most individual investors allow emotions to get in the way of making good decisions. On the one hand, buying a security is easy. On the other hand, selling it requires discipline most individuals don't have. For instance, if the investment is going up, then inexperienced investors often believe the trend will continue. As a result, they fail to capture gains by selling positions because they do not want to pay taxes on the gains. And if it's going down, they're reluctant to sell because doing so is recognition of failure, or they believe it will eventually

SCHEDULE D
(Form 1040)

Department of the Treasury
Internal Revenue Service (99)

Capital Gains and Losses

▶ Attach to Form 1040 or Form 1040NR.
▶ Information about Schedule D and its separate instructions is at *www.irs.gov/scheduled.*
▶ Use Form 8949 to list your transactions for lines 1b, 2, 3, 8b, 9, and 10.

OMB No. 1545-0074

Name(s) shown on return
James R & Natalie C Smith

Your social security number
123-44-5678

Part I   Short-Term Capital Gains and Losses—Assets Held One Year or Less

See instructions for how to figure the amounts to enter on the lines below. This form may be easier to complete if you round off cents to whole dollars.	(d) Proceeds (sales price)	(e) Cost (or other basis)	(g) Adjustments to gain or loss from Form(s) 8949, Part I, line 2, column (g)	(h) Gain or (loss) Subtract column (e) from column (d) and combine the result with column (g)
1a Totals for all short-term transactions reported on Form 1099-B for which basis was reported to the IRS and for which you have no adjustments (see instructions). However, if you choose to report all these transactions on Form 8949, leave this line blank and go to line 1b .				
1b Totals for all transactions reported on Form(s) 8949 with **Box A** checked	312,325.	304,135.		8,190.
2 Totals for all transactions reported on Form(s) 8949 with **Box B** checked				
3 Totals for all transactions reported on Form(s) 8949 with **Box C** checked				

4 Short-term gain from Form 6252 and short-term gain or (loss) from Forms 4684, 6781, and 8824 .	**4**	
5 Net short-term gain or (loss) from partnerships, S corporations, estates, and trusts from Schedule(s) K-1	**5**	
6 Short-term capital loss carryover. Enter the amount, if any, from line 8 of your **Capital Loss Carryover Worksheet** in the instructions	**6** (32,875.)
7 **Net short-term capital gain or (loss).** Combine lines 1a through 6 in column (h). If you have any long-term capital gains or losses, go to Part II below. Otherwise, go to Part III on the back	**7**	-24,685.

Part II   Long-Term Capital Gains and Losses—Assets Held More Than One Year

See instructions for how to figure the amounts to enter on the lines below. This form may be easier to complete if you round off cents to whole dollars.	(d) Proceeds (sales price)	(e) Cost (or other basis)	(g) Adjustments to gain or loss from Form(s) 8949, Part II, line 2, column (g)	(h) Gain or (loss) Subtract column (e) from column (d) and combine the result with column (g)
8a Totals for all long-term transactions reported on Form 1099-B for which basis was reported to the IRS and for which you have no adjustments (see instructions). However, if you choose to report all these transactions on Form 8949, leave this line blank and go to line 8b .				
8b Totals for all transactions reported on Form(s) 8949 with **Box D** checked	238,310.	253,000.		-14,690.
9 Totals for all transactions reported on Form(s) 8949 with **Box E** checked				
10 Totals for all transactions reported on Form(s) 8949 with **Box F** checked.				

11 Gain from Form 4797, Part I; long-term gain from Forms 2439 and 6252; and long-term gain or (loss) from Forms 4684, 6781, and 8824	**11**	
12 Net long-term gain or (loss) from partnerships, S corporations, estates, and trusts from Schedule(s) K-1	**12**	
13 Capital gain distributions. See the instructions	**13**	3,500.
14 Long-term capital loss carryover. Enter the amount, if any, from line 13 of your **Capital Loss Carryover Worksheet** in the instructions	**14** (67,140.)
15 **Net long-term capital gain or (loss).** Combine lines 8a through 14 in column (h). Then go to Part III on the back	**15**	-78,330.

For Paperwork Reduction Act Notice, see your tax return instructions.

Schedule D (Form 1040)

Schedule D (Form 1040)   Page **2**

Part III	**Summary**	

16 Combine lines 7 and 15 and enter the result . . . . | **16** | -103,015.

> - If line 16 is a **gain,** enter the amount from line 16 on Form 1040, line 13, or Form 1040NR, line 14. Then go to line 17 below.
> - If line 16 is a **loss,** skip lines 17 through 20 below. Then go to line 21. Also be sure to complete line 22.
> - If line 16 is **zero,** skip lines 17 through 21 below and enter -0- on Form 1040, line 13, or Form 1040NR, line 14. Then go to line 22.

17 Are lines 15 and 16 **both** gains?
☐ **Yes.** Go to line 18.
☐ **No.** Skip lines 18 through 21, and go to line 22.

18 Enter the amount, if any, from line 7 of the **28% Rate Gain Worksheet** in the instructions . . ▶ | **18** |

19 Enter the amount, if any, from line 18 of the **Unrecaptured Section 1250 Gain Worksheet** in the instructions . . . . ▶ | **19** |

20 Are lines 18 and 19 **both** zero or blank?
☐ **Yes.** Complete the **Qualified Dividends and Capital Gain Tax Worksheet** in the instructions for Form 1040, line 44 (or in the instructions for Form 1040NR, line 42). **Do not** complete lines 21 and 22 below.

☐ **No.** Complete the **Schedule D Tax Worksheet** in the instructions. **Do not** complete lines 21 and 22 below.

21 If line 16 is a loss, enter here and on Form 1040, line 13, or Form 1040NR, line 14, the **smaller** of:

- The loss on line 16 or
- ($3,000), or if married filing separately, ($1,500)   } . . . . | **21** |(3,000.)

Note. When figuring which amount is smaller, treat both amounts as positive numbers.

22 Do you have qualified dividends on Form 1040, line 9b, or Form 1040NR, line 10b?

☒ **Yes.** Complete the **Qualified Dividends and Capital Gain Tax Worksheet** in the instructions for Form 1040, line 44 (or in the instructions for Form 1040NR, line 42).

☐ **No.** Complete the rest of Form 1040 or Form 1040NR.

Schedule D (Form 1040)

come back if they just hold on long enough. By doing so, they ignore **opportunity costs**, which are the potential benefits given up when selecting one alternative over another.

For the most part, the vast majority of individual investors sell when markets are down because they fear losing more money, they cannot tolerate losing, or they have a *hope strategy,* which illustrates the powerful role emotions play when it comes to money. They *hope* the market goes back up. When it doesn't, they sell once the pain is greater than the perceived reward of holding on. These investors often sell when they're afraid and buy back after the markets are recovering because they don't want to miss out on investment opportunity. The result is they tend to buy high and sell low, which makes it very difficult to be profitable.

"Do you know what happened to the proceeds from all the transactions?" Patrick asked.

Natalie didn't have an answer.

He then referred to Schedule D and pointed to the short-term loss of $24,685 on line 7 and a long-term loss of $78,330 on line 15, for a total loss of $103,015 on this year's return as shown on line 16, page 2 of Schedule D.

He explained that the losses could be part of a **loss carry-forward**, which is an accounting strategy that is used when the amount of losses from an investment transaction exceeds the capital gains from other investment transactions. If the net result is a loss that exceeded $3,000, it could be "carried forward" in future tax years to offset future capital gains.

Patrick added that only up to $3,000 of the losses could be used to offset ordinary income in the current tax year and offset capital gains up to the amount of any unused losses. If a balance remained after offsetting gains and taking $3,000 against ordinary income, then the balance would be **carried forward** to the next tax year to offset future capital gains (again, up to $3,000 of ordinary income until the losses were fully deducted).

The net effect was a current deductible loss of $3,000 and a carryforward of just over $100,000 to next year's tax return. This meant they had another marital asset Jim did not identify on his spreadsheet. The $100,000 loss carryforward could be used to offset future gains from investment sales, thereby saving them taxes on those sales. As a result, it was an asset that could be divided by each person claiming his or her share on his or her own tax returns following the divorce.

SUPPLEMENTAL INCOME AND LOSS

Next, they reviewed **Schedule E: Supplemental Income and Loss.**

On line 3, the rental income was $39,600, and on line 20, the amount of expenses totaled $39,466. This left a net income of just $134, which was reflected on line 21.

But Patrick pointed out that evaluating the cash flow provided a different perspective. Adding lines 9 through 16 resulted in a total cash deduction (which reflected expenses paid) of $22,375.

In order to determine the positive cash flow, Patrick subtracted the total cash deduction ($22,375) from the rents received (line 3: $39,600), which resulted in a positive cash flow of $17,225.

Using the positive cash flow figure, Patrick then subtracted the amount of principal repayment to the rental property's mortgage to determine the real net cash flow.

Last year, the couple had principal payments totaling $9,425. By subtracting the principal payments from the positive cash flow, he was able to determine the *real net cash flow:*

$$\begin{array}{r} \$17,225 \text{ positive cash flow} \\ - \quad \underline{\$9,425 \text{ principal payments}} \\ \$7,800 \text{ real net cash flow} \end{array}$$

Thus the property was actually generating tax-sheltered income. Patrick pointed out Jim's spreadsheet didn't include this tax-sheltered cash flow.

SCHEDULE E **(Form 1040)**	**Supplemental Income and Loss**	OMB No. 1545-0074

SCHEDULE E
(Form 1040)

Department of the Treasury
Internal Revenue Service (99)

Supplemental Income and Loss
(From rental real estate, royalties, partnerships, S corporations, estates, trusts, REMICs, etc.)
▶ Attach to Form 1040, 1040NR, or Form 1041.
▶ Information about Schedule E and its separate instructions is at *www.irs.gov/schedulee.*

OMB No. 1545-0074

Name(s) shown on return

James R & Natalie C Smith

Your social security number

123-44-5678

Part I — Income or Loss From Rental Real Estate and Royalties Note. If you are in the business of renting personal property, use Schedule C or C-EZ (see instructions). If you are an individual, report farm rental income or loss from **Form 4835** on page 2, line 40.

A Did you make any payments in 2014 that would require you to file Form(s) 1099? (see instructions)   ☐ Yes ☒ No
B If "Yes," did you or will you file required Forms 1099?   ☐ Yes ☐ No

1a Physical address of each property (street, city, state, ZIP code)

A	Great Owl Circle Reston VA 20190
B	
C	

1b	Type of Property (from list below)	2 For each rental real estate property listed above, report the number of fair rental and personal use days. Check the **QJV** box only if you meet the requirements to file as a qualified joint venture. See instructions.		**Fair Rental Days**	**Personal Use Days**	QJV
A	1		A	365	0	☐
B			B			☐
C			C			☐

Type of Property:
1 Single Family Residence   3 Vacation/Short-Term Rental 5 Land   7 Self-Rental
2 Multi-Family Residence   4 Commercial   6 Royalties   8 Other (describe)

Income:	Properties:		A	B	C
3	Rents received	3	39,600.		
4	Royalties received	4			
Expenses:					
5	Advertising	5			
6	Auto and travel (see instructions)	6			
7	Cleaning and maintenance	7			
8	Commissions.	8			
9	Insurance	9	1,200.		
10	Legal and other professional fees	10			
11	Management fees	11			
12	Mortgage interest paid to banks, etc. (see instructions)	12	14,875.		
13	Other interest.	13			
14	Repairs.	14	1,800.		
15	Supplies	15			
16	Taxes	16	4,500.		
17	Utilities	17			
18	Depreciation expense or depletion	18	17,091.		
19	Other (list) ▶	19			
20	Total expenses. Add lines 5 through 19	20	39,466.		
21	Subtract line 20 from line 3 (rents) and/or 4 (royalties). If result is a (loss), see instructions to find out if you must file **Form 6198**	21	134.		
22	Deductible rental real estate loss after limitation, if any, on **Form 8582** (see instructions)	22	( )	( )	( )

23a	Total of all amounts reported on line 3 for all rental properties	23a	39,600.
b	Total of all amounts reported on line 4 for all royalty properties	23b	
c	Total of all amounts reported on line 12 for all properties	23c	14,875.
d	Total of all amounts reported on line 18 for all properties	23d	17,091.
e	Total of all amounts reported on line 20 for all properties	23e	39,466.
24	**Income.** Add positive amounts shown on line 21. **Do not** include any losses	24	134.
25	**Losses.** Add royalty losses from line 21 and rental real estate losses from line 22. Enter total losses here	25	( )
26	**Total rental real estate and royalty income or (loss).** Combine lines 24 and 25. Enter the result here. If Parts II, III, IV, and line 40 on page 2 do not apply to you, also enter this amount on Form 1040, line 17, or Form 1040NR, line 18. Otherwise, include this amount in the total on line 41 on page 2	26	134.

For Paperwork Reduction Act Notice, see the separate instructions.   Schedule E (Form 1040)

"That shocks me because Jim always told me we were breaking even," Natalie said.

"That's true on an after-tax basis but not on a **real net cash flow** basis."

"What does that mean?" she asked.

Patrick explained the income from the property paid for all of its ongoing expenses including the mortgage. In the end, about $7,830 remained, which is why he referred to it as *real net cash flow*. This could be used to save for future expenses, invested separately, or spent.

On the tax return, however, the couple could deduct all actual cash expenses incurred maintaining the property plus its depreciation, which is not a cash item. Therefore, the couple could have a cash surplus of $7,830, but due to the depreciation, they only had to report about one hundred dollars of income to the IRS.

He added that **depreciation** meant the IRS would allow the couple to take a tax deduction for an investment of real property based upon its expected useful life. For residential real estate, the depreciation is 27.5 years on the improvements. Commercial real estate has a 31-year depreciable life. Both residential and commercial real estate depreciation do not include land value because land cannot be depreciated. Other depreciable property may include vehicles, machinery, and other appliances, all of which have different depreciation schedules.

"I had no idea about the rental property and never realized it had excess cash we could have saved. What do you think happened to that money?" Natalie asked.

"I don't know. But it's definitely a question we need to ask when Kathleen requests additional information from Jim," Patrick said.

Lastly, he noted the couple was subject to **alternative minimum tax (AMT)**, which increased their tax liability. After the divorce was final, the AMT would most likely not apply to Natalie.

He explained that Congress enacted AMT in order to make sure high-income taxpayers (the top 5 percent of income earners) would have to pay a minimum amount of taxes. Generally speaking, it is a 26 percent flat tax for individuals.

AMT was established in 1971. Today, AMT has undergone several significant changes that have affected many middle-income earners, taxpayers that would not be considered the top 5 percent of income earners.

INTEREST AND DIVIDEND INCOME

Patrick and Natalie then reviewed the couple's bank statements and brokerage accounts. Using the tax return as a reference, he took statements from each account and noted income they had generated. He compared the information on the statements with what was reported on **Schedule B: Interest and Ordinary Dividends**.

The bank accounts had generated very little interest (line 4). But several larger amounts of dividends and capital gains distributions appeared at the bottom of the schedule on line 6.

By calculating the income on the tax returns and cross-referencing it with the account statements, Patrick could determine if any accounts were missing or if any accounts had not been identified.

"Overall, how do I know if Jim accurately reported everything here?" Natalie asked.

"Do you know the difference between *tax avoidance* and *tax evasion?* Answer: five to ten years in prison! That's why most people aren't willing to intentionally lie on tax returns," Patrick said.

"Next, we'll review the entries on the spreadsheet Jim provided and compare them with the statements you obtained. The bank account statements appear to match what's on the spreadsheet. With that said, the real estate values are an estimate. I'd suggest you pay an appraiser to take a look at both your residence and the rental property."

"Jim will probably balk at the idea of paying for that," Natalie said.

SCHEDULE B (Form 1040A or 1040) Department of the Treasury Internal Revenue Service (99)	Interest and Ordinary Dividends ▶ Attach to Form 1040A or 1040. ▶ Information about Schedule B and its instructions is at *www.irs.gov/scheduleb*.	OMB No. 1545-0074

Name(s) shown on return	Your social security number
James R & Natalie C Smith	123-44-5678

Part I

Interest

(See instructions on back and the instructions for Form 1040A, or Form 1040, line 8a.)

Note. If you received a Form 1099-INT, Form 1099-OID, or substitute statement from a brokerage firm, list the firm's name as the payer and enter the total interest shown on that form.

		Amount
1	List name of payer. If any interest is from a seller-financed mortgage and the buyer used the property as a personal residence, see instructions on back and list this interest first. Also, show that buyer's social security number and address ▶	
	WFB	50.
2	Add the amounts on line 1	50.
3	Excludable interest on series EE and I U.S. savings bonds issued after 1989. Attach Form 8815	
4	Subtract line 3 from line 2. Enter the result here and on Form 1040A, or Form 1040, line 8a . . . . ▶	50.

Note. If line 4 is over $1,500, you must complete Part III.

Part II

Ordinary Dividends

(See instructions on back and the instructions for Form 1040A, or Form 1040, line 9a.)

Note. If you received a Form 1099-DIV or substitute statement from a brokerage firm, list the firm's name as the payer and enter the ordinary dividends shown on that form.

		Amount
5	List name of payer ▶ Schwab	3,200.
	E-Trade	500.
6	Add the amounts on line 5. Enter the total here and on Form 1040A, or Form 1040, line 9a . . . . ▶	3,700.

Note. If line 6 is over $1,500, you must complete Part III.

Part III

Foreign Accounts and Trusts

(See instructions on back.)

You must complete this part if you **(a)** had over $1,500 of taxable interest or ordinary dividends; **(b)** had a foreign account; or **(c)** received a distribution from, or were a grantor of, or a transferor to, a foreign trust.

		Yes	No
7a	At any time during 2014, did you have a financial interest in or signature authority over a financial account (such as a bank account, securities account, or brokerage account) located in a foreign country? See instructions		×
	If "Yes," are you required to file FinCEN Form 114, Report of Foreign Bank and Financial Accounts (FBAR), to report that financial interest or signature authority? See FinCEN Form 114 and its instructions for filing requirements and exceptions to those requirements		
b	If you are required to file FinCEN Form 114, enter the name of the foreign country where the financial account is located ▶		
8	During 2014, did you receive a distribution from, or were you the grantor of, or transferor to, a foreign trust? If "Yes," you may have to file Form 3520. See instructions on back		×

For Paperwork Reduction Act Notice, see your tax return instructions.   Schedule B (Form 1040A or 1040)

"This is for your protection. After all, how can you make a decision about one of your largest assets without verifying its value first? Next, I see all the investment statements except the E*Trade account. We need to figure out this account's cost basis and also note if any trading has been done that would indicate redirection of the assets," Patrick said.

Patrick explained that a **cost basis** is what Jim and Natalie paid for a particular security plus any additions from dividends and capital gain reinvestments.

He added that cost basis was important to understand when an investment holding was sold. For example, a **low-basis investment** (purchased at low price compared to current price) will have a higher tax liability because there will be a taxable gain to report on their tax return. The resulting tax liability reduces the real value of the asset. In dividing assets, especially if they were not equally split, Natalie needed to be aware of the basis to determine the net value of the asset. Normally, brokerage statements will show the cost basis information. This is why it is important to obtain a copy of the entire statement.

"I know we've covered a lot so far. How are you feeling?" Patrick asked.

"Completely overwhelmed. Even more than when we first met," Natalie said.

"I've worked with countless clients who have felt just as you do right now. In many cases, their doubts reflect they have relied on their spouses to take on the finances, which leaves them feeling vulnerable and uncertain about the future," Patrick said.

"Wouldn't it be easier to make minor adjustments to Jim's spreadsheet, like add the fact that I want to keep the house and all the tweaks you recommend, and then follow it?"

"I'm sure Jim was attempting to be as straightforward as possible with his spreadsheet. He probably developed it from a 'let's just get this divorce done and over with' mentality. But as far as we know, he didn't consult an attorney, which is obvious, based on the rookie mistakes I've pointed out to you so far. The errors in his calculations and assumptions would have a significant negative impact on your financial future. The bottom line is following his outline will fuel your fears of becoming a bag lady," Patrick said.

Throughout his career, Patrick had worked with individuals and couples where a financial imbalance existed. One spouse maintained financial control, which left the other spouse with little knowledge about how money was being invested and spent. While this division of labor may have worked throughout a marriage, it puts one spouse at a severe disadvantage in the event of divorce or death of the other spouse. Numerous clients who knew little about their finances had counted on Patrick to shed light on aspects of their financial lives that, for years, had been shrouded in obscurity.

"Now that you've pointed out all these areas of concern, I don't have a clue about next steps," Natalie said.

"What you're feeling is natural. The whole reason you're here is to make decisions that are in your best interest. That's why you hired Kathleen and me. You definitely don't need to be an expert in finance or family law, but you do need to be aware of the issues in your divorce—blindly following anyone's advice is hazardous to your fiscal health. We're here to develop strategies that will protect you," Patrick said.

Patrick raised one more issue: Was Jim's company healthcare plan covering Natalie's kids, or was her school district's policy covering them?

"We are all covered under Jim's plan. But will this still be the case?" she asked.

He explained it would depend upon the PSA. Jim could continue providing health insurance for the kids. But as far as Natalie was concerned, she would need to obtain coverage either on her own or through the school system.

She had one other temporary option. Under COBRA, she could continue under Jim's plan for up to thirty-six months, but she would have to pay for it herself. **COBRA** stands for Consolidated Omnibus Budget Reconciliation Act. It provides temporary health insurance to employees, spouses, and dependent children if they lose coverage for various reasons.

Natalie still had time to explore her options in order to make the best decision once the divorce was settled.

"We've gone over everything I planned to review with you today. After our meeting, Cullen will send you a straightforward summary of everything we've talked about, which will include next steps. Don't hesitate to call or email any questions to us. Do you have any questions right now?" Patrick asked.

"I think I'm okay for now," Natalie said.

Natalie was experiencing information overload. Even if she did have questions, she had no energy to ask them.

The three concluded their appointment. After Natalie left, Patrick and Cullen reviewed the meeting notes. Cullen was now tasked to prepare two summaries, one for Natalie and one for Kathleen. Natalie's summary would include a list of any additional information she would need to gather. Kathleen's summary would include an overview of the meeting notes, along with Patrick's comments. She would be able to use this summary during her next meeting with Natalie.

On Natalie's to-do list, she was to obtain the following items:

- ◘ Updated statements for Jim's E*Trade account including the cost basis

- ◘ Copies of his option grants

- ◘ Jim's old employer pension benefit statement

- ◘ Information on her spending or cash flow for her living expenses

- ◘ An appraisal of their home and the rental property

Patrick also scheduled a conference call with Kathleen to discuss the marital and non-marital assets. He planned to prepare an updated list of all assets broken down into the marital and non-marital categories. This would most likely be an area of contention for Jim because either he was not aware of the separation between marital and non-marital assets or he chose to ignore the difference. In his list, Patrick would also include information about the possible pension benefit, the loss carryforward, and alternative division of the assets, which would provide a better financial situation for Natalie.

NATALIE PHONES KATHLEEN

After her meeting with Patrick, Natalie contacted Kathleen's office. She spoke with her lawyer about her conversation with Samantha.

"If you can provide proof of his infidelity, then we may be able to use it as ammunition," Kathleen said.

She provided examples of the type of proof the courts would accept that demonstrated infidelity.

"Jim's cheating may not affect the legal aspects of the PSA because this isn't going to be a litigated court case. But it could certainly be used to our advantage if Jim has any guilty feelings about his cheating," Kathleen said.

Natalie decided the time was right to hire a private investigator.

CHAPTER 12

PATRICK MEETS WITH NATALIE, FOLLOWED BY A THREE-WAY MEETING

Two weeks later, Natalie had a follow-up appointment with Patrick. The purpose of the meeting was to review Patrick's new summary that reflected the division of marital and non-marital assets. It included information from Jim's original spreadsheet, financial documents Natalie had provided Patrick, and changes that came about after Natalie and Patrick last met.

"Keep in mind financial data is outdated the moment I receive it—that's the nature of the beast. So what you see will continually evolve," Patrick said.

"First, let's review the major changes in this spreadsheet. You'll notice it is set up differently from the one Jim created. I use specialized software designed for dividing marital assets. For now, we'll keep this spreadsheet between the three of us. We'll use it as a tool to help you prepare for mediations. Plus, we don't want Jim to get suspicious or nervous about it at this stage."

Division of Property: Patrick's Spreadsheet

	JIM'S AMOUNT	NATALIE'S AMOUNT	TOTAL AMOUNT
NON-RETIREMENT ASSETS			
REAL ESTATE EQUITY			
Residence	$285,500	$285,500	$571,000
Total Value $900,000			
1st Mortgage $275,000			
Expense of Sale $54,000			
Marital Equity $571,000			
Rental Property	$200,000	$0	$200,000
Total Value $550,000			
1st Mortgage $350,000			
Marital Equity $200,000			
TOTAL REAL EST. EQUITY	**$485,500**	**$285,500**	**$771,000**
CASH & INVESTMENTS			
Joint WFB	$5,000	$20,000	$25,000
Jim's WFB	$10,000	$0	$10,000
Jim's E*Trade	$181,500	$43,500	$225,000
SSI Vested Stock Options	$112,000	$112,000	$224,000
Natalie's Schwab	$0	$0	$0
Loss Carryforward	$50,000	$50,000	$100,000
TOTAL CASH & INVESTMENTS	**$358,500**	**$225,500**	**$584,000**
PERSONAL EFFECTS			
Natalie's Personal Property	$0	$1	$1
Jim's Personal Property	$1	$0	$1
Sailboat	$30,000	$0	$30,000
BMW	$35,000	$0	$35,000
Subaru	$0	$15,000	$15,000
TOTAL PERSONAL EFFECTS	**$65,001**	**$15,001**	**$80,002**

	JIM'S AMOUNT	NATALIE'S AMOUNT	TOTAL AMOUNT
TOTAL NON-RETIREMENT ASSETS	**$909,001**	**$526,001**	**$1,435,002**
RETIREMENT ASSETS			
IRA/401(k)s			
IRA	$75,000	$75,000	$150,000
401(k)	$187,500	$187,500	$375,000
403(b)	$0	$85,000	$85,000
TOTAL RETIREMENT ASSETS	**$262,500**	**$347,500**	**$610,000**
TOTAL ASSETS	**$1,171,501**	**$873,501**	**$2,045,002**
DEBTS			
Credit Card	$0	($25,000)	($25,000)
BMW	($15,000)	$0	($15,000)
TOTAL DEBTS	**($15,000)**	**($25,000)**	**($40,000)**
TOTAL ASSETS	**$1,171,501**	**$873,501**	**$2,045,002**
TOTAL DEBTS	**($15,000)**	**($25,000)**	**($40,000)**
TOTAL PROPERTY	**$1,156,501**	**$848,501**	**$2,005,002**

"During mediations, we recommend you use Jim's as a guide," said Patrick.

Patrick's updated information addressed the personal property and the Schwab account. He identified the non-marital account, which was Natalie's inheritance, as well as the non-financial aspects of the personal property, which included personal possessions such as furniture and clothing. The furniture and clothing most likely didn't have a current real financial value. As a result, Patrick believed the two items should not be included in the property division.

In Jim's original spreadsheet, the amount of personal property he allocated to Natalie was used to offset other actual financial assets, which put her at a disadvantage. Therefore, Patrick believed the couple should remove the personal possessions from the outline, or at least minimize them until they could be divided accurately and fairly.

As a result of removing the Schwab account and personal property from Natalie's side of the ledger and adding the value of Jim's deferred compensation and the loss carryforward, the bottom line of the spreadsheet showed about a $308,000 difference between two of them. This meant Natalie would need about $154,000 more in order to bring her side of the ledger into balance with Jim's.

"That's amazing news for me. But Jim's going to blow a fuse over this," she said.

"I agree this will be a huge surprise to him, which is why I think you should only bring up these two items, the personal property and the inherited Schwab account, and nothing else in the first mediation. I'll show you other bombshells in our future meetings—ones you'll present to him in subsequent mediations," Patrick said.

"Under 'Personal Effects,' why does 'Personal Property' appear twice?" Natalie asked.

"I did this to separate your personal property from Jim's personal property," Patrick said.

Patrick identified other assets that would also greatly impact the division of marital assets. For example, the couple would identify their primary residence as a hybrid property (in other words, it would contain both marital and non-marital equity). Based on Patrick's evaluation, the home's equity would be the most significant asset they would divide, and it would have the greatest impact on Natalie's future financial well-being.

Patrick reminded her of the essential divorce questions, which would be particularly helpful now:

1. How much financial and emotional currency am I willing to spend?

2. Will the settlement allow me—both with my children and independent of them—to be financially secure now and in the future?

"Fighting for what you're entitled to in regards to your primary residence may not be easy," Patrick said. "But by doing so, you'll increase the likelihood your settlement will allow you to be financially secure. So, in this instance, it will be worth the financial and emotional currency you'll need to leverage. I'm also confident I can find even more ways to improve your situation, and I'll work on them as we move forward. Overall, from a financial perspective, I think you'll be fine," he said.

"You'll be fine" were comforting words Natalie couldn't hear enough times. Although with every meeting she felt more secure in her financial future, the thought of being on her own terrified her.

At the end of their meeting, Patrick told Natalie that he would make sure Kathleen had the necessary financial information in order to make wise decisions about Natalie's property settlement. He also assured Natalie that he would continue to e(
how to maintain her financial independence post-di

Natalie left her appointment with Patrick lool
to her first three-way meeting with Kathleen and I

would solidify the strategy for the first mediation and pour the foundation for future ones. She was both excited to hear Patrick's news and sad her years of marriage would boil down to nothing more than a cold financial agreement, one that would leave her starting all over again.

THREE-WAY MEETING: NATALIE, KATHLEEN, AND PATRICK

A few days later, Natalie and her team met at Patrick's office to prepare Natalie for her first mediation. Her lawyer and financial adviser had developed their strategy, which was summarized in an outline. They also planned to describe what to expect during the mediation and answer her questions.

"Now that your mediation is coming up, how do you feel?" Kathleen asked.

Natalie described her anxiety and trepidation. At the same time, she was eager to dismantle her husband's spreadsheet and witness his reaction to the hours she had spent preparing her points.

"Overall, our strategy is to play it safe during the first mediation. In other words, be agreeable to Jim's spreadsheet," Kathleen said.

"But there's so much wrong with it," said Natalie.

"Definitely," Patrick said. "But first allow yourself to become acquainted with the mediation process, which is brand-new to you; get to know Courtney; and save the critical and most controversial aspects of Jim's spreadsheet for subsequent mediations. Trust us; play nice now—he'll be in for a real surprise later."

"Next, we'll share key mediation principles that will set you up for success," Kathleen said.

MEDIATION PRINCIPLE 1: Timing Is Key

Natalie needed to present her most compelling and important arguments at the right time. If revealed prematurely, she ran the risk of losing out on opportunities to create a more favorable settlement. In addition, poorly timed arguments could derail her team's plans and create more problems than they would solve. Thus Natalie should avoid bringing up potentially inflammatory issues during the first full mediation session.

"Let Jim do most of the talking initially; you want him to feel he's in control," Kathleen said.

MEDIATION PRINCIPLE 2: The Process Is a Marathon, Not a Sprint

"Slow is best," Patrick said. "The key is to avoid presenting issues prematurely. While Jim may be tempted to resolve everything as quickly as possible, you want to avoid this mindset."

Rather than disclose her most compelling arguments against Jim's spreadsheet all at once, Natalie should strategize when to present each item. If done too quickly, Jim might call off the mediation altogether or hire an attack-dog-style attorney or do both in order to protect his interests that were now at risk. Kathleen and Patrick would help her determine the pace and sequence in which she should present her arguments.

They also advised her to follow Courtney's lead. She would address each of the four mediation steps one-by-one: **identification**, **clarification**, **valuation**, and **decision**.

"Courtney will go over each in depth with you and Jim during your first mediation," Kathleen said.

During the mediation process, the couple would jointly uncover various disagreements about their assets. By identifying assets together, they would avoid "blame games" and encourage an awareness of the issues. This process would also cause Jim to see why he would need an attorney to help him understand the legal aspects of their divorce.

MEDIATION PRINCIPLE 3: Understand the Interests of Each Party and Build Consensus as You Move through the Process

Developing consensus between disagreeing parties is an important mediation aspect, particularly at the beginning. This sets a positive tone for future meetings. Thus finding common ground and agreeing on the division of a few easy-to-resolve assets as quickly as possible would engender early goodwill during an otherwise unpleasant process. The couple would also be able to assess how far apart they were on various issues and where they would need to allot the most effort to reach a compromise.

As far as Jim and Natalie were concerned, in order to build consensus, they would need to identify the least contentious assets first and save the most difficult ones for later discussion. The following is a list of major items to be resolved during the meditation and divorce process:

1. Custody

2. Marital and non-marital assets

3. Investment and retirement assets

4. Home equity and hybrid property

5. Spousal support

6. Child support

Kathleen explained that, in general, spousal and child support were the last areas to address because they were the most contentious. Also, custody needed to be resolved before any child support calculations could be made. And before addressing spousal and child support, all income from assets had to be identified first. This meant the division of property needed to be resolved before addressing spousal and child support.

Kathleen would spearhead figuring out the spousal and child support amounts because these were considered a legal matter that required her input. In the meantime, Patrick would provide preliminary calculations for spousal and child support using a special software program designed to make the calculations. These would be placeholders until Kathleen could determine the final amounts.

"What specifically does child support cover?" Natalie asked.

"Child support is designed to provide, food, clothing, shelter, and other basic living needs for minor children living with a parent," Kathleen said.

"And how is support determined?" Natalie asked.

Kathleen explained that support was set by looking at all income sources each parent has (including any spousal support, earned and unearned income, and deferred income). Based on these income sources, Kathleen would apply the statutory guidelines to calculate the child support amount that one parent would pay the other.

Furthermore, additional expenses for the children, such as before- and after-school activities, childcare, health insurance, summer camps, tutors, private school tuition, doctors, dentists, and therapists, could also influence the support amount.

PRIMARY FOCUS OF FIRST MEDIATION

"So are there any issues you recommend I focus on first?" Natalie asked.

Her team recommended she limit the first mediation to the following:

1. Personal property

2. Inheritance (Schwab account)

"These are basic and can easily be resolved and confirmed by any attorney that would represent Jim," Kathleen said.

The three of them then discussed *how* to present the personal property and inheritance, given Natalie's general unease regarding how the first full mediation meeting would go.

Personal Property

"One of our goals in the first meeting is to keep Jim's defenses down. So I'd recommend playing innocent at first," Kathleen said. "I'd frame the two issues as questions. For example, when Jim presents his spreadsheet, say, 'I'm curious. Why are you allocating so much of the personal property to me?"

Kathleen encouraged Natalie to explain it was her attorney who raised this concern. Typically personal property listed would be items of great value, such as fine art and antiques, and the couple had neither of these. She could then suggest removing the personal property from the spreadsheet and address its division later, outside of any discussion regarding financial assets.

Inheritance (Schwab Account)

In regards to the inheritance, Kathleen suggested Natalie once again bring up her attorney by saying she learned the inheritance *was not* a marital asset. Thus it shouldn't be part of the division.

"Jim will definitely object to anything about my inheritance," Natalie said.

Her husband had always questioned why Natalie wanted to keep the inheritance separate. Jim insisted his name be added to it. To him, her refusal demonstrated she didn't trust him. He believed it was *their* money because they'd use it to support their children and make home improvements. Most of his irritation, however, was rooted in his determination to control how it was invested.

"If tackling that subject will rattle his nerves, then perhaps you can simply ask Courtney what she thinks about the inheritance being a separate account," Patrick said.

Her team believed Courtney's response would include a general overview of marital versus non-marital assets. She would then suggest both of them receive specific recommendations from their respective attorneys.

Patrick reassured her that regardless of how the Schwab account was registered, according to his research, no marital monies had been added to the account, and withdrawals were used only for the down payment and home improvements.

PRIMARY RESIDENCE

"When should I bring up my intentions to keep the house? As I've shared before, I want it at least until Rachel graduates from high school and ideally college," said Natalie.

"After doing my research, I think presenting that option won't cause additional issues in regards to its valuation. In fact, doing so would actually increase Jim's equity because we would not include the cost of sale in the calculation. But keep in mind the cost of ownership for a house could become very expensive. If the agreement includes the fact of selling the property and splitting the proceeds, then it will be whatever that amount turns out to be. But if you want to retain the house as part of the agreement, then you'll need an appraisal to use as the valuation," said Patrick.

He added that if she planned to retain the house, it could possibly cause long-term cash flow problems that could be detrimental to her financial independence.

"You suggested that during the mediation I tell Jim, 'My attorney brought up X, Y, Z concerns,' which relates to my next question: How do I disclose I'm working with both of you?" Natalie asked.

"Early on, Courtney will most likely ask you and Jim about legal representation. In that case, feel free to mention me. You most likely won't be asked about a financial adviser. I'd avoid bringing up Patrick for now," said Kathleen.

"I'm not sure what will upset Jim more: the personal property and inheritance or the lawyer part. I tend to give in when he gets upset. Any recommendations about what I should do if he blows up?" Natalie asked.

"The good news is the mediator's role is to oversee the meeting. If Jim loses his cool, don't react. Just let Courtney take charge. She has been trained to address tense situations. Strategies she'll use include reminding all parties of the process and calling a time-out if necessary," Kathleen said.

Patrick then explained how Courtney would introduce the mediation process to Natalie and Jim. This included what would take place during their first and subsequent meetings. After each meeting, the couple would have homework assignments to complete in preparation for their next meeting. This would keep the process moving forward. Examples of homework include the following:

◘ Topics to discuss with Kathleen regarding marital and non-marital assets and child and spousal support

◘ Obtaining the necessary financial and legal data

◘ Sharing financial statements with each other, such as the 401(k), IRA, and E*Trade statements; this is part of the financial discovery, which requires that spouses show supporting documents to one another

◘ Addressing any conclusions they've drawn during mediation, such as having the home appraised and accurately identifying assets

"By the way, did you end up hiring a private investigator?" Kathleen asked.

"Yes. His calendar's booked this week. He said he would start next week. Maybe I'll have some news to share with Jim during our first mediation," Natalie said.

"Promise me you'll call me first if you find anything out before your first mediation. I know what he's done is very hurtful. But we want to make sure all your actions support the outcome you seek, so we want to avoid any hasty moves that could compromise our strategy," Kathleen said.

"And based on all we've uncovered and planned so far, you won't regret holding your cards close to you," Patrick said.

Natalie agreed to follow her team's advice.

CHAPTER 13

FIRST MEDIATION

Natalie sat in the reception area of Courtney's office. She had arrived fifteen minutes early for her first mediation and was thumbing through the notes on her iPad. Every day since her last meeting with Kathleen and Patrick, she had reviewed the talking points her divorce team had provided her and rehearsed her answers.

At 1:00 p.m., Courtney's administrative assistant invited her to the conference room, and Natalie took a seat. The mediator entered shortly after and introduced herself.

"Great to finally meet you in person," Natalie said.

"Likewise," Courtney said. "Jim just phoned our office; he said he'll be here in a few minutes."

Natalie was relieved her husband was running late. This allowed her to avoid the awkward silence of waiting with him in the reception area.

After Jim arrived, Courtney invited him to take a seat. From his briefcase, he pulled out a file folder containing his division of assets spreadsheet and other divorce documents he had prepared. Courtney stood by the large flip chart located at the head of the conference room table. She began the meeting.

"As you know, I'm a lawyer and a trained mediator. Throughout our time together, I'll put on my mediator hat. In other words, I'm not here to legally represent either of you or provide legal advice."

Courtney wrote "RESPECT" at the top of the flip chart. She explained that throughout the process, everyone must uphold the meaning of this word. The couple would most likely run into areas where they would disagree. But despite divergent perspectives, they must always maintain respect, which meant giving the other person an opportunity to speak and respond to questions without interruption and refraining from making personal attacks or threatening gestures. The meetings were to be a safe place to discuss differences and find solutions together for their joint best interest.

She then summarized her role, which was to:

- Set the parameters of how they would work
- *Not* provide financial or legal advice
- Ensure all key conflicts are identified
- Help resolve key conflicts
- Maintain neutrality throughout the process
- Ensure everyone follows the mediation process and stays on track toward solving disagreements
- Keep everyone apprised of next steps, including homework assignments each would need to complete between mediations
- Note areas the couple disagrees about and that need more work to resolve

"You may already be aware of the mediation process. But I always like to make sure we're all on the same page, so I'll briefly explain the parameters of how we'll work together," Courtney said.

She described that during each mediation, all individual items they identified would appear on a flip chart; some items might be easily dealt with while others might require additional investigation to determine how best to make a decision about the disposition.

Select items might require outside financial consulting in order that the couple better understand the consequences of their decisions. Writing information down on the flip chart keeps everyone focused. It ensures the mediation process respects each of their perspectives, including what they're most concerned about, and it sets the stage for how they'll deal with issues important to each of them as they move toward an agreement.

Courtney then described each mediation step.

FOUR STEPS OF MEDIATION

STEP 1. IDENTIFICATION

The couple would develop a list of all the assets and liabilities and identify the ownership of each. This would give them a clear understanding of assets that might be subject to division or be retained by one of them.

STEP 2. CLARIFICATION

Once they identified assets, they would address each one and determine when it was acquired, if it was subject to division, the tax consequences of the asset, and who was liable for any debts associated with it.

In the eyes of a husband or wife, the emotional attachment to a particular asset—such as sporting equipment, a family piano, or the pet dog—can trump its financial value. Thus identification and clarification bring an understanding of how each party feels about specific items or issues. This step may be helpful in how they decide on the division. Once assets have been identified and clarified, negotiations begin. This involves the next two steps.

STEP 3. VALUATION

The couple may need to obtain appraisals for assets that require them. They may also collect financial statements that begin from the date of separation and extend to current time. These include closing documents for real property, tax returns, and current pay stubs. Documentation is the key to identifying values. Furthermore, having statements of the various financial accounts enhances the ability to verify values and make decisions about the division of assets. In addition, the couple may need to obtain documentation for assets acquired prior to the marriage.

STEP 4. DECISION

The couple would make decisions jointly and based on items they had identified, clarified, and valued. Coming to agreement and making decisions together demonstrated an important objective of the mediation process: **self-determination.** Self-determination *increases* the likelihood each will follow through with the PSA and *decreases* the possibility of non-compliance after the divorce.

ADDITIONAL CONSIDERATIONS

As the couple addresses their assets and liabilities, they will have discussed related issues, such as tax consequences and whether or not assets have equal values, especially when making decisions about trading one asset for another. This is another example where having an outside financial consultant would benefit both of them.

"At the end of each mediation, you'll be assigned tasks to complete before the next meeting. I'll also email you a summary of the meeting for your review," said Courtney.

She added the mediation process would provide a format to address each item they identified. They would come to a decision quickly about certain items. Meanwhile, they would set other items aside that would require additional attention. Also, some steps would probably overlap. For instance, an asset may be identified and they may quickly agree on a value, and then the actual or final decision can be made.

The four steps work nearly in conjunction in this instance. But as far as assets that are difficult to clarify or value, they will likely require more discussion before a decision can be made.

THE MEDIATION BEGINS

"I know I've covered a lot of ground so far. Are there any questions I can answer?" Courtney said.

Although he didn't say it, Jim saw little value in her overview. He thought muddling through each step was excessive and delaying the task at hand—to move the divorce to a quick resolution. In fact, Jim felt an urgency to address step 4, decision, as soon as possible. After all, the sooner they divided their assets, the faster their marriage would end, which would save him money and allow him to focus on life post-divorce.

"Thank you for your introduction," Jim said. "Now that's out of the way, Natalie and I have reviewed a spreadsheet I created that outlines the division of assets. You'll see the spreadsheet covers three steps: identification, clarification, and valuation. At the bottom of my spreadsheet, I've equally divided the assets. So why don't we dive right into step 4, *decision*? That way we can agree on the division of assets, wrap things up, and save ourselves unnecessary expense and time."

"I appreciate your preparation," said Courtney. "I assure you there is a time and place to address your spreadsheet. Specifically, it aligns perfectly with the first step, identification. It will also serve as a solid starting place for valuation. But we follow a particular order for a reason—the methodology is based on decades of trial-and-error refinement of the mediation process by experts in the field. Unfortunately, skipping steps compromises the process and creates more problems than it solves. The goal is to not jump to any conclusion before its time. So we need to understand the assets and liabilities, first, from when and how they were acquired, next, what their values were at the time of separation, and then, their current values."

Jim expressed that because they just separated a few months ago, the values of their assets would not be much different from what appeared on his spreadsheet. Rather than slow the meeting down arguing over this, he decided to drop his current agenda to push the mediation to step 4. But he did express he didn't want to spend much time on identification, which simply reviewed what he already knew.

Natalie was relieved Courtney reined in her husband and took control and appreciated how the mediator addressed Jim's tendency to dominate conversations, particularly ones between the two of them. Left to the couple's own devices, Natalie would have allowed him to move forward with his initial plan.

"At what point will we know how many meetings we'll need to have?" asked Natalie.

"It depends on you and Jim and your ability to reach agreement on the issues. I'm here to provide an environment that will allow you to disagree in a way that is conducive to finding solutions," Courtney said.

"I really thought we could hammer this out in just a couple of meetings," Jim said.

Courtney then asked if either of them had retained a lawyer.

"Doesn't mediation make a lawyer unnecessary?" Jim asked.

"Yes, mediation can be a means to avoid hiring a lawyer to represent you in court. But it's still highly advisable to have an attorney in order to ensure the decisions you make are complying with the law and in your best interest—particularly when you'll be required to sign a legally binding agreement, such as an MOU or the PSA," Courtney said. "And Natalie, how about you?"

She took a deep breath dreading Jim's reaction to what she was about to say. "Yes, I have one," Natalie said. "Kathleen Weber."

"What?! How long have you been spending *our* money—*my* money—on lawyers? Don't you realize we'll each get less if we're paying crazy legal fees?" Jim asked.

"From what I understand, hiring attorneys to help with mediation is normal and often necessary. Isn't that true, Courtney?" Natalie asked.

In her opinion, Courtney explained no one should sign a legal document without proper representation. In addition, the extent to which they would require a lawyer depended on their individual needs. Because divorce was complicated and confusing, she recommended each spouse hire a lawyer. Their respective attorneys would review the memorandum of understanding (MOU) before they signed it. They would also help them make objective, prudent decisions throughout the mediation process. In addition, lawyers would help determine spousal and child support because these are legal matters. Spousal support is negotiated, but child support is determined via the statutory guidelines.

Courtney knew Natalie's lawyer. Because Kathleen was also trained in the collaborative divorce process, Courtney believed Natalie's attorney would be an important ally in the mediation process.

"So far I haven't found any compelling reason for me to hire a lawyer. I guess we could just use Natalie's to close up any loose ends concerning required legal notices. I'm paying her legal fees, after all," Jim said.

"Jim, as we forge ahead with the mediation, I think you'll find having your own legal counsel will benefit you immensely. There are many nuances when it comes to the law, and you should have independent representation before you sign anything," Courtney said.

She then suggested they begin addressing each asset. They would use the four-part mediation process as their guide.

STEP 1. IDENTIFICATION

"Why don't we use my spreadsheet as a starting point?" asked Jim.

"What are your thoughts, Natalie?" Courtney asked.

"As a starting point, I'm okay with it. But I've reviewed it with my attorney, and she identified several items that probably need to be changed before we consider any division. Two items stand out: my Schwab account, which is my inherited asset, and the personal property, which really has no financial value. I'd like the Schwab account removed because it's non-marital, and I'd like to remove or set the personal possessions aside because they shouldn't play a role in the financial aspects of the property settlement," Natalie said.

"Wait. You're taking apart my spreadsheet? What the hell is going on here?" Jim asked as he abruptly stood up from his chair. "See what happens when you involve lawyers? I deal with them all the time at work. They're just paid to stir up trouble so they can charge more," Jim said.

Courtney calmly asked Jim to sit down and reminded him of their agreement to be respectful and not make any threatening gestures. She explained that Natalie had a right to obtain legal counsel to help her make decisions. She asked Jim if he was familiar with how to identify marital and non-marital assets.

From what he understood, marital assets were ones they had accumulated during their marriage. Because they had used the inheritance for marital purposes, he believed it was part of their overall assets. In addition, he thought all assets were marital because they had been married for twenty-five years.

Courtney provided a general description of marital and

non-marital assets as the terms were understood in Virginia family law. These rules, with slight variations, were similar to ones in other states as well. *Non-marital assets* were those acquired prior to the marriage, received by inheritance, gift, or bequest from someone other than the spouse and those acquired post-separation. Meanwhile, *marital assets* were all other assets acquired during the marriage. Identifying assets as marital or non-marital was not always easy. In addition, there was hybrid property, which was where both types of assets have been commingled.

"Keep in mind assets are subject to interpretation because numerous factors could impact what constitutes marital and non-marital. This is where an attorney would play an important role," Courtney said.

In regards to the personal property, Jim maintained Natalie, not he, would receive most of it.

"What many people don't realize is the actual amount you first paid for personal possessions is irrelevant," Courtney said. "With the exception of art and antiques, whose worth you can quantify through an appraisal, most personal possessions have little value. Thus they usually don't play a role in the division of the financial assets."

"I'm happy to discuss dividing personal possessions once we settle the financial issues. And if you think they have value, by all means, consider selling them," Natalie said.

Courtney then tore a sheet from the flip chart and taped it to the wall. She titled it "Future Discussion" and then wrote "Schwab account" and "Personal property." She also noted the following:

> Natalie believes the Schwab account is non-marital because it was an inheritance. Jim believes it's marital because it has been used for marital purposes. We may need to determine what value the personal property has at a later time and how it may affect the final division of property.

"Let's put these aside for now because they'll require further input by legal counsel to determine their status in the division of assets. Be assured we're not making any decisions regarding these assets yet. We're simply identifying and seeing which ones we agree on and which we have a difference of opinion about," Courtney said.

Her conciliatory comment alleviated Jim's concerns that Courtney was favoring Natalie during the proceeding. At the same time, he began to realize he probably needed to hire a lawyer and prepare more for the next mediation.

After identifying Natalie's Schwab account and the personal property, they continued identifying assets. Using Jim's spreadsheet as a guide, they went through the remaining assets one-by-one:

- Joint Wells Fargo Bank account (WFB)
- Jim's WFB
- Primary residence
- Rental property
- Jim's E*Trade
- Jim's 401(k)
- Jim's IRA
- Natalie's 403(b)
- SSI stock options
- Cars
- Sailboat
- Credit card debt

STEP 2. CLARIFICATION

"Now that we've identified assets, we're ready to have a more in-depth discussion about them. In the clarification phase we'll verify ownership of assets and how they're titled. Either one of you or both of you can own an asset. For instance, the loan on your house may be co-signed. This information would appear on your monthly mortgage statement," Courtney said.

They then addressed the following for each item:

1. Ownership

2. Preference for division

3. Notes that included purchase dates and associated debt if applicable

4. Estimated value

In regards to estimated values, in the event they didn't agree on one value, Courtney noted a range that reflected both perspectives. For the next three hours, the couple worked using the four-step process for each asset and liability they identified. The following is a summary of what appeared on the flip-chart pages and were taped to the wall. The large sheets of paper demonstrated the result of their hard work:

Courtney's Spreadsheet Based on Mediation Discussion

Items	Ownership	Estimated Value	Notes
Joint WFB	Joint	$10,000 to $25,000	Bill pay account
Jim's WFB	Jim	$5,000 to $10,000	Business and personal expenses
Primary Residence	Joint	$900,000 to $975,000	Purchased 1998 Natalie: Down payment, 20% and paid for improvements later. Mortgage balance $275k? Natalie expressed she seeks to retain the house until Rachel graduates from high school.
Rental Property	Joint	$500,000 to $600,000	Prior residence Purchased 1991 for $150k, refinanced. Mortgage balance $350k? Jim expressed he wants to retain the rental property.
Jim's E*Trade	Jim	$225,000	Jim's trading account in stocks. Jim seeks to retain the E*Trade.

Items	Ownership	Estimated Value	Notes – Jim (J), Natalie (N)
Jim's 401(k)	Jim	$375,000	Maximum contribution Plus match
Jim's IRA	Jim	$150,000	Old 401(k)
Natalie's 403(b)	Natalie	$85,000	Contributes 10% plus match
SSI Stock Options	Jim	$375,000 to $400,000	Need clarification to determine net after-tax value. Jim expressed he wants to keep these.
Cars	Joint	J: $35,000 N: $15,000	J: BMW, to keep; N: Subaru, to keep
Sailboat	Joint	$30,000	No debt, J to retain
Credit Card Debt	Joint	$25,000	J says it's N's responsibility because expenses incurred after separation. N says she used it for family holiday spending and to meet general needs.

Based on Courtney's initial observation, she thought the couple could easily clarify the joint checking accounts. So she recommended they begin with them.

"What's the purpose of the accounts?" Courtney asked.

"I deposit my teaching salary into the joint account, and Jim deposits enough to cover all current common bills," Natalie said.

"I've also opened a new bank account I use to pay for personal living expenses ever since I moved out," Jim said.

Courtney noted the following on the flip chart:

> Joint checking at WFB for household and living expenses, and Jim has separate account to meet his personal living expenses. Agreed to use the joint account to pay all current expenses associated with the residence and both would continue to deposit their paychecks into the joint account until the MOU was signed.

She then asked if they had additional information they wanted to add. Neither of them did, so she moved on.

Cars

"Earlier, both of you agreed to keep your respective cars. As a result, you'll need to determine how they were titled; you'll need to transfer titles to your own names if they don't appear that way right now," Courtney said.

The couple both jotted this down in their notes.

Primary Residence

Courtney asked if they had agreed upon how they'd dispose of their residence. Jim indicated he wished to sell it as soon as possible. Meanwhile, Natalie wanted to retain the house at least until Rachel graduated from high school.

"I'm willing to give up other assets to offset the equity in the house that Jim would otherwise be receiving," Natalie said.

"And Jim, what are your thoughts on Natalie keeping the house?" Courtney asked.

"Natalie can keep the house if I can keep the rental property and most of my investment accounts," Jim said.

Courtney asked Natalie if she was receiving expert advice to help her make her decision since retaining the house might have a big impact on her finances going forward. Thus she believed it was in Natalie's best interest to consider the pros and cons of her decision. Also, if she planned to keep it, Courtney told Natalie she would need to obtain an appraisal, which would be used in the valuation stage.

"I see how I could benefit from outside expertise here," Natalie said.

Natalie chose her words carefully. She recalled her team's advice to avoid bringing up Patrick's role—at least for now. They then moved on to the rental property.

Rental Property

"For now, you have estimated the rental property's value at $550,000 to $600,000 with a mortgage balance of around $350,000, which leaves a net equity of $200,000 to $250,000," said Courtney.

Courtney referred to the following, which appeared on Jim's original spreadsheet:

	Jim	Natalie
Rental Property	$167,000	$0

"When I look at your original spreadsheet, Jim; you have your net equity shown as $167,000 on your side of the ledger. Can you tell me how you arrived at that value?" asked Courtney.

"My calculation included the cost of the sale," Jim said.

"If I'm not mistaken, didn't you say you intended to retain the rental property?" asked Courtney.

Jim replied yes.

Courtney then suggested he add this to the list of questions to ask his attorney noting that the cost of sale may not be an allowed reduction of the value if Jim plans to retain the property.

"Do you know when it was originally purchased and how much it cost?" Courtney asked.

Jim said he purchased it the year after they married. They were able to finance it 100 percent and only had to cover its closing costs. They bought it for $150,000.

"Is the property titled in Jim's name alone? And is one or both of you on the mortgage?" asked Courtney.

"It's titled jointly, and both of us are on the mortgage," said Jim.

"How long did you live there, and did you ever refinance it?" Courtney asked.

Natalie said they lived in the property until they purchased their current home. After that point, they turned it into a rental. They had refinanced it in order to obtain a lower interest rate before it became a rental property. They also used some of the equity to help pay for their kids' college expenses.

Courtney then asked when and how much money they pulled out of the rental property for college. Although Jim didn't have the precise figure, he thought it was about $50,000 the first time around. They also refinanced the house again when interest rates dipped a few years ago. At that time, they didn't pull out any money.

"Do you still have copies of the HUD-1 settlement documents from when you purchased the house as well as the last time you refinanced it?" the mediator asked.

Jim believed he still had them and wrote a note to himself to look for them. These statements would help in determining the amount of equity that had been created during the periods between the original purchase and each refinancing.

"How much rental income do you receive, and what are the current expenses on the rental property?" Courtney asked.

Jim said the rent was $3,300 per month. He jotted down a reminder to review the previous year's tax return and note the amount of expenses.

"Do you have a current mortgage statement?" Courtney asked.

"Yes. I'll be sure to look for it," Jim said.

This was needed to evaluate and verify the actual mortgage balance, the current interest rate, and the monthly mortgage payment. In addition, the statement showed the amount of any escrow payments for real estate taxes and homeowner's insurance premiums.

"Since we're on the subject of rental property, I have a question," Natalie said. "Jim oversees the property now, but we both did some improvements over the time we lived there. Does the fact we refinanced it impact the division of its equity?"

Courtney explained it *would not* likely have an impact if it met the following conditions:

1. They purchased the property as their primary residence after they were married, and rather than selling it, they later turned it into a rental property.

2. They *did not* contribute non-marital monies to it.

3. No non-marital assets were used for improvements.

"Although I advise you run this by your attorney first, from what I see, it appears the rental property equity would be 100 percent marital. Do you both agree?" Courtney asked.

"But I manage the rental property. Doesn't that count for something?" Jim asked.

"And do I get credit for the gardening and painting I've done over the years?" Natalie asked.

Courtney used both questions to illustrate why they both needed their own legal counsel. Generally efforts they each performed would not be considered as adding non-marital or separate contributions. Then again, exceptions to most everything exist. Their lawyers would be the best to address their concerns.

The mediator then recommended a fifteen-minute break.

After their much-needed rest, they continued clarifying other assets and liabilities, which appeared on sheets of paper covering the conference room walls.

"The two big-ticket items on our list are your primary residence and rental property. Does either of you have any ideas about how to determine their value?" Courtney asked.

"Isn't the property tax bill enough?" Jim asked. "I used that when I prepared my spreadsheet. And I also have the amounts that appear on Zillow and Redfin—popular real estate websites. I hear their estimates are pretty accurate too."

"Those can certainly be resources. Does either of you have any other ideas? How was the property valued when you did the refinancing?" asked Courtney.

"If you're suggesting we get an appraisal, I'm against needlessly spending money. I don't think the market has changed significantly since we did the last refinance so we should be able to use the ones we already have," said Jim.

"What do you think, Natalie?" Courtney asked.

"I'm not sure. Are there any benefits to getting an appraisal now?" Natalie asked.

Courtney explained if they were planning to sell one or both properties, then having a formal appraisal done at the moment might not be as critical because they would end up dividing the net proceeds. If, however, one of them planned to retain one or both of the properties, then a formal appraisal would be more important in order to determine the amount to allocate under the PSA.

Natalie then said she would take care of the primary residence appraisal if Jim would do the same for the rental property. They each agreed to obtain the necessary appraisals by the next mediation session.

Spousal and Child Support

"Jim has spousal and child support amounts on his spreadsheet," Natalie said. "But from what I understand, it's too early to determine any support. First, we need to agree on the division of assets; next we have to identify all sources of income. Also doesn't child support follow statutory guidelines?" asked Natalie.

"Yes, we have groundwork to cover before we can figure out support. Also, I always advise clients to consult with their attorneys because determining support is one of the most complicated aspects of divorce and agreeing upon an amount typically requires negotiation and an understanding of the law," Courtney said.

"Fine. Let's take it off for now. I just thought I'd offer an amount that would be fair for Rachel and us. But Natalie's suddenly an expert and wants to complicate everything," Jim said.

After an arduous four hours (which actually felt like ten to both of them) since they had first met in Courtney's office, their meeting drew to an end. At the mediation's close, Natalie's biggest concern hadn't changed: She was still worried about her and her children's financial futures.

Meanwhile, Jim was concerned about the cost of Natalie's attorney and how powerless he felt reining her in. And the thought of his having to retain an expensive lawyer made him regret deciding to mediate in the first place. "Why mediate when I have to hire a lawyer anyway?" he thought to himself.

"I want to thank you for respecting the process. By identifying and clarifying most assets, we definitely got off to a great start and set a solid foundation for future meetings," Courtney said.

She reviewed their homework assignments, which were as follows:

1. Obtain documentation to further clarify identified assets.

2. Receive valuations and appraisals for the real property that was being retained.

3. Collect copies of investment accounts, mortgage refinancing, and HUD-1 statements for property from time of purchase and each refinancing.

By this point, Jim conceded he needed a lawyer and told the group he'd find one before the next mediation. The three then reviewed their calendars. In order to keep the process moving, they decided to schedule the second mediation in three weeks.

Jim offered to obtain his year-end IRA, 401(k), mortgage, HUD-1s, and E*Trade account statements and a copy of their joint tax return and send copies to Courtney and Natalie.

"You don't need to bother sending me any of those. In fact, I've already got them ready to go. Would you like me to send them to you?" Natalie asked Jim.

Her quick offer to take charge surprised Jim, who was certain she couldn't know what those documents were—let alone be ready to send them to him. But he now wondered if he had underestimated her resilience and determination.

POST-MEDIATION REFLECTION

Courtney went to work preparing a mediation summary. In it, she included Jim's spreadsheet with two simple revisions: First, she placed a question mark next to the item "Natalie's Schwab," which was Natalie's inheritance. This indicated that it still needed clarification as to being marital or non-marital. Second, Courtney placed another question mark next to the personal property. This indicated the concerns Natalie expressed regarding the valuation of these items. This served as a placeholder and indicated it would be subject to division later. She emailed the summary report to Kathleen, Natalie, and Jim.

After their first mediation wrapped up, Natalie and Jim left Courtney's office. Jim phoned Claudia.

"I feel I got punched in the gut for the past four hours," he said. "Do you mind if I come over now?"

What Jim thought would be a mediated divorce requiring two sessions—three max—he now realized would require more meetings, more lawyers, more expense, and more time than he had anticipated.

Meanwhile, Natalie's private investigator sat in his car, waiting for Jim to leave Courtney's office. He trailed his suspect to Claudia's house. Once Jim arrived, the PI took photos of Jim parking his car and Claudia greeting him at the front door. This evidence would confirm his client's biggest fear.

Jim and Claudia made love that night. Afterwards, as his lover lay asleep, Jim lightly kissed her on the cheek and quietly left the bedroom. He sat on the living room couch, opened his laptop, and began the arduous task of finding a lawyer. He knew Natalie had already met with her lawyer—*God only knows how many times!*—and had developed her strategy. He believed she was way ahead, which left him scrambling to catch up.

From hiring a plumber to discovering the best car deal, Jim reflected on the many times he had counted on his wife to make important household decisions. This time, however, he knew he couldn't rely on her help. Over the next two days, he narrowed his search and scheduled introductory appointments. At the same time, he felt resentment regarding the need to pay for representation, particularly because he believed he could find most answers to his legal questions online. "If they just followed my spreadsheet, this would be so easy. Lawyers ruin everything!" he insisted.

If the couple were dancing, Natalie had just taken the lead and changed the tempo. Although she felt exhausted, she left the meeting exhilarated after skillfully executing her well-rehearsed moves. She was confident this process, which Jim had initiated, would respect and encourage her point of view. She knew the next few weeks and months would require the same amount of focus and time she had already committed. When she arrived home, she collapsed on the couch.

CHAPTER 14

NATALIE DEBRIEFS WITH HER TEAM AND MEETS WITH PATRICK

The next afternoon, Natalie and her team had a 3:30 p.m. conference call to discuss how the first mediation went.

Natalie described the following to Kathleen and Patrick:

- ◘ She felt confident and well prepared throughout the mediation.

- ◘ Courtney was a skilled listener and reined in Jim when he wanted to rush through the mediation and his temper flared.

- ◘ Courtney explained the process, and they identified all assets on Jim's spreadsheet.

- ◘ They agreed to set aside the personal property and her Schwab account for now.

- ◘ When they reached the clarification phase, they discussed their rental property and primary residence, both of which might require an appraisal.

- ◘ Jim was surprised and irritated to learn Natalie had hired a lawyer.

- ◘ Jim reluctantly agreed to hire an attorney.

- ◘ Courtney provided them homework assignments.

- ◘ Courtney had created a chart that summarized their assets, who owned them, their estimated values, and notes, which included the following:

  - ◘ *They agreed to retain their current cars and to use their joint account for all living expenses with the exception of Jim's apartment, which he would pay for on his own.*

  - ◘ *Jim felt strongly about retaining his company stock options and the E*Trade account.*

Natalie added that Jim planned to retain the rental property and she wanted the primary residence for now. She wanted her team's input regarding whether keeping the house was financially responsible. Natalie also told them that custody was a significant issue for her, and full custody was the only option she would consider.

"How and when will custody be resolved?" she asked.

Kathleen responded it would be necessary to make that decision before they could make any of the final support calculations. She recommended that Natalie and Jim reach an agreement on custody as soon as possible so they could begin to look at the support issues. If they could not reach an agreement on their own, then Natalie would need to consider going to court to resolve the custody issue.

At the end of their conference call, Patrick confirmed Natalie's meeting with him that would take place Thursday afternoon.

NATALIE'S MEETING WITH PATRICK

The moment Patrick saw Natalie, he could tell she was preoccupied. They left his reception area and took a seat in his office.

"Is everything okay?" Patrick asked.

Natalie held a large envelope in her hand. She pulled out a photo and handed it to Patrick. The picture showed Jim embracing a woman while they both stood in the entrance of a house.

"Is this the evidence from the PI?" Patrick asked.

"Unfortunately for me, yes. Everyone's suspicions about Jim were right. How could I have been so naïve? But at least now I have an explanation for his erratic behavior," Natalie said.

In the private investigator's report, he identified the woman in the photo as Claudia. She was forty-two years old, single as far as he could tell, had no kids, earned her PhD, and was a researcher specializing in hospital medical identity theft. The fact Claudia wasn't a mom provided Natalie slight relief knowing her husband's affair was ruining only one family.

At this point, Natalie didn't know who she despised more, Claudia or Jim. She also felt foolish for not acting on her suspicions about his infidelity sooner and for being betrayed by his lies.

"I'm sorry about the photos. It takes your divorce to a completely different emotional level. But it's better to know now rather than later—I know that does little to make you feel better. Just know you're not responsible for his irresponsible behavior," said Patrick.

"I spent last night crying wondering what I did or didn't do right. I feel as if I'm on a merry-go-round and can't get off. What are the kids going to think?" she asked.

"Your kids are lucky to have a mom that cares so much. Sadly, Jim's probably in his lust phase, which means he's operating with blinders and not thinking about how his actions are affecting you and the kids. If you haven't told Kathleen already, I recommend you let her know A.S.A.P. so she can deal with any legal matters that may arise as a result of the affair. As far as my role is concerned, I'm here to support you and keep us focused on ensuring you have a solid financial future," Patrick said.

As he had previously explained to Natalie, the affair probably wouldn't have a significant financial impact on the settlement. If Jim had any remorseful feelings, Natalie might be able to guilt him into providing minor concessions.

"I called my sister Barrett last night before I cried myself to sleep. She told me to go out for blood."

Patrick reassured Natalie her team would be as aggressive as possible. At the same time, he reminded her that during negotiations, maintaining balance between acting aggressively and passively was key. Over-escalating the tension between her and Jim could create a negotiation impasse, which could lead to litigation.

"Plus, a contentious divorce may adversely impact your kids and your long-term relationship with Jim," he said.

"What do you mean by 'long-term relationship'? It's over between him and me!" Natalie said.

"Because you have kids, your lives are forever connected. You'll be jointly involved with them through birthdays, holidays, and special events like graduations, weddings, and maybe even grandkids. At the moment, Jim probably doesn't realize how much harm his actions are causing his family, but he will eventually. When will you speak with your therapist?" he asked.

"I meet with Dr. Michaels next week," Natalie said.

"She'll provide valuable insight for sure. In the meantime, I have an idea. Why don't we shift the conversation in another direction? In fact, I have some good news. But before we move on, did I ever share the quote my sister told me after her divorce?"

"No, what is it?"

"'A woman needs a man like a fish needs a bicycle,'" he said.

Natalie chuckled, which provided her with much-needed relief.

Patrick then pointed to a goal he had written on the wall for all his divorce clients:

To become financially self-sufficient
so they will never be dependent on a spouse again.

As he explained, that way, in the future, if his clients chose to remarry or live with their partner, they would experience peace of mind knowing they could manage on their own under nearly any circumstances.

"Become financially self-sufficient? I love that idea! But how do I do it?" Natalie asked.

Her team had already begun the process by setting her inherited assets apart from her marital assets and removing personal possessions from the joint financial accounting. These two moves would benefit her bottom line immensely but not nearly as much as identifying her separate interest in their house.

"During our time together today, I'd like to focus on the residence. If you recall, there are marital, non-marital, and hybrid assets," Patrick said.

"Because we bought the house with both separate and marital contributions, it's a hybrid asset, right?" Natalie asked.

"Precisely. We're now tasked with identifying what part of the equity is your separate asset and what part is marital," Patrick said.

He explained the most complicated asset to divide would be the home's equity. While Jim's spreadsheet showed an equal division of the equity in the residence, it did not include Natalie's separate non-marital contribution for the down payment or for improvements.

"Sounds as if what you're saying is I'm entitled to more than what currently appears on his spreadsheet," said Natalie.

"Yes," he said.

Patrick explained how he typically went about dividing a residence's equity:

- Identify the price paid to buy the house and the source of the down payment.

- Identify amounts spent to make home improvements and the sources of those payments.

- ◘ Add in any amounts removed as a result of refinancing or taking out home equity loans.

- ◘ Determine the amount of equity accrued as a result of paying down the mortgage over the period of ownership.

- ◘ Based on the above information, calculate the total amount of marital equity.

Based on what Patrick had uncovered so far, Natalie had used her inherited assets to make contributions to the acquisition and improvements to their home.

He identified the following:

- ◘ When they bought the house, Natalie provided a $90,000 down payment from her Schwab account.

- ◘ A couple of years later, she provided another $50,000 for home improvements.

"Because you previously provided me the documents I needed, such as your HUD-1 statement, I see you've contributed $140,000 of your separate monies toward the purchase and improvement of your current residence. As a result, you've got a powerful legal precedent on your side," said Patrick.

"I like what I'm hearing so far!" said Natalie.

"The state courts have used several methodologies to determine how to divide a home's equity when both separate and marital contributions create a hybrid property. One of the most widely used is the **Brandenburg formula**," Patrick said.

He explained this was also known as a "source of funds" rule (SOF). The Brandenburg formula, based on a Kentucky divorce case in 1981, has been widely accepted in Virginia as well as other eastern states. It is an established way of splitting hybrid property such as Jim and Natalie's primary home. In Natalie's case, the Brandenburg formula would provide her a greater interest in their home's equity due to her separate contribution into the property.

Previously, Kathleen and Patrick had reviewed the strengths and weaknesses of different formulas for determining Natalie's separate interest in the home's value. One of the roles of the other methodologies was to create *fairness*. In other words, the other formulas narrowed wide gaps in the equity division of the marital residence that sometimes took place when using the Brandenburg formula.

Patrick explained that in states where the Brandenburg formula didn't apply, other methodologies were used. And some states didn't recognize hybrid property at all.

"For instance in Colorado, *all property appreciation* is marital, even separate property," Patrick said.

He added this meant hybrid property was never an issue. If Natalie and Jim were divorcing there, Natalie would simply receive the amount she contributed. The couple would then divide the rest.

In *community property* states like California, all assets and income received during a marriage were considered community property and would be divided equally.

Because Virginia recognized hybrid property, Kathleen and Patrick determined the Brandenburg formula was the best for Natalie, and they had preliminary numbers using it.

Based on the Brandenburg calculation, Patrick told Natalie the following good news: *Her portion of their home's equity would be better than fifty-fifty.*

"In other words, you're entitled to a separate credit for your non-marital contribution," Patrick said.

"Does that mean if we have, say, $600,000 of proceeds from the house, I'll get back my $140,000, which was my contribution, some interest on my contribution, and then split the rest?" asked Natalie.

"Yes. And it gets even better. It's not just interest you'd be receiving but a portion of the property appreciation over the period of ownership too," said Patrick.

"This falls into the 'too good to be true' category because I don't see Jim going along with any of this," said Natalie.

"He will once he meets with his attorney, who will explain what I've told you about hybrid property. There's no way around it—you're entitled to it in Virginia. I'm sure he and his lawyer will try to come up with alternative calculations that are more favorable to him," said Patrick.

THE BRANDENBURG FORMULA: A CASE STUDY

The following is a summary of Natalie and Jim's home equity division using the Brandenburg formula:

Property Description		Year Purchased	1998
Residence		Price of Property	$450,000
		Present Fair Market Value	$900,000
		Cost of Sale	$54,000
		Present Mortgage Balance (1st+2nd)	$275,000

Itemized Investments	Husband	Wife	Marital	Borrowed
Initial down payment in 1998		$90,000		
Renovations in 2002		$50,000		
Mortgage pay down			$149,000	
Refinancing proceeds				

CALCULATED RESULTS   **NET EQUITY** | $571,000

Investment Summary	Amount	
Husband's Separate Investment		How to Divide
Wife's Separate Investment	$140,000	Marital Portion
Marital Investment	$149,000	Husband Receives — 50%
Total Investment, Separate + Marital	$289,000	Wife Receives — 50%

Distribution of Equity	Percent	Amount	If marital portion is divided as set forth above, then total distribution of fund is
Husband's Separate Interest			
Wife's Separate Interest	48.4%	$276,609	
Marital Interest	51.6%	$294,391	**Husband** — **Wife**
Total	100.0%	$571,000	$147,196 — $423,804

From the data Natalie provided Patrick, the couple bought the house in 1998 for $450,000 and used $90,000 from her inheritance as the down payment. This left $360,000 ($450,000 - $90,000), which is the amount they financed.

Then, in 2002, they completed renovations to the kitchen and bathrooms. They used another $50,000 from her inheritance to pay for those improvements. Thus Natalie's total separate contribution using her inheritance was $140,000.

In 2004, they refinanced to realize a lower interest rate. From 1998 to 2004, they had paid down $35,000 of the original mortgage, which meant the payoff of the mortgage balance at that time was $325,000:

$$\$360,000 - \$35,000 = \$325,000$$

The $35,000 they paid down would count as their marital contribution. The refinance included $7,000 in closing costs, which brought the new mortgage balance to $332,000.

From 2004 to 2010, they had paid down $37,000 of the second mortgage, or first refinance, which meant the payoff of the mortgage balance at that time was $295,000:

$$\$332,000 - \$37,000 = \$295,000$$

In 2010, the couple refinanced again and withdrew $50,000 to pay for educational expenses for Ben and miscellaneous other household items. The refinance included the $50,000 of equity they withdrew and another $7,000 in closing costs:

$$\$295,000 + \$50,000 + \$7,000 = \$352,000$$

According to Patrick's research, Jim had exercised some of his stock options in 2012 and used $25,000 of those proceeds to pay down the mortgage. As a result, the current mortgage balance, including the equity created from the mortgage payments and the additional principal reduction was now $275,000. This meant they had paid down another $77,000 of the mortgage. The total of all mortgage equity was:

$$\$35,000 + \$37,000 + \$77,000 = \$149,000$$

The total of Natalie's separate contribution was $140,000 and the marital contribution was $149,000.

The end result was the Brandenburg formula that indicated Natalie would receive just over $423,000 of home equity while Jim would receive about $147,000.

Natalie was thrilled to hear this. She would earn credit for the amount she had contributed that was a non-marital asset, as well as the appreciation of that contribution and the marital portion. This would allow her to retain a much larger portion of the overall equity in the property.

The news diminished her fears she would be losing her house and not have anywhere to live. Now she was being told not only that could she keep the house but also that Jim would have to pay her much more than he had anticipated.

"Not that I'm complaining, but it doesn't seem fair I'd get back so much more compared to Jim. So what you're saying is the combination of my paying for the down payment and the home improvements with non-marital assets will provide me a larger percentage of the equity?" asked Natalie.

"That's right," said Patrick.

"During the mediation, Courtney suggested I go over with you the pros and cons of keeping the house. With this news, I think I'll stay—at least until Rachel graduates from high school. I also love that place; it's where my kids grew up," Natalie said.

Patrick informed her if she decided to keep their primary residence, the equity in the house would be split without considering the cost of sale. Therefore, Jim would receive a higher amount than if they sold it because there would be no offset for the cost of sale. Under these circumstances, Natalie would have to buy Jim out to the tune of about $160,000 in order to keep the house.

As a result, she would also have to ask herself, "How will I come up with the money required to pay Jim his share of the equity in order to buy him out?"

"Doing so might be as simple as having Jim retain more of another asset to balance the division," Patrick said.

"When Jim hears about this during the next mediation, he's going to go crazy! If it weren't for your calculation, I'd have *no idea* I'd be entitled to receive any growth on my separate investment into the house," Natalie said.

"Where are you in regards to the home's appraisal?" Patrick asked.

"I contacted an appraiser recommended by my friend. The appraiser's scheduled to be at the house next week," Natalie said.

Natalie and Patrick then reviewed other areas of the new outline he had developed for the division of the marital assets. At the end of their meeting, Patrick reassured her that he would be working with Kathleen on these new numbers, which would be ready in time for her next mediation.

NATALIE MEETS WITH DR. MICHAELS

A few days after her meeting with Patrick, Natalie had an appointment with Dr. Michaels. During their session, Natalie updated her therapist regarding the private investigator's photos.

"I've had a week to process Jim's infidelity. I'm still feeling terrible about it. But lately my concern has been mostly about my kids. How's this going to affect them?" Natalie asked.

"Are you referring to the cheating or the divorce?" Dr. Michaels asked.

"Both!" Natalie said.

The two spent time talking about how she was dealing with the news about Jim and Claudia. They then discussed strategies that would help Natalie heal from the trust that was broken between her and Jim.

Later in their session, Natalie asked about parenting plans. She definitely wanted one; however, at the top of her priority list was to have full custody of Rachel. But she was concerned Jim would object.

Dr. Michaels listened to Natalie's worries. She then provided guidance regarding next steps. Dr. Michaels based the advice she gave on her years of counseling divorcing parents and their children. Because Rachel was fifteen years old and Natalie and Jim had a relatively amicable relationship, the therapist proposed the following option: Natalie could arrange an informal face-to-face meeting with Jim to discuss child custody.

"If taking this direction makes sense to you, I have some additional suggestions: When you talk to Jim, make sure you emphasize it's all about Rachel and that's the only reason you're suggesting a meeting. That way, you'll minimize any fears he has about having to defend himself against any curveballs unrelated to your discussion about custody," Dr. Michaels said.

The therapist provided Natalie the following guidelines for their discussion:

- Focus only on custody, nothing else.
- Listen to the other's perspective and how each expresses his or her concerns about Rachel.
- Respect how each parent intends to spend time with Rachel.
- Determine if the two could come to an agreement that, in principle, would place Rachel's needs first.
- Consider having a parenting plan drawn up as an addendum to the PSA.

Dr. Michaels's recommendations provided Natalie with the information she needed to have a productive conversation with Jim regarding her wish to have full custody of Rachel. She knew the timing of the custody discussion was key. Thus rather than push for the conversation right away, she would wait until Jim was ready to listen to her perspective.

CHAPTER 15

NATALIE AND KATHLEEN DISCUSS CHILD AND SPOUSAL SUPPORT

Two weeks after Natalie's appointment with Patrick, she met Kathleen in her office. Kathleen provided her client an update. She had received Patrick's new spreadsheet with the Brandenburg formula that reflected Natalie keeping the house. His data also uncovered the loss carryforward, which would help Natalie with future income taxes.

"Patrick and I went over your income. As a result, I have ideas regarding spousal and child support. But before I explain what I've come up with, is there anything you'd like to talk about first?"

Natalie handed Kathleen the PI's photos and explained what she knew about Claudia and their affair.

"I'm so sorry you had to learn about it this way. As painful as this news is, we'll use it to our best advantage. Layering guilt about his transgressions may motivate him to be more conciliatory. For instance, if we were to hit a negotiations impasse and have to resolve your divorce using the courts, Jim's infidelity would probably come up at some point. From there, it would become a matter of public record. I'm sure disclosing his cheating for everyone to see forever is the last thing he wants. By mediating, his infidelity will stay off the record, so it's in his best interest to stick with the process and to be a team player."

"The farther I go down the divorce path, the more I realize what a fool I've been. This has been a wake-up call. I really need to take control of my affairs—no pun intended," Natalie said.

Kathleen added that infidelity was less of an issue in present-day divorces than it had been in the past. At the same time, when it came to negotiating spousal support, she would try to leverage it if it would benefit her client. Natalie knew she would never earn as much money as Jim, so she would gladly take any negotiation advantage she could get her hands on.

CHILD AND SPOUSAL SUPPORT OVERVIEW

"Before we can calculate child support, we need to know what your custody arrangement will be. If I recall correctly, you indicated wanting sole custody of Rachel but were willing to share legal custody," said Kathleen.

"Definitely. As long as Jim is with that home wrecker, I don't want my children to be exposed to his bad behavior!" said Natalie.

"Got it. Then I'll run the numbers assuming you'll have sole custody," said Kathleen.

With this information, Kathleen would calculate child support using the following formula:

1. Divide marital assets and determine total income for each spouse.

2. Determine spousal support.

3. Calculate child support using guidelines.

Child Support

Kathleen reminded Natalie child support was paid only until the child was emancipated. Because Natalie's son, Ben, had graduated from college and Ryann was a college freshman, Kathleen didn't include them in the child support calculation.

In addition, child support was calculated using the statutory guidelines, and amounts were always modifiable. In other words, they were subject to change in the event of a significant income increase or decrease of either spouse. For instance, if Jim experienced an income spike, Natalie could ask the court to increase the support payment.

In reality, Jim would most likely be the last person to disclose any higher earnings that took place after their divorce, and Natalie might never actually find out about it. As far as Natalie was concerned, she was less concerned about any income increase or decrease because child support would terminate for her in three years, which was when their youngest daughter, Rachel, would turn eighteen years old.

Spousal Support

Kathleen explained that spousal support was always negotiated. In other words, unlike child support, no specific guidelines must be followed. Formulas, however, do exist for calculating temporary support, and these are sometimes used as a basis for determining long-term spousal support.

Unlike child support, spousal support may or may not be subject to modification, and the terms are variable. In most cases, when a marriage has been twenty years or more, the support term would be longer than if the marriage lasted less than ten years.

Kathleen described the following variables that play a role in determining spousal support:

■ **Age of parties**—how much time remains before normal retirement age?

- **Work history**—what is the spouse who is receiving support qualified or capable of doing?

- **Education level**—will the spouse who is receiving support need training or more education to obtain a decent job? This is especially important if the spouse has been out of the workforce for a period of time.

- **Health issues**—does the spouse who is receiving support have a medical condition that would prevent him or her from working?

- **The cost of living for each**—what is the needed cash flow for each party to maintain his or her standard of living?

In addition, spousal-support terms varied from case to case, and divorcing couples could propose and agree upon nearly any realistic scenario.

"We'll be negotiating the amount and the terms of the payments. Experience has taught me that practically no one wants to pay support and anyone who does wants the shortest term possible. There are many cases where the paying spouse has the financial means to provide a lump sum and is willing to do so if it means he or she doesn't have to cut a monthly support check," Kathleen said.

Death, Disability, and Support

Support will terminate upon the death of the spouse who is paying support. This is a critical but often an overlooked support component.

"I'll ask Patrick to calculate the amount of life insurance you should own on Jim so you'll be protected in the event of his premature death," said Kathleen.

"I would definitely have *never* made the life insurance-support connection," said Natalie.

Kathleen added that disability on Jim's part could present the greatest threat to Natalie's financial well-being.

A term life insurance policy on Jim could protect Natalie's financial future in the event of his early demise. But disability insurance, unlike most life insurance, was difficult to obtain. Thus Kathleen believed the best way to protect Natalie's future income was to have spousal support be *non-modifiable* for an extended period. This meant Jim would still be required to pay Natalie's support even if he became disabled. As a result, the onus would be on Jim to maintain disability insurance to cover the risk.

College Tuition

"How about the kids' college tuition? I was hoping Jim would have to pay for that," said Natalie.

Kathleen explained that college expenses were not part of the PSA unless both spouses agree to include it. This is because the court doesn't rule on parental obligations once a child is emancipated.

"We'll make sure we address your college tuition concern in the mediation and final settlement," said Kathleen.

The Support Calculation

"I have a much better understanding regarding how support works. Now it's the amounts I'm worried about," said Natalie.

With the information Patrick had provided, Kathleen made preliminary projections of what support might look like.

First, based on Natalie's budget, her expenses were about $10,000 per month.

"I don't have any information regarding Jim's expenses, so we'll leave that for him to figure out. Once he hires his lawyer, that person will help him calculate the amount for him," Kathleen said.

Natalie knew she took home $2,500 per month, so the $10,000 expense figure, resulting in a $7,500 monthly shortfall, scared her. She then thought about the options Patrick provided her, such as selling the house.

"I told Patrick I'd like to keep the house. Patrick's developing a plan that addresses selling the house in three years and moving into a less expensive one afterwards, which would cut my living expenses," said Natalie.

"Great idea. I've seen way too many cases where the wife keeps the house and goes broke trying to maintain it. Let me show you what else I've come up with," Kathleen said.

Kathleen used a widely accepted computer program that determined support amounts based on laws in Virginia. Part of the calculation required inputting the gross income amount from all sources.

"What's really nice about this software is once we input the spousal support data, it will also automatically calculate child support. In your case, I understand you want sole physical custody of Rachel. However, I've also included a shared support calculation so we have that information and would not be surprised if Jim presents it," Kathleen said.

Kathleen reached her support findings by identifying the couple's total income from the summary report from Patrick, which was based on last year's tax return, W-2s, 1099s, and all investment account statements. Sometimes income was easily identifiable. What was not easily identifiable, however, was when an executive, such as Jim, had benefits that might reduce income, such as deferred compensation, which wouldn't necessarily show up on a tax return.

The following was Jim and Natalie's income summary:

	Jim	Natalie
Base salary	$325,000	$47,000
Unearned income	$5,000	$6,000
Annual bonus	$50,000	n/a
Stock options	$25,000	n/a
Net rental income	$7,800	0
Total annual income	$412,800	$53,000
Total monthly income	$34,400	$4,417

Their combined income was $465,800, and Natalie's income represented just 11.4 percent of the total. Kathleen used the *pendente lite* formula to determine temporary support. From there, Natalie could propose whatever amount she felt was reasonable and could be supported.

Temporary Support Calculation

"During our first meeting," Kathleen said, "I explained there were two temporary support formulas. Now that I have the necessary financial information, I can go over each formula."

She explained the formula that applies to a couple's particular circumstances depends on whether or not the dependent spouse will be receiving child support. Kathleen prepared results for Natalie using both formulas.

FORMULA 1

If a spouse is receiving child support, then temporary spousal support is calculated by the following, which uses gross monthly income:

1. Multiply the higher income by 28 percent.

2. Multiply the lower income by 58 percent.

3. Subtract the result of step 2 from step 1, which is the monthly amount.

Using this formula yielded the following results for Natalie:

1. $34,400 x 28% = $9,632

2. $4,417 x 58% = $2,562

3. $9,632 - $2,562 = $7,070

FORMULA 2

If there is no child support, the temporary spousal support formula is as follows:

1. Multiply the higher income by 30 percent.

2. Multiply the lower income by 50 percent.

3. Subtract the result of step 2 from step 1, which is the monthly amount.

Using this formula yielded the following results for Natalie:

1. $34,400 x 30% = $10,320

2. $4,417 x 50% = $2,208

3. $10,320 - $2,208 = $8,112

"Does higher spousal support impact child support?" Natalie asked.

"The higher the amount of spousal support you receive, the lower your child support will be," said Kathleen.

With the two calculations, her team was able to establish an initial range from which they could make adjustments. Kathleen's recommendation would be to seek $8,000 of spousal support while receiving child support and raise it to $9,000 per month once Rachel turned eighteen. If Jim disagreed, it would be up to him and the attorney he hired to prove why Natalie should receive less. Although the final figure might be different from this range, Kathleen believed the amount would not be significantly lower.

"But since the calculations indicate I receive only about $7,000 of spousal support per month during the period in which I receive child support and $8,000 of spousal support after child support ends, how will we obtain higher amounts?" Natalie asked.

"Spousal support is negotiated, and the amount we calculated is based upon a temporary support guideline. For long-term support, we need to take into account your actual cash flow needs, which Patrick has identified. According to his findings, you'll need $7,000 per month in spousal support after taxes. This means that because you're in a 20 percent tax bracket, you'll need to receive about $9,000 of gross support."

Support and Taxes
Spousal support is taxable income to the recipient (Natalie) and is a tax deduction for the payer (Jim).

Child support, on the other hand, would not be taxable income to Natalie and would not be tax deductible by Jim.

Support Length and Terms
Given that Natalie and Jim were married for twenty-five years, Kathleen's plan was to request spousal support to last until she reached age seventy. Although the length might be rejected, Kathleen believed it was worth proposing. In the end it might end up closer to her normal retirement age of sixty-seven.

Child Support: Custody
Jim traveled throughout the year for work. Natalie believed Rachel wouldn't want to live with him given his frequent absences. Plus, she didn't want Rachel exposed to Jim's love life. Thus Natalie was emphatic about having sole physical custody, but she was willing to consider joint legal custody. She was uncertain whether Jim would agree to the arrangement.

Sole physical custody would mean Rachel would live full-time with Natalie. In exchange, Natalie would agree that Jim would have liberal visitation under a schedule that included holidays and vacations.

Due to Rachel's age, however, she would have more input into how much time she would spend with her father than she would if she had been a younger girl.

Legal custody meant both Jim and Natalie would be able to make decisions on Rachel's behalf until she was emancipated. They would also jointly agree to anything having an impact upon Rachel's well-being but not regarding her day-to-day life.

"We may need to keep your firm position under a hat for now because we don't want Jim to know our point of view regarding important divorce matters until the time is right. Also, maintaining flexibility and timing your agenda items prudently may motivate him to agree to the arrangement you seek," said Kathleen.

"I'll also talk to Rachel and get her perspective. I'm completely horrified thinking about my daughter seeing Jim with that woman," Natalie said.

Following the child support guidelines, Kathleen calculated Natalie would be entitled to $1,150 per month, which would continue until Rachel reached age eighteen. The spousal support they would ask for during the time Natalie was receiving child support would be $8,000 per month.

PRELIMINARY SUPPORT SUMMARY

INCOME SOURCES	Per month	Per year
Work	$3,917	$47,000
Unearned income	$500	$6,000
Spousal support	$8,000	$96,000
Child support	$1,150	$13,800
Total	$13,567	$162,800

The key for Natalie would be to cover her living expenses without depleting her investments. She needed to build them up to meet her income needs after spousal support ended. Kathleen also reminded Natalie to wait to present any support figures until after the property division was completed.

"Patrick will guide you through the steps you'll need to maintain your financial well-being. He's already told me that, based on the division of property he's developed so far, you should be fine over the long term—as long as you continue to live within your means," Kathleen said.

"I'll spend the weekend reviewing everything you shared about my living expenses. So what happens next?" asked Natalie.

Kathleen said she would confer with Patrick. Afterwards, and prior to her second mediation, the three would have a conference call. During their talk, Kathleen and Patrick would walk her through the mediation.

In particular, Natalie was nervous about Jim's reaction to the Brandenburg formula. As a result, her team would help her develop her strategy regarding how to effectively express her stance and address his counterarguments.

"You've come a long way. I know it's tough going through all of this. But you will survive this ordeal without ever having to worry about being a bag lady," Kathleen said.

"I'm trying to be strong because most of the time I just want to start crying. I feel as if I'm under a microscope having to disclose so many details of my life to people I've just met. I have *no idea* how couples go to court and air their dirty laundry for everyone to see," said Natalie.

CHAPTER 16

JIM MEETS WITH HIS ATTORNEY

After conducting his lawyer research, Jim decided to hire Al Stephenson. Al had been practicing family law in Virginia for over twenty years, and Jim appreciated his extensive background in mediation, collaborative divorce, and litigation.

During their first meeting, Jim summarized how the first mediation had gone. He also told Al about Kathleen and Courtney. The local family law community was small, and Al knew both of them well. He spoke highly of their experience and reputations.

Toward the end of their introductory appointment, Al informed Jim that he billed $450 per hour and required a $10,000 retainer. In his work, Jim hired lawyers on a regular basis. Therefore, Al's rate didn't surprise him. This time around, however, SSI's coffers would not be covering legal fees. Signing the retainer agreement and cutting the check filled Jim with resentment toward Natalie, who thwarted his otherwise perfect divorce plan.

After their meeting, Jim emailed Al the summary Courtney had prepared. In it, she had revised Jim's first spreadsheet. First, she had placed a question mark next to Natalie's Schwab account because Jim needed to follow up about this with his lawyer regarding whether it was marital or non-marital property. Second, she had valued the item "personal property" at $1, which served as a placeholder until they agreed upon its division.

JIM'S SECOND APPOINTMENT WITH AL

Prior to seeing Al for today's substantive meeting, Jim was filled with uncertainty and anxiety after feeling cornered into hiring his own counsel and being put on the defense during the first mediation. At the same time, he looked forward to receiving Al's input regarding how best to protect his interests.

At 10:00 a.m., Jim arrived at Al's office. An administrative assistant warmly greeted him and escorted him to a small conference room. She asked if Jim wanted something to drink. He politely declined—his nerves suppressed any thirst.

Shortly after, Al entered the room. The two shook hands, and he took a seat across from Jim at the round table. Al preferred round rather than square and rectangular ones, which often created head-of-the-table hierarchies.

"The information you emailed me was very helpful. After reviewing it, I'm really glad you contacted me because doing this on your own would have probably created more headaches down the road than you could imagine," said Al.

"It's ironic you say that because my motivation to mediate and spend hours working on a preliminary division of assets was to save us time and money. Natalie didn't have a clue or interest in anything to do with household finances, so I was shocked when she came at me during the mediation like an attack dog. Now, one of my biggest worries is this divorce will blow up in terms of legal fees," said Jim.

"Although I can't make any promises, I will say that after doing this for twenty years, I've witnessed how meditation with a solid team saves money in the long term—especially when compared to litigation. You can count on Courtney to do most of the heavy lifting. Meanwhile, I'm here to support and advise you and help you understand the legal issues involved and reach a reasonable settlement under the mediation format," Al said.

As far as Al could tell from his research, he didn't see any major roadblocks in the couple's case, as long as they were willing to negotiate fairly and make decisions based on their common interests.

"I took some pretty heavy blows during the first mediation, and I don't want to get blindsided again," Jim said.

"From what you told me, you went over your spreadsheet during the first mediation. Natalie disputed the marital versus non-marital assets. Do you know the difference between the two?" Al asked.

"After having my spreadsheet torn apart during the mediation, I do now. Natalie argued her inherited assets and personal property shouldn't be counted. I can't believe she's suddenly an expert!" Jim said.

Al said it was highly likely Natalie was well coached by a financial adviser. He came to this conclusion because Kathleen regularly recommended her clients work with one—especially when they were less informed about financial matters. Jim was incensed to hear this. He now felt even more duped and foolish.

"The timing of my question may not be ideal, and I think I know the answer already, but do you have a financial adviser helping you with the divorce?" Al asked.

"No. I've always managed to take care of our finances and don't see the need to hire another person. I'm confident I can conduct my own research," said Jim.

"I won't tell you what to do, but I will say experience has taught me that working with a financial expert can be very helpful when you're dealing with the issues we will be talking about today. I'm certainly confident in the law and have all the legal resources I'll need at my disposal. But I'm not a financial expert and don't have the specialized tools at my disposal that financial advisers do. I'm just asking you to consider hiring a financial expert familiar with the divorce process," said Al.

"I'll give it some thought. Two lawyers, two financial advisers, this is looking more like collaborative divorce every day," Jim said.

"Let's continue our discussion about assets," Al said.

Personal Property

Al explained that in regards to the personal property, whether it was a marital or non-marital asset depended on how and when it was acquired and if it had any verifiable monetary value. If it didn't, then most couples divided their personal household, which usually didn't require a mediator's input. On occasion, however, some couples wasted time and money bickering over possessions that could otherwise easily be replaced.

"Do you have any items you think have real financial value and are important for you to retain?" asked Al.

Jim said his half-hull sailboat model collection and nautical paintings and collectibles were the only items that had any real meaning to him, and he wanted to keep those.

Most of the other items, however, were easily replaceable. At the same time, he wondered if he was entitled to receive at least some of the furniture such as a few chairs, a sofa, and their bedroom set.

"Right now, I feel like I'm in my twenties again. Back then, I just had a waterbed and bookshelves made of cinderblocks and 2x4s," said Jim.

"I'll note the nautical items. And yes, I think you should be able to retain some of the household items in order to get reestablished on your own. Overall, my suggestion is that you and Natalie divide the personal property by mutual agreement," Al said.

He noticed Jim had a bulleted list on his legal pad. Al asked if he wanted to address any of the items.

Jim replied by questioning Al about Natalie's inherited property (her Schwab account). He wanted to know if it was a marital or non-marital asset.

Marital and Non-marital Property

Al informed Jim that Natalie's Schwab account probably wouldn't qualify as part of the marital property division. If, on the other hand, it generated income, that income would be used to calculate support.

"During the first mediation, Natalie told me she wanted to keep the house. I was okay with that as long as I keep the rental property and my retirement accounts," Jim said.

"I'll note this, and we'll discuss this in depth later. What's next on your list?" Al asked.

"Is there anything her team might pull out of their bag of tricks that will significantly change the overall division of assets? I definitely don't want to be humiliated during the next mediation," said Jim.

"I'm glad you asked. When you researched marital and non-marital property, did you come across anything about hybrid property?"

"Yes. I read up on it. I know Virginia recognizes hybrid property and not all states do. I didn't think it applied to me because aside from the Schwab account, all the other property seems to be marital," said Jim.

"How did you cover the down payment on your current residence?" Al asked.

"From an inheritance she received. When she first received it, we opened a money market account and stuck it all in there. Of course, I wanted to invest it in something that would grow. But she's so risk averse, I just let her park it there. She also took out money from that same account to pay for some home improvements a few years later," Jim said.

"Unfortunately, the money market account sounds as if it may technically be a separate asset. If she used it for the down payment and the home improvements, she's likely eligible to receive credit for the amounts she contributed. The courts have established formulas to determine the non-marital and marital portion of the equity in a hybrid property, which your house might be. Is this the same account that is referred to as the Schwab account?" asked Al.

"Yes, and I think I've factored her contribution in already. She'll get back her $140,000 before we split the balance," Jim said.

Al broke the news that Jim's calculation oversimplified how hybrid properties were divided. Multiple court cases have been accepted and used to protect a spouse's separate interest and treat both parties fairly. In addition, various factors, such as personal contributions when someone has actually participated in the construction or improvement of the property, may play a role in dividing a hybrid property.

Because of this, Al explained Natalie might be entitled to a greater proportion of the home equity as a result of paying for the down payment and for the home improvements out of her inheritance—even if they jointly owned the house.

"I don't know the exact amount Natalie would be eligible for. But from what I've figured out so far, she made a significant contribution. Thus she would likely receive a disproportionate amount of the home's equity. Once I gather the necessary data on the house, I'll be able to make calculations to ensure the division is fair and complies with the law. I know this comes as unwelcome news," Al said.

"After all I've done for her. If it weren't for me, she'd be living off a teacher's salary! Will I receive *any* credit for the countless hours I've put maintaining the house while Natalie sat back and watched?" asked Jim.

"I promise you I'll look into all the issues and facts and make sure everyone is playing by the rules," said Al.

"Well these damn rules are clearly tipping in her favor. So far during this meeting, I've learned I'm not entitled to any of her Schwab account and I'm getting screwed over in regards to the home's equity. What about my retirement accounts and investment portfolios—money I've generated through my own hard work? Can her team dig their claws into those too?" Jim asked.

Qualified and Non-qualified Assets

Al explained Jim was referring to two different asset types. His retirement accounts were *qualified* assets because the money in them had not been taxed and would only be taxed upon distribution. Meanwhile, his investment portfolios were *non-qualified* assets because they were accounts he had invested in with after-tax money—he could access non-qualified assets before retirement without penalty. They also have different tax structures. Thus, even if the qualified and non-qualified assets had the same balance, their net after-tax values would be significantly different. Withdrawing from non-qualified assets would allow him to take advantage of favorable capital gains tax rates versus ordinary income tax rates.

Jim stated that he would like to keep as much of his retirement accounts as possible because they were based on income he had earned and he had been the sole contributor.

Also, because his E*Trade account comprised individual stocks, he believed Natalie would not know how to manage them so he should retain them. In addition, after Al had explained the differences between qualified and non-qualified accounts, Jim was concerned about dividing the individual stocks and how to offset one type of investment account with another.

Grouping Assets for Division

"My suggestion is to bundle similar assets in separate groups when making choices about their division," Al said.

Al recommended dividing retirement separately from other assets. By keeping similar assets in separate groups, the couple would avoid complications that arose when calculating and off-setting the after-tax effects net of retirement assets and non-retirement assets.

By *not* doing so, however, unfair trades could result.

"For instance, using your hard-earned retirement assets to offset the home's equity may benefit you because you don't have any expenses associated with retaining your retirement accounts. Meanwhile, there are lots of costs for home ownership. However, the retirement assets have not been taxed while the home equity might be obtained with little or no tax liability," said Al.

Stock Options

Jim then brought up his stock options. Since they would be in-come he would receive in the future, he asked if they would be marital or non-marital assets.

Al explained stock options could be a mixture of marital and non-marital assets. The type of marital asset they were would depend on when the stock options were granted and their vest-ing schedule. In most instances, if Jim were to have stock op-tions granted to him during his marriage and a portion of those vested after separation, they would be considered hybrid assets. Meanwhile, stock options obtained during the marriage and fully vested before separation would be considered marital.

"So if I understand you correctly," Jim said, "if we were to identify the individual stock option grants, Natalie would be en-titled to a portion of the fully vested options *and* some of the partially vested options too."

"That's correct," Al said.

"That really sucks!"

Jim went on to explain that SSI was a closely held business that hadn't gone public yet, so its stock valuation was not adjusted daily. Instead, it was adjusted quarterly, based upon what the company's board of directors decided. Because of this, Jim believed the stock could become very valuable if the company either was acquired or went public. As a result, a win for Jim would be retaining his company's stock and stock options after the divorce. In order to be able to do this, he planned to hide his intentions from Natalie and Courtney.

MEETING WRAP-UP

"Any other questions?" Al asked.

"This hybrid property news is *really* stressing me out. What additional information will I need to calculate Natalie's share of the home's equity and to update the property division?" Jim asked.

Al recommended Jim gather everything he had offered to obtain at the end of the first mediation as well as documents that indicated the current value of assets.

"When is your second mediation?" Al asked.

"Two weeks. Does that give us enough time?" Jim asked.

"Not completely, but it should be enough to prepare you to avoid getting caught off guard again. How about we meet in one week? In the meantime, email or fax me the statements and other documents you used to generate your updated spreadsheet so I can refer to them specifically," said Al.

The two concluded their appointment.

JIM AND AL PREPARE FOR THE SECOND MEDIATION

A week later, Jim and Al met to review the summary Al had prepared. He informed Jim that the overall division of the marital assets did not appear to be an issue. But because the primary residence would be a hybrid property, it might create more challenges.

He also confirmed that Jim planned to retain the rental property and was willing to either sell the primary residence or allow Natalie to retain it if she was able to pay him his fair share of the equity.

Al added that more than half of the equity would likely be allotted to Natalie for the residence due to its hybrid nature. Al had run a preliminary calculation, which indicated the equity could end up being a 70 percent, 30 percent split. Before proposing this ratio, however, he wanted to see what Kathleen would put forth. If Al could challenge her offer, he would.

Jim expressed frustration over the home equity. If Al's assumptions were correct, he wondered if he would have enough money to buy a new place of his own.

Al believed if Jim could offset the equity in the rental property with the equity in the residence and use some of his non-retirement assets as well he could balance out his financial assets. This could provide Jim a means to retain the majority of his retirement accounts. He also felt they would be able to negotiate Jim's retaining the stock options, which was Jim's intention.

After their meeting, Jim went to work generating a new spreadsheet based on Al's expert feedback. Although Jim didn't have all the data he needed yet, his next spreadsheet would reflect the following significant changes: Natalie's inherited property (the Schwab account) would be a non-martial asset so it wouldn't be part of the property division, Natalie would keep the house, and she would retain a large portion of the primary residence's equity, which would provide Jim offset opportunities. This could make it simpler to balance the marital assets.

CHAPTER 17

SECOND MEDIATION

It was 12:45 p.m., and Natalie sat in Courtney's reception area reviewing her mediation notes. Ten minutes later, Jim arrived.

Aside from Natalie emailing Jim reminding him of bills that needed to be paid, the two hadn't communicated with each other since the first mediation.

"So, what surprises do you have in store for me today?" he asked as he took a seat across from her.

"I really hope we can work on reaching a resolution so we can both move on with our lives. By the way, have you hired a lawyer yet?" she asked.

"Yes. His name's Al Stephenson, and he knows your lawyer. He thought we could reach a fair settlement without going to court. He was impressed with the financial research you'd done. I told him you'd never been interested in finances before, so he wanted to know if you were receiving financial advice. Are you?" Jim asked.

"Yes. Patrick's been an invaluable resource. My lawyer made the recommendation and referral. Did yours recommend a financial adviser?" she asked.

"Yes. But I passed. At least one of us needs to make sure we don't go broke doing this. Al's all I need," Jim said.

With reception-area tensions between them mounting, Natalie wished Jim had arrived late for this mediation as he'd done for the first one.

Fortunately, a few moments later, Courtney greeted the couple and then escorted them to the conference room. Jim and Natalie took a seat, and Courtney stood in front of the flip chart.

"I appreciate both of you completing the homework assignments from our last meeting," she said.

She reviewed the following items, which they had discussed at the end of the first mediation:

- ◘ Obtain documentation to clarify identified assets.

- ◘ Receive valuations for the real property that was being retained.

- ◘ Collect copies of investment accounts, mortgage, refinancing, and HUD-1 statements for each property from time of purchase and each refinancing.

"I received your updated information. Any questions before we begin?" Courtney asked.

Jim told the group about hiring Al who had advised him about the Schwab account. Jim had also prepared a new spreadsheet that removed that account and the personal property.

"Here is my updated spreadsheet that reflects the changes we previously discussed and additional revisions after meeting with Al," Jim said.

He set his new spreadsheet on the table.

Jim's Revised Spreadsheet

Account	Value 12-31	Jim	Natalie
ASSETS			
Joint WFB	$25,000	$0	$25,000
Jim's WFB	$10,000	$10,000	
Residence	$900,000		$625,000
Rental Property	$550,000	$200,000	
Natalie's Schwab	$125,000		
Jim's E*Trade	$225,000	$112,500	$112,500
Household	$200,000	$0	$0
Subaru	$15,000		$15,000
BMW	$35,000	$35,000	
Sailboat	$30,000	$30,000	
Jim's IRA	$150,000	$130,000	$20,000
Jim's 401(k)	$375,000	$250,000	$125,000
SSI Stock Options	$222,800	$222,800	
Natalie's 403 (b)	$85,000		$85,000
Total Assets	**$2,947,800**	**$990,300**	**$1,007,500**
LIABILITIES			
Residence Mortgage	$275,000	$0	
Rental Mortgage	$350,000	$0	
BMW	$15,000	$15,000	
Credit Cards	$25,000		$25,000
Total Liabilities	**($665,000)**	**($15,000)**	**($25,000)**
NET BALANCES	**$2,282,800**	**$975,300**	**$982,500**

"My lawyer told me there might be some offset for the down payment Natalie made on the house and the amount she contributed to the improvements. Will we address these matters today?"

"We can discuss whatever both of you agree to talk about. At the same time, since we were able to identify all assets during our last meeting, I suggest we continue clarifying the remaining items on the list before we get into valuing anything more substantial," Courtney said.

She added they would continue with the four-step process: identification, clarification, valuation, and decision.

CLARIFICATION: Loss Carryforward

Natalie brought up the loss carryforward of about $100,000 and how it would reduce future tax liability.

Jim acknowledged the loss carryforward existed, but because it didn't have a current value and it could only be used to offset future investment gains, he didn't think it should be part of the division. He also thought Natalie didn't need to worry about it because her tendency was to invest conservatively. As a result, her investments wouldn't generate much in gains. Also, the value wasn't in the amount of the carryforward. Rather, it was only in the amount of tax savings.

Natalie argued, however, it needed to be identified because it might reduce her taxable income and gains. Both she and Jim would be able to retain half the balance on their individual tax returns.

Jim reminded Natalie if the divorce was not final by year's end, then for the current tax year they would file jointly, which would allow them to save on taxes. Once they were divorced, however, they would file individually and split the loss carryforward.

Courtney recommended they add the loss carryforward with a value of $100,000 on the flip chart. She would place a question mark beside it because the couple wouldn't know the precise amount until they filed their current year's tax returns.

They agreed with her suggestion. Nevertheless, the loss carryforward discussion frustrated Jim—it was yet one more item that would require consensus, which meant additional negotiations accompanied by additional expenses.

"In the interest of time, could we move on and continue using my revised spreadsheet, so we can get the clarification and valuation out of the way as soon as possible?" Jim asked.

"That's fine. But I'm in no hurry to make decisions without understanding their consequences. That's why I've been working with my lawyer and financial adviser," said Natalie.

"Clearly, you're in no hurry. Meanwhile, every minute we're stuck hammering out our disagreements means less money for both of us. You don't seem to understand the cost of paying for expert advice. Or maybe you just don't care that your team loves spending our money," Jim said.

"I'm not going to argue about this. Let me remind you you're the one who filed for divorce in the first place," Natalie said.

"Jim, you mentioned you wanted to make a note about certain personal possessions. What are they?" asked Courtney.

"As far as personal possessions are concerned, my list is short. I want the nautical things and artwork and some living room furniture. That's about it," said Jim.

Courtney noted his items on the flip chart under "Personal Possessions." The three agreed to address these later during their personal property discussion.

"We've now gone through identifying and clarifying most all assets on the spreadsheet, except the home equity. Shall we continue with the home equity next?" Courtney asked.

CLARIFICATION: Real Estate Equity

Natalie took a deep breath knowing the consequence of what she would disclose. She drew strength by reminding herself of her team's support.

"The amount Jim has shown on his spreadsheet for my home equity does not include credit for my separate contribution and doesn't reflect any credit for the investment return on my contribution," she said.

She placed a spreadsheet on the table that Patrick had prepared.

It had the Brandenburg calculation. Jim saw the following figures:

Equitable Distribution of Hybrid Property
Using the Brandenburg Formula

Property Description		Year Purchased	1998
Residence		Price of Property	$450,000
		Present Fair Market Value	$900,000
		Cost of Sale	
	Present Mortgage Balance (1st+2nd)		$275,000

Itemized Investments	Husband	Wife	Marital	Borrowed
Initial down payment in 1998		$90,000		
Renovations in 2002		$50,000		
Mortgage pay down			$149,000	
Refinancing proceeds				

CALCULATED RESULTS   **NET EQUITY** $625,000

Investment Summary	Amount		
Husband's Separate Investment		How to Divide	
Wife's Separate Investment	$140,000	Marital Portion	
Marital Investment	$149,000	Husband Receives	50%
Total Investment, Separate + Marital	$289,000	Wife Receives	50%

Distribution of Equity	Percent	Amount	If marital portion is divided as set forth above, then total distribution of fund is	
Husband's Separate Interest				
Wife's Separate Interest	48.4%	$302,768		
Marital Interest	51.6%	$322,232	**Husband**	**Wife**
Total	100.0%	$625,000	$161,116	$463,884

Jim's eyes bulged as he focused on four of the figures:

- ◘ **Natalie's separate interest: $302,768**
- ◘ **Natalie's total equity: $463,884**
- ◘ **Marital interest: $322,232**
- ◘ **Jim's total equity: $161,116**

"This is absurd! What I proposed on my spreadsheet is based on my meeting with my lawyer. You realize you're asking for *more than* double what you paid. There's no way in hell I'm going to agree to that," he said.

Even though Jim's attorney had already determined Natalie would be entitled to more than half of the home's equity, the amount she proposed was much higher than what Jim had expected. Seeing this figure in print made him fume.

"Keep in mind Natalie's calculation—the Brandenburg formula—is just one methodology among many that determines separate interest in hybrid property. I encourage you to go back to your attorney and discuss your options," Courtney said.

"You're damn right I'm going to go back to my attorney! Al gave me a heads-up about it being disproportionate, but Natalie's numbers are ridiculous," Jim said.

Courtney asked Natalie to provide Jim the data she used to determine the amount. She told them that even if they both used the same formula, the end results might not be the same because they would depend on the variables involved in each refinance and value of the actual home improvements.

She added that there were a few items that might affect the calculations under the Brandenburg formula. For example, withdrawals made during a refinance that might require an offset to the non-marital interest, or the appreciation from home improvements paid from separate contributions might need to be determined.

Courtney encouraged them to come up with a range of answers together and select the outcome they could both agree on.

"I can tell you this right now: The amount she's showing isn't going to happen. Natalie, how do you expect me to buy another place on my own with the numbers you and your supposed team of experts came up with?" he asked.

Courtney posted a sheet of chart paper on the wall with a note about the couple's home's equity division and how it required further review.

In the spreadsheet Natalie and Patrick developed, as offsets, they used a combination of Jim's investment accounts, the equity in the rental property, and his keeping the boat and car. But Jim disputed this. He recalled how they agreed to forego personal possessions as financial offsets. In addition, his car had a loan whereas hers was paid off.

"During our previous mediation, Natalie, you intended to keep the house, and Jim, you intended to keep the rental property. Is this still the case?" asked Courtney.

"Yes, I still want the rental property," said Jim.

"I went over the pros and cons with my team, as you suggested. Yes, I still want to keep it," Natalie said.

"But," said Jim, "in light of today's conversation, I won't agree to anything until we resolve the issues of our home's equity division. You can keep the house—the maintenance is going to break the bank, so don't say I didn't warn you—but I'm not going along with your financial adviser's ridiculous proposal on the amount of equity you get to keep. And don't forget, I want to hold onto my investment accounts."

"Maybe Al and Kathleen can discuss the issues with you individually. Then you can come to terms agreeable to both of you," Courtney said.

"Yeah, and how much will it cost us to pay for all this expert advice?" Jim asked.

Courtney noted the differences in their perspectives. She suggested they come back to the issue once they had clarified other property division areas. She then asked them to consider alternatives that would not negatively impact what they had already accomplished.

"Jim, you're retaining most of the retirement accounts and your stock options already," said Natalie. "The bottom line on your proposal shows you with the majority of the assets. If we use the numbers for the residence Patrick came up with, that brings our overall balance closer. Meanwhile, you'll be able to keep most of your precious retirement accounts and stock options. So if I offer you more equity from the house, what would you give up in return?"

"I'll need to discuss with Al and see what he thinks," Jim said.

CLARIFICATION, VALUATION, AND TENTATIVE DECISION:
Retirement Accounts

Courtney moved onto the retirement accounts. Employment income had funded the retirement accounts, and taxes were deferred on those accounts until monies were withdrawn.

The taxes Jim and Natalie paid on their retirement withdrawals would be dependent upon their tax bracket at the time of withdrawal. In most cases, they would be taxed at a lower rate during their retirement years because the couple would have less income compared to their working years.

During previous meetings the couple had with their respective lawyers, their attorneys had told them retirement accounts should be treated separately and divided equally. Also, Jim had much more in his retirement accounts, and Natalie was entitled to these. Patrick had suggested they spilt Jim's 401(k) equally and use his IRA as a way to offset any imbalance once they divided the retirement assets.

In some instances, they could divide their overall retirement without actually dividing each retirement account. If this were the case, they would follow a simple three-step process:

1. Take the total value of all retirement accounts.

2. Divide the total value in half.

3. Use one account to transfer assets in order to bring the overall total into balance.

"When I reviewed Natalie's spreadsheet she sent me and compared it to mine, we roughly came up with the same numbers. At the same time, it's absurd I have to give up so much of my retirement when I earned it and saved it from my salary," Jim said.

"Speaking of retirement, I was meaning to ask: Did you have a retirement account from your old company?" Natalie asked.

"I have no idea what you're talking about. I rolled over my old 401(k) into my first IRA. It was a minor amount because I didn't start contributing until after we were married," Jim said.

"But I remember you also telling me about having a pension plan there," Natalie said.

"Maybe I did, but it's been years since I mentioned anything about that. I think I'm getting something when I turn sixty-five. But it won't be much because I only worked there for about eight years—starting right out of college," Jim said.

"If you could, please find out about this pension plan. It might need to be identified, along with the other assets," Courtney said.

"Is that really necessary? It's something I started before we were married, after all," Jim said.

Courtney replied while it may have no impact, the pension still needed to be identified and clarified in order to evaluate all assets.

Before the next mediation, Jim agreed to contact his old employer in order to obtain a statement about his pension.

"My financial adviser also noted there was a $25,000 amount on your W-2 under deferred compensation," said Natalie.

"Yes, I also have an option to make contributions to the company's deferred compensation program until I leave or retire, but the amount isn't guaranteed, which is why I left it off the spreadsheet," Jim said.

"What do you mean it's not guaranteed? You always told me it would be for retirement income once you reached sixty-five, and you never expressed any doubt about it," Natalie said.

"Technically it is not guaranteed because there's a forfeiture clause, which means I would lose the benefit if I'm terminated for cause," Jim.

"And since when have you been worried about a termination and a forfeiture clause? I guess once you realized I may be entitled to some of it, suddenly it became an item that isn't subject to division," Natalie said.

Jim told the group he would discuss his retirement accounts with his attorney. He would seek Al's input regarding their division.

CLARIFICATION: Credit Card Debt

Jim was concerned about the credit card debt Natalie had amassed since they had separated.

"In November and December, I bought presents for kids and family members," Natalie said. "I've always been in charge of gifts, so I knew Jim wouldn't object to that. Then in January, after the holidays and Jim telling me he wanted a divorce, I did some retail therapy—bought some clothes, went to the spa, nothing crazy. I needed some relief from the news. He'd clearly been preparing for divorce for months. Meanwhile, I had days to start making sense of all this. So yes, I did use the credit card to gain some peace of mind. And I've also been seeing a therapist that doesn't bill through insurance," Natalie said.

"The credit card balance is $25,000. How much did the Christmas gifts cost? Jim asked.

"I'm not sure. Probably around $10,000," Natalie said.

"So you're telling me you spent $15,000 on clothes and spa treatments?" Jim asked.

"No, I also covered other expenses while you were out of town. I'd be happy to account for all of it—every penny was spent on the kids and on my sanity after you announced wanting a divorce. Meanwhile, I don't think you can claim the same degree of transparency for your debt," Natalie said.

"What do you mean by that?" Jim asked.

"It seems you've been doing your share of entertaining lately," Natalie said.

"It's all business related. You know that. And I get reimbursed," Jim said.

"I'm sure you're really well reimbursed for entertaining," Natalie said.

Courtney recommended they discuss the credit card conflict with their attorneys. Their lawyers would shed light on the responsibilities each had regarding the balance.

FIRST AND SECOND MEDIATION SUMMARIES

Courtney then referred to Jim's spreadsheet to review what they had covered so far in the first and second mediations.

First Mediation

During the first mediation, they had identified, clarified, and valued most of the minor assets and noted the necessary steps to take for the larger items including the boat. This included the following:

- **WFB Accounts:** They agreed Natalie would retain the joint account and Jim would keep his separate account.

- **Cars:** They agreed to retain their own cars. Jim had a loan balance, and Natalie did not. Each would remove the other from his or her car title and the loan.

- **Boat:** They agreed Jim would keep the sailboat. He would also retitle it to his own name. Jim was now in charge of appraising it because the value on his spreadsheet was an estimate.

They were each responsible to gather the necessary data on the other assets so they could be addressed in the next mediation.

Second Mediation

During the second mediation, they had identified and clarified the following:

- **Schwab Trust:** Jim had confirmed with his attorney that this was Natalie's separate account. As a result, it wasn't part of the division.

- **Rental Property:** They agreed Jim would retain the rental property. They needed to remove Natalie from the loan itself and still had to confirm its actual net income. Jim was charged with obtaining an appraisal.

- **Loss Carryforward:** They agreed they would share the balance equally after filing the current year's tax returns.

- **Retirement Accounts:** During the first mediation, they identified, clarified, and valued these. In the second mediation, they developed a tentative division of the retirement accounts, but they still needed to explore the deferred compensation and pension.

Still Pending

The following items remained still pending on their list:

- **Residence:** For now, they agreed Natalie would retain it. But the marital and non-marital equity still needed to be confirmed because Jim opposed Natalie's Brandenburg calculation. Natalie would have Kathleen provide Al information on the Brandenburg calculation so Jim and Al could evaluate it. Also, Natalie had ordered an appraisal, and she expected to have it ready by the next mediation session.

- **E*Trade:** The investment holdings in the E*Trade account might be spilt in such a way as to balance the equity in the residence.

    They still needed to receive the cost basis information.

If their investment holdings would be split equally, then it wouldn't be an issue. But if their investment holdings would be split unequally, then the E*Trade might become a source of disagreement because the tax basis of the assets would indicate the actual net value, which could be significantly different from the gross value.

The E*Trade, a non-retirement asset, could be easily valued and cashed out as necessary. At the same time, its value could change quickly with the stock market's ups and downs. During Natalie's meetings with Patrick, he suggested that Jim sell some of the investment holdings in the portfolio in order to decrease current risks associated with their fluctuating value.

◘ **SSI Stock Options:** They still needed to clarify and value this. Jim dreaded addressing this item. His intention was to keep them, but he had to act as if he were still open to dividing the options he believed he had rightfully earned.

They planned to address it in the third mediation. Jim reluctantly agreed to provide the grant letters detailing the options provided. The stock options might be used as an offset for other assets.

◘ **Deferred Compensation:** The topic concerned Jim because he wanted to keep as much of his deferred compensation plan as possible.

Courtney asked Jim to provide a balance of the account and a description of the plan. That way, Natalie could review it with her lawyer. As much as he was reluctant to do so, Jim agreed to gather information from the company's website, which contained the deferred compensation plan information and annual statements.

◘ **Personal Property:** While this had been identified and clarified, it still needed further discussion. It would not play a role in the financial division. But Jim noted he wanted the nautical items, including several prints and knick-knacks, and some of the furniture, which would allow him to settle into his new apartment.

◻ **Retirement Accounts:** Need clarification regarding Jim's prior employer pension plan.

◻ **Debts:** During the second mediation, they had identified various debts. But they still remained in the clarification stage. Jim would retain his car loan, but they had not yet agreed who was responsible for the credit card debt. This was a contentious issue and would require further discussion.

"We've had another very effective meeting," Courtney said. "It appears you agree on a number of important issues. We just need some clarification and calculations to resolve what remains. We've built great momentum. I'd like for us to meet again in about a week or two so we can keep on track with resolving the remaining issues."

They pulled out their smartphones, coordinated their calendars, and agreed upon a date.

NATALIE'S LAST WORD

Courtney thanked the couple for their participation and adjourned the meeting. Jim and Natalie collected their belongings and walked toward the exit. As was his habit, he held the door for Natalie.

She glanced at him. "How's Claudia?" she asked.

Without waiting for his response, Natalie continued down the hall. As much as she wanted to, she refused to turn around to see his expression. She didn't care—or at least she wanted him to think she didn't care. Instead, she proceeded on her path, satisfied with the verbal blow she had just dealt him.

Jim held the door, frozen, dumbstruck by her question.

"Is everything okay, Jim?" Courtney asked as she walked by him. The mediator's words snapped him out of his silent stupor.

"Yes, yes. Fine. I just know I have a lot of work ahead of me," Jim said.

He left the office. As he walked toward his car in the parking lot, he left Al a voicemail:

> Just wrapped up the mediation. She's getting way more help than I thought. I need you to make sure I don't get totally screwed by this divorce.

CHAPTER 18

NATALIE'S THIRD MEDIATION PREPARATION

The day after the second mediation, Natalie contacted her team and updated them regarding what had taken place during the meeting. Based on this information, Kathleen and Patrick developed the strategy for Natalie's third mediation. They all met at Patrick's office the following week.

"How do you feel about the process?" Kathleen asked.

"I can tell Jim and I are covering more and more difficult topics because with each mediation the tensions are rising, particularly over Brandenburg. And I only fueled the hostility last time by asking Jim about Claudia—totally caught him off guard," Natalie said.

"I would have loved to have seen the look on his face," Kathleen said.

"That makes two of us—I said it in passing as I walked out of the meeting and didn't turn around," Natalie said.

"I'm sure he had no idea that was coming. Probably even more surprising than your Brandenburg bombshell," Patrick said.

Kathleen and Patrick had been working on Natalie's new spreadsheet. They believed the couple was close to reaching an agreement.

On the conference room wall, Patrick projected the spreadsheet that appeared on his laptop. This would allow everyone to view and revise it together in real time. At the conclusion of their three-way meeting, Natalie would have a new spreadsheet, which she would use for her third mediation.

Patrick described the following five items on today's agenda:

1. Refine the Brandenburg formula.

2. Review Jim's deferred compensation plan, the pension plan, and calculate the pension benefit using the Qualified Domestic Relations Order (QDRO) formula.

3. Review stock options.

4. Review investment income.

5. Review child custody and discuss child and spousal support.

"As I shared earlier with Patrick, I was able to obtain the home appraisal. It came in at $950,000. I think the new value will impact the numbers we have been using to determine the equity division," Natalie said.

'That's good news. I can easily make the changes to the Brandenburg calculation and the property division spreadsheet," Patrick said.

"We're sure Jim will bring his own updated spreadsheet to the next mediation. Hopefully, Al will have educated Jim enough so he'll know what we're proposing is reasonable. No doubt, there will be disagreements. But overall, we're not expecting any major roadblocks," said Kathleen.

"Based on my preliminary calculations, I think you and the kids will be in solid financial shape," said Patrick.

"Your reassurance is the best news I've heard all day. Can I see the numbers?" Natalie asked.

"Hold tight; you'll see them soon—Kathleen and I still need to refine the spousal and child support amounts in order to make the final projections," Patrick said.

"In order to best prepare you for the next mediation, let's address each item on the agenda. As we cover each item, please don't hesitate to ask questions—we want you to have a clear understanding of everything we discuss, and there is a lot to cover," said Kathleen.

BRANDENBURG AND OTHER FORMULAS

"This Brandenburg impasse Jim and I are dealing with is really stressing me out. And it's certainly rattling his nerves. When I started questioning whether it was worth fighting for, I reminded myself of the essential divorce questions:

1. How much financial and emotional currency am I willing to spend?

2. Will the settlement allow me—both with my children and independent of them—to be financially secure now and in the future?

"Jim said the amount I was receiving was ridiculous. He didn't understand why I should be entitled to so much for my separate contribution. He thought—as I had—that we would just calculate the equity, subtract my separate contribution, and then divide the balance. But now I know better. As you suggested earlier, I'm willing to spend as much financial and emotional currency as I need on this because it will increase the likelihood the settlement will allow my children and me to be financially secure now and in the future," Natalie said.

"I'm glad you're using the essential divorce questions to add objectivity to your decision making. Keep in mind Jim's lawyer might present other court-accepted formulas regarding hybrid property. Or he might propose different calculations using Brandenburg," said Patrick.

Patrick presented Natalie a preliminary calculation based on the following worksheet:

Property Description		Year Purchased	1998
Residence		Price of Property	$450,000
		Present Fair Market Value	$950,000
		Cost of Sale	
		Present Mortgage Balance (1st+2nd)	$275,000

Itemized Investments	Husband	Wife	Marital	Borrowed
Initial down payment in 1998		$90,000		
Renovations in 2002		$50,000		
Mortgage pay down			$149,000	
Refinancing proceeds				

CALCULATED RESULTS   **NET EQUITY** $675,000

Investment Summary	Amount		
Husband's Separate Investment		How to Divide	
Wife's Separate Investment	$140,000	Marital Portion	
Marital Investment	$149,000	Husband Receives	50%
Total Investment, Separate + Marital	$289,000	Wife Receives	50%

Distribution of Equity	Percent	Amount	If marital portion is divided as set forth above, then total distribution of fund is
Husband's Separate Interest			
Wife's Separate Interest	48.4%	$327,000	
Marital Interest	51.6%	$348,000	**Husband** / **Wife**
Total	100.0%	$675,000	$174,000 / $501,000

1. The couple's home was worth $950,000.

2. From $950,000, Patrick subtracted $275,000, which was the home's mortgage balance, and $327,000, which was Natalie's non-marital interest.

3. What remained was about $348,000, which was the marital interest.

4. Patrick divided $348,000 by two, which would result in each of them receiving $174,000 in marital interest.

5. Thus Natalie's total interest in their home would be $327,000 for her separate interest plus $174,000 for her marital interest for a total of $501,000.

Patrick noted his calculation might have to be refined yet again to include an amount to offset a portion of Natalie's non-marital interest due to the withdrawals the couple took during their last refinance. Furthermore, the amount of appreciation from home improvements they paid with separate contributions might affect his calculations.

In regards to home improvements, they might need to demonstrate how they increased the property's value in order to justify the amount of additional separate interest calculated.

"As a result, the final amount of your separate interest may be lower than this current calculation. However, I feel confident you'll end up with somewhere between $300,000 and $350,000 of separate interest and your share of the total interest in the home equity will be near $500,000," Patrick said.

Natalie was pleased with Patrick's preliminary numbers because having $500,000 of equity would allow her to keep the house.

RETIREMENT:
DEFERRED COMPENSATION AND PENSION

"Jim was surprised when I brought up the $25,000 on his W-2. I'm sure he knew Patrick was behind it. If we were playing good cop-bad cop, you would definitely be the bad one in his eyes," Natalie said.

"As long as you're receiving your fair share, that's fine with me," said Patrick.

"He supposedly didn't include it on the spreadsheet because he thought it wasn't guaranteed and not currently available to him. But I don't believe anything he says anymore. He just wants to keep as much as possible to support his new love interest," Natalie said.

Kathleen had asked Al for the balance on Jim's deferred compensation plan. He reported that it had a current value of $150,000. Patrick would add this to the spreadsheet. Her team was confident Natalie would receive a benefit, in one form or another, from Jim's deferred compensation.

"I've done some calculations regarding the pension Jim received at the first job he had when you were married. The news will also rattle his nerves," Patrick said.

Patrick explained that according to his research, Jim was fully vested in the pension he earned from the first job he had out of college. Once he reached sixty-five years old, he was due to receive $1,800 per month ($21,600 per year) for life, adjusted for inflation. Natalie was entitled to a portion of it, or she could use the pension to offset other assets.

"But he participated in the pension before we were married, so why am I entitled to any of it?" she asked.

"Yes, he had worked in the company for three years prior to your marriage. But he also worked there for five years *after* you were married. In other words, he earned part of the pension while you were married, so it now becomes a hybrid property," said Patrick.

PRESENT VALUE AND QDRO

Natalie asked if Patrick would use the Brandenburg formula to determine her separate interest in the pension.

Patrick explained that he wouldn't use the Brandenburg formula because it was mostly used for real property. Instead, he had two other options:

- ◘ Present Value (PV)

- ◘ Qualified Domestic Relations Order (QDRO)

PV translates future dollars into their current value. It is based on the idea that a dollar today is worth more than a dollar in the future because you can invest today's dollar, and it will grow over the years.

For Jim's pension, which would be available in the future, Patrick would calculate what amount today would be equivalent to that pension in those future years, based on an assumed interest rate. The downside of using PV is that changes in the interest rate and inflation rate assumptions will have a significant impact on the results.

Patrick explained in Natalie's case, the PV would be based in part on Jim's projected life expectancy after he reached age sixty-five, as well as the inflation rate and interest rate, which is technically known as a discount rate. Patrick would then take that number to calculate the PV at Jim's present age. That PV would be used in the spreadsheet as an alternative to the QDRO formula. The value would also change if the pension included an inflation benefit.

"I ran a preliminary calculation and came up with a current marital value of about $133,500 for the pension with no inflation benefit and about $220,400 if we used a 2 percent annual inflation rate on the pension benefit. I'm going to use the $133,500 as a placeholder on my summary spreadsheet for the division of property. However, I think we can either use it as a trade-off or get you part of the pension using the QDRO," Patrick said.

He added that, on the other hand, **QDRO**, was a fairly simple formula.

Patrick would follow these steps:

1. Identify the number of years Natalie was married while Jim worked for the company.

2. Divide the result of step 1 by the number of years Jim worked for the company.

3. Multiply the result of step 2 by 50 percent. This is Natalie's marital interest in the pension.

Using this formula yielded the following results for Natalie:

1. The couple was married for five years while Jim worked for the company.

2. Jim worked for the company for eight years. Five divided by eight is 0.625, or 62.5 percent.

3. Natalie's interest in the pension is 0.625 x 50 percent = 31.25 percent.

Natalie would be entitled to 31.25 percent of Jim's pension when he turned sixty-five years old. This could translate to $562.50 per month or $6,750 per year.

In general, the courts have favored QDRO over PV because QDRO is the more straightforward of the two calculations. A change in the assumptions used in a PV calculation can lead to a wide range of results, which can create more conflicts than solutions.

"We can ask Jim to provide you your share of the pension *or* use Patrick's PV calculation to show the pension's current value, so we can offset it with other retirement accounts," Kathleen said.

AN ADDITIONAL RETIREMENT ACCOUNT IDENTIFIED

In Patrick's research, he recently found another account that would count as a marital asset. Jim and Natalie each had a Roth IRA. This type of retirement account is tax deferred and tax free when withdrawn in retirement. Another benefit is it can be passed down tax free to beneficiaries. The account balances weren't enough to significantly change the overall division of assets. Nonetheless, Patrick did need to account for them. He included the Roth IRAs on the latest spreadsheet.

STOCK OPTIONS

Natalie remembered Jim didn't want to discuss his SSI stock options during the second mediation. She realized his discomfort about the topic might have reflected his desire to keep them.

Patrick explained part of her strategy could include allowing Jim to have the stock options. This is where the first essential divorce question is helpful:

How much financial and emotional currency are you willing to spend?

By giving up the stock options, Natalie was deciding to *not* spend much financial and emotional currency on it. This would provide Jim a feeling he had experienced a victory. By giving Jim the stock options, she would direct her focus on other assets that could be more easily identified and valued. In the end, this would play a role in her strategy to develop a settlement that would allow her to be financially secure. But rather than concede the stock options right away, Patrick suggested Natalie express moderate resistance and then eventually give Jim what he wanted.

INVESTMENT INCOME

Patrick told Natalie that **investment income** was also called "unearned income" and it included dividends, interest, and net rental income. Depending on multiple factors within the divorce, it could be included when calculating support. This would be the case regardless of whether or not the income was spent or reinvested into a portfolio or savings account.

His preliminary estimate was $6,000 per year of investment income for Natalie's Schwab account. Add that to her $47,000 salary, and she would have a total of about $53,000 of income that would be used in the support calculations.

On the other hand, Patrick projected Jim's investment income from the rental property would be $7,800 and $5,000 from his E*Trade portfolio. These would be added to his salary, bonus, deferred compensation, and the exercise of his stock options. Combined, he calculated Jim's total income for determining support would be $412,800.

"Wow! I never realized just how much money he was making. No wonder he was trying to get me to agree early on for the support amount he proposed—before I caught on that it was lower than what I was entitled to! So what does this mean as far as my support overall is concerned?" asked Natalie.

"That's exactly what we're going to go over next," said Kathleen.

CHILD CUSTODY

Kathleen asked Natalie for updates regarding any custody discussions she might have had with Jim.

"I worked with Dr. Michaels on this. With her guidance, you'll be glad to hear Jim and I hammered out custody," she said.

"What a fantastic surprise. How'd you do it so quickly?" Kathleen asked.

Natalie described how she brought up her custody concerns with Dr. Michaels during one of their therapy sessions. "I told her that, more than anything else, I wanted full custody of Rachel. I also asked for her recommendations regarding the next steps. She provided a step-by-step plan. Part of it required Jim and me to meet in person," said Natalie.

Bolstered by her therapist's guidance, Natalie developed her strategy. She had rehearsed what she would propose to Jim. After she felt confident she could effectively present her points and provide compelling counterarguments to his objections and believed the timing was right, she gave Jim a call to schedule a meeting.

When Jim saw Natalie's name appear on his phone's screen, he experienced a sense of relief. He felt immense guilt after she had confronted him about Claudia at the end of their previous mediation. He had no idea what she thought of his infidelity at the moment, and he had no intention of asking her about it, but he could immediately tell by the calm sound of her short "Hi, Jim, it's me" that she wasn't calling in anger. During their conversation, she described her session with Dr. Michaels and leveraged her therapist's advice in order to lend credibility to her pitch.

"My therapist suggested we meet informally to share our thoughts in regards to Rachel's future and maybe even come to some kind of agreement," said Natalie.

"I've been thinking about Rachel a lot too. At the same time, if we meet, I don't want this to turn into a mediation about the divorce," said Jim.

"I'm just as concerned as you are about that. I think if we agree to stick to the topic of Rachel's well-being and save everything else for formal mediations, we'll both stay on track," said Natalie.

Jim agreed to meet Natalie at the end of the week at the town park near their home. But before fully committing, he wanted to speak to his lawyer first.

Reaching out to Al for his input about Natalie's proposal, Jim wanted to know what his custody options were, if agreeing to meet was prudent, and if so, what he should say.

Al said the meeting was an approach many couples took. Overall, he found nothing objectionable about it. He coached his client and provided his recommendations.

NATALIE AND JIM DISCUSS CHILD CUSTODY

Natalie brought her iPad to their meeting. On her screen was an outline based on the information Dr. Michaels had provided. Natalie planned to use this to generate talking points. She started with item number one on her list.

"My general feeling is I think it's in Rachel's interest if you and I figured out custody together and then presented Rachel with a unified position," said Natalie.

"I don't think that's necessary. My attorney said Rachel being fifteen means she is old enough to tell us what she wants to do. A judge would probably go about it in the same way too," said Jim.

Natalie was relieved she had prepared a counterargument for what Jim proposed.

She told him that placing the custody decision on Rachel could make her feel as if they were asking her to choose which parent she wanted to live with. Any subsequent guilt she felt over picking one parent over another could result in emotional issues for her later.

To avoid this, Natalie recommended they share what each wanted. Using this information, they could come to an agreement based on what was in their daughter's best interest. Once they developed a preliminary plan, they could arrange to meet with Rachel. They would present what they'd come up with and receive her input in order to form a final plan.

"According to my therapist, one of the benefits of this approach is it would be an open and transparent means to work out custody. By developing a plan and receiving her input, we would reassure Rachel we both wanted what was best for her, we'd continue to be equally involved in her life, and her opinion mattered," Natalie said.

Although Natalie's strategy was something he hadn't thought of before, it seemed reasonable. He agreed with Natalie's observation that leaving the decision up to Rachel could cause her to feel pressured to pick sides. And the emotional toll such a decision would take concerned him.

"Your plan makes sense. So where do we go from here?" Jim asked.

"How about we each share what we want? You start," Natalie said.

Jim expressed his biggest concern had to do with his relationship with Rachel. He had always had a close connection with her, and he feared the divorce would put their bond at risk. He wanted to continue to participate in her life, which included her extracurricular activities. He also sought to play a role in the decisions that would affect her. He didn't want the divorce to turn him into a bystander.

When it was Natalie's turn, she described having the same fears as Jim. She added her biggest concern was Jim's intense work travel. He was gone about two weeks every month. As a result, she believed it was in Rachel's best interest to call one place her primary home.

"I get your point about my travel making scheduling custody a challenge. But I still want to see her as much as possible. Could we have a flexible arrangement instead of a fixed schedule?" Jim asked.

"How about this: Would you consider giving me primary custody and we'd share joint legal custody?—I'm all for co-parenting. I'd also go along with you having a flexible schedule with Rachel whenever you were at home," Natalie said.

"As long as anything we decide doesn't restrict me from seeing Rachel, then I could agree to that," Jim said.

An emotional weight lifted off Natalie's shoulders. Having full custody of Rachel was at the top of her wish list.

"Thank you, Jim. I know what we agreed to is best for her. I promise you, I'll never interfere with her time with you. And given her busy schedule, both of us are seeing a lot less of her these days anyway. I know she loves being with you," she said.

She input their tentative agreement in her iPad. Natalie then glanced at her notes. The next item on her outline was the parenting plan.

"My therapist suggested we consider working on a parenting plan. Dr. Michaels gave me a list of mental health professionals with special expertise in divorce mediation. We'd hire one of them to draft the parenting plan. Once we decided on a therapist, we would schedule a meeting with him or her. My therapist also recommended a joint meeting with Rachel to show her what we came up with today," Natalie said.

"Al told me about parenting plans. He said they were a way to improve our relationship post-divorce because it would benefit how we communicate about Rachel and address issues we'll come across in the future. I know we'll be dealing with graduations and hopefully weddings and grandchildren in the future. I'm actually okay going along with it as long as the cost is reasonable and it doesn't delay our mediations," said Jim.

"So it's settled. Where should we meet with Rachel and present her what we've come up with?" asked Natalie.

"She loves Nino's Pizza downtown. How about there?" Jim asked.

"Great idea," Natalie said.

Jim offered to phone their daughter and set up the dinner. They agreed to meet with Rachel the next evening.

"If she asks, what should I say we're getting together for?" Jim asked.

"Hmm. Not sure. What if you keep it simple and say it was a family discussion—nothing too serious," said Natalie.

JIM AND NATALIE PRESENT THEIR PLAN TO RACHEL

While waiting for their pizza order, Natalie told Rachel about the plan she and Jim had agreed upon.

Rachel's response was thoughtful and expressed wisdom beyond her fifteen years of age. She said she was sad about the divorce. As she loved both her parents, one of her biggest concerns was the breakup would adversely affect her relationship with them. She was particularly concerned about her dad because he had already moved out and she wasn't sure how they would maintain their close connection.

"I'm also relieved you thought it was a good idea for me to stay in one place. The thought of living in two homes and keeping track of two bedrooms doesn't really appeal to me. Plus, Dad's apartment is farther away from school than our house. At the same time, I'm glad I can see Dad as often as possible. That's super important to me," she said.

Tears welled in her eyes as she thought about the inevitable consequence of the divorce: Her dad would never move back home again.

Jim and Natalie reassured Rachel the divorce didn't mean either one of them would be leaving her. They also said they wanted Rachel to be able to express herself and to talk openly and honestly about any issues she had. Overall, her input would be important and something they'd take seriously.

After dinner, Natalie and Rachel returned to the house. Natalie went to work drafting the custody outline based on what they had discussed at Nino's Pizza:

- Natalie would retain primary custody.

- They would share joint parenting (in other words, joint legal custody) and responsibility for Rachel.

- Jim would commit to having Rachel with him at least two weekends per month. He also wanted to have dinners with her and attend her activities whenever he was in town.

- They would all share a Google calendar. Each person would be responsible to input any activities and travel that would affect the others' schedules. Also, by knowing Rachel's schedule, both parents would be able to determine which activities they would attend. They agreed that both or one parent could show up to events without restrictions.

Afterwards, Natalie emailed Jim her bulleted summary.

DRAFTING THE PARENTING PLAN

The following week Natalie and Jim met with one of the therapists Dr. Michaels recommended. Dr. Michaels told her that in most instances, lawyers draft parenting plans. In Natalie's case, she decided to reach out to Dr. Fredericks. In addition to being a marriage and family counselor, Dr. Fredericks specialized in parenting plans. His rate was reasonable (which pleased Jim), and his credentials were solid (which pleased Natalie), so they agreed to hire him.

After they met with Dr. Fredericks, he took Natalie's summary and included her points in the parenting plan he developed. His parenting plan, like most, covered topics relevant to a child's well-being, such as medical, mental health, scheduling, travel, and communication:

1. **Medical and Mental Health:** Rachel would remain on Jim's health insurance plan, and any medical issues related to Rachel would be accessible to both parents. They agreed to allow Rachel to see a therapist in order to provide her an independent and private place to share her feelings. What she discussed during therapy would remain private—neither parent would have access to the information unless Rachel authorized it.

2. **Scheduling and Travel:** They identified holidays, vacations, birthdays, camps, and any other events that might require joint participation, as well as separate travel with Rachel. They agreed to remain flexible in regards to the timing of these events. The only requirement was, if either traveled with Rachel away from the area, he or she would provide the other parent an itinerary and contact information.

3. **Communication:** All agreed to keep each other informed of their schedules and about any issues such as last-minute changes to planned events or schedules. Open communication would prevent conflicts from arising. In the event of an unresolved conflict, the parents agreed to obtain help from a neutral party, such as Courtney or Dr. Fredericks, to resolve the matter respectfully.

Natalie showed Kathleen and Patrick the bulleted summary she drafted, as well as the parenting plan Dr. Fredericks created.

"You've got a great daughter," Kathleen said. "And I'm glad you included Rachel in the decision-making process so she doesn't feel left out."

This was the outcome Kathleen had hoped for. She had been concerned a separate mediation would be necessary to resolve the custody issue and had known this additional step and its cost would frustrate Jim. The couple's custody agreement removed what could otherwise have been a significant roadblock in reaching a divorce settlement.

"I was happy with the result too," said Natalie.

"Unfortunately, we're not out of the woods yet. Although custody's out of the way, support is usually *the most* contentious aspect of the mediation process. The intense emotional issues surrounding support and its long-term financial implications are probably the two biggest reasons why resolving it is so difficult," Kathleen said.

"It's also one of the last issues to address because a couple can't calculate support until they divide their assets and know all income amounts including income from separate assets," Patrick said.

Due to the complexity of the spousal and child support discussion, Natalie's team planned to address support in depth during her next three-way meeting with them. Between now and then, Patrick would verify the income data and complete an updated income and expense spreadsheet for Natalie. This would provide him the information he needed to determine Natalie's real cost of living. From there, he and Kathleen would calculate the support amount Natalie would need and develop a long-term plan for her.

"So here's my summary of what Jim and I still need to work out," said Natalie.

- ◘ **Residence:** Continue to refine the Brandenburg calculation. My team is eager to see how Al responds and what he proposes.

- ◘ **E*Trade:** Might be used as an offset to balance the primary residence's equity.

- ◘ **SSI Stock Options:** Clarification and valuation—plan to allow Jim to retain.

- ◘ **Personal Property:** Clarification, valuation, and jointly make a decision once the real property assets have been divided.

- ◘ **Retirement Accounts:** Add together all retirement accounts except the pension and then balance the amount overall using one primary account instead of dividing each account individually.

- ◘ **Debts:** Determine who would be responsible for credit card debt. The goal is to have the balance shared equally.

"We've taken an exhaustive look into your entire financial life as a couple. Barring something completely off the wall coming from Jim and his lawyer, I'm confident we're close to a resolution," Kathleen said.

"I'll print out the spreadsheet we revised during our meeting today," Patrick said. "Make sure you review it and take it to your third mediation."

CHAPTER 19

THIRD MEDIATION

With each mediation, the balance of power between the couple shifted. In the divorce dance, Jim initially took the lead. But now, their roles have reversed: As Natalie became more confident, Jim's uneasiness grew. At the same time, working with Al had given him the legal counsel he needed to address his greatest concerns:

- ◘ Having to pay an exorbitant amount of support for decades to come
- ◘ Not having enough money left to buy a new home
- ◘ Being able to maintain his current standard of living

Natalie and Jim sat in the mediator's conference room.

"How are things going with Al?" Courtney asked Jim. "Has he helped clarify what we've covered so far?"

"As much as I hate to admit it, I should have retained him earlier. He's developed his own calculations for Brandenburg and dividing the remaining assets. I emailed it to you yesterday," Jim said.

"And I'll project it so Natalie can see it. How about you, Natalie? Any updates?"

"I also emailed you my latest spreadsheet. Is it ready to go?"

"Yes, we'll see both," Courtney said.

Before their meeting, Courtney had taped the flip-chart notes she'd recorded from previous mediations around the room's periphery. She also projected a spreadsheet on the wall showing what they had covered and what they would address during the third mediation.

The following was Courtney's summary:

Item	Disposition
Bank Account	Natalie to retain joint account and Jim to retain his own account
Cars	Each retain own, Jim responsible for loan on his BMW
Sailboat	Jim retains
Residence	Natalie retains, using Brandenburg formula, $325k to $350k separate interest of Natalie?
Rental Property	Jim retains, removes Natalie from loan, agreed value to be $550k pending appraisal
Household	Jim retains nautical items and divide the rest equitably
Child Custody	Natalie retains custody and joint parenting
E*Trade	Use margin and liquidity for balancing
SSI Options	Jim retains all options
Schwab	Natalie's separate asset
Loss Carryforward	Split for future tax returns
Jim's IRA	Final amount to be determined but likely used to offset other assets
Jim's 401(k)	Use for balancing, overall goal is to balance the retirement amounts equally

Item	Disposition
Natalie's 403(b)	Natalie to retain
Credit Card Debt	Agree to split?
Spousal Support	To be determined by attorneys?
Child Support	Statutory guideline

"Since we started with Jim last time, I think it's Natalie's turn. Do you have anything you'd like to address first?" Courtney asked Natalie.

"The appraisal is done. It came in at $950,000, which is a bit higher than we had expected. I still have some concerns about the stock options. Maybe Jim can tell us why he wants to keep them," Natalie said.

"I want them because they're going to be difficult to manage and aren't going to be easy to divide," Jim said.

"That's fine with me as long as we can use the E*Trade account to balance the division," said Natalie.

"I like the idea, but to be completely honest, I don't think you want the E*Trade because it's all penny stocks," said Jim.

"My financial adviser suggested you might be able to retain most of the E*Trade account by using a margin line of credit," Natalie said.

"Hmmmm. Interesting approach: I'd be able to keep most of the current stock I've purchased and pay off the margin loan as I make future transactions. How much did you determine was your share?" Jim asked Natalie.

"My spreadsheet shows $157,500. Courtney, can we see the spreadsheet?" Natalie asked.

Courtney projected it on the wall.

	JIM'S AMOUNT	NATALIE'S AMOUNT	TOTAL AMOUNT
NON-RETIREMENT ASSETS			
REAL ESTATE EQUITY			
Residence	$0	$348,000	$348,000
Total Value	$950,000		
1st Mortgage	$275,000		
Sep. Property	$327,000		
Marital Equity	$348,000		
Rental Property	$200,000	$0	$200,000
Total Value	$550,000		
1st Mortgage	$350,000		
Marital Equity	$200,000		
TOTAL REAL EST. EQUITY	**$200,000**	**$348,000**	**$548,000**
CASH & INVESTMENTS			
Joint WFB	$0	$25,000	$25,000
Jim's WFB	$10,000	$0	$10,000
Jim's E*Trade	$67,500	$157,500	$225,000
SSI Vested Stock Options	$224,000	$0	$224,000
Natalie's Schwab	$0	$0	$0
Loss Carryforward	$50,000	$50,000	$100,000
TOTAL CASH & INVESTMENTS	**$351,500**	**$232,500**	**$584,000**
PERSONAL EFFECTS			
Natalie's Personal Property	$0	$1	$1
Jim's Personal Property	$1	$0	$1
Sailboat	$30,000	$0	$30,000
BMW	$35,000	$0	$35,000
Subaru	$0	$15,000	$15,000
TOTAL PERSONAL EFFECTS	**$65,001**	**$15,001**	**$80,002**

	JIM'S AMOUNT	NATALIE'S AMOUNT	TOTAL AMOUNT
TOTAL NON-RETIREMENT ASSETS	$616,501	$595,501	$1,212,002

RETIREMENT ASSETS			
IRA/401(k)s			
IRA	$37,500	$112,500	$150,000
401(k)	$187,500	$187,500	$375,000
403(b)	$0	$85,000	$85,000
Non-qualified Deferred Comp.	$150,000	$0	$150,000
Pension PV	$66,750	$66,750	$133,500
Non-marital PV Pension	$0	$0	$0
TOTAL IRA/401(k)s	$441,750	$451,750	$893,500
DEFINED BENEFIT PENSIONS			
IBM/Pension	$0	$0	$0
TOTAL PENSIONS	$0	$0	$0
TOTAL RETIREMENT ASSETS	$441,750	$451,750	$893,500

TOTAL ASSETS	$1,058,251	$1,047,251	$2,105,502

DEBTS			
Credit Card	($12,500)	($12,500)	($25,000)
BMW	($15,000)	$0	($15,000)
TOTAL DEBTS	($27,500)	($12,500)	($40,000)

TOTAL DEBTS	($27,500)	($12,500)	($40,000)

TOTAL ASSETS	$1,058,251	$1,047,251	$2,105,502
TOTAL DEBTS	($27,500)	($12,500)	($40,000)
TOTAL PROPERTY	$1,030,751	$1,034,751	$2,065,502

According to Patrick's calculations, the E*Trade account was valued at $225,000. The margin loan had a 50 percent limit, so Jim would receive only about $112,500.

Natalie's proposal considered the following:

1. Jim sells one-third ($75,000) of the E*Trade account.

2. This would leave him with a balance of $150,000 ($225,000 - $75,000 = $150,000).

3. Jim would obtain a $75,000 margin line of credit on the balance of $150,000 (50% of $150,000).

4. The total created from the sale and the margin would be $150,000, and any remaining balance needed could come from other cash assets.

"That gets us pretty close to the total of $157,500 that appears on my spreadsheet. You keep the stock options, and we use the E*Trade account to balance. Does that work for you, Jim?" asked Natalie.

Jim said he would discuss the E*Trade alternative with Al. If his lawyer agreed to the arrangement, the end result would mean Jim would retain the remaining E*Trade account and Natalie would receive her share in cash rather than stock.

Courtney added the following to the flip chart:

> E*Trade as a possible offset to stock options and home equity using margin, Jim to review the information with Al to reach a decision.

CLARIFICATION: Retirement Accounts (Pension)

"Now that you've provided the information on your old pension plan," Natalie said to Jim, "Patrick came up with a QDRO formula to determine the marital share, which is 31.25 percent of your pension."

"That pension was from before we were even married. How are you entitled to any of it, let alone 31 percent? And what the hell is a QDRO formula?" Jim asked.

"Jim, was the pension earned entirely while you were single? Or did it start when you were single and continue after you married?" Courtney asked.

"So because we were married for part of the time I was earning my pension, I take it that it's considered a marital asset. Natalie's team of asshole experts strikes again—I'm hemorrhaging assets and apparently can't do a damn thing about it," Jim said.

Courtney reminded Jim of their agreement to use no profanity and to be respectful. She then explained the QDRO formula to Jim.

"Nothing's set in stone yet. Run the pension scenario by Al, and see what he says," said Courtney.

"Is it really worth fighting for, Natalie? I can't imagine it being much money—maybe worth a cup of coffee," Jim said.

"That would be a very big cup of coffee, to the tune of $1,800 per month once you turn sixty-five," said Natalie.

"There's no way it's worth that much! Besides, sixteen years from now, the company may not even be around anymore," Jim said. He was incensed. Part of him hoped the company would burn to the ground so he wouldn't have to pay Natalie another penny.

Courtney added the pension to the summary draft of her spreadsheet. She also told Jim the pension was the company's liability, but the Pension Benefit Guarantee Corporation insured them, so Jim would most likely receive a benefit, even if the company went bankrupt.

Next, the couple addressed the primary residence.

VALUATION AND DECISION: Brandenburg Formula

Natalie believed the only property issue remaining was her separate interest in the primary residence. The amount her team had calculated was based on her retaining the house and Jim keeping the rental property.

While Jim agreed to use the Brandenburg formula, he wanted to prorate the withdrawals they made with Natalie's separate interest. Prorating would reduce her separate interest because a portion of the withdrawals would be considered a return of her separate interest.

They had used the withdrawals to pay for home refinances, college tuition, expenses on the boat, and other expenses Jim hadn't defined.

Natalie disagreed. She didn't believe it was fair to reduce her separate interest in the equity merely because Jim decided to pull out cash for other expenses.

"You realize that cash wasn't just for me or the withdrawal a decision made only by me," said Jim. "If you recall, *we* decided to withdraw the cash."

"Is there an amount you could both agree upon that would allow you to resolve this?" Courtney asked.

"I could agree to the separate amount being $300,000," said Jim.

Natalie, however, would go no lower than $325,000.

"If you think about it, your numbers are pretty close," said Courtney.

She recommended recording both amounts on the flip chart. They could then revisit the issue after determining other items that needed to be adjusted. The couple agreed to table the Brandenburg formula discussion for now and focus on the other remaining items.

Courtney wrote the following on the flip chart:

> Natalie's separate interest in home equity:
> $300,000 to $325,000

VALUATION AND DECISION: Rental Property Appraisal

Jim provided the appraisal results on the rental property. He had hoped for the appraisal to come in at $550,000 or below. To his chagrin, the amount was actually $575,000. He said he planned on obtaining another appraisal in order to verify its accuracy.

"You picked the appraiser, so why do you need a second opinion? If you're still not satisfied with the second one, will you want a third? Heck, maybe I should have one done too," Natalie said.

"Of course you'd want your own. After all, spending our money isn't a problem for you," said Jim.

For argument's sake, Courtney suggesting using the $575,000 appraisal to see how it would impact the property division balances.

By using $575,000 rather than the $550,000 appraisal Jim sought, his side of the balance sheet would increase by $25,000. In this case, Natalie would be entitled to a $25,000 offset somewhere else.

"Does either of you have any suggestions as to which asset to use to offset?" Courtney asked.

"If—and right now this is purely speculation—Natalie was entitled to an offset, I think she could receive a larger share of the E*Trade account," Jim said.

"But," said Courtney, "in order for that to work, it would most likely require forfeiting the margin line of credit proposal. The reason is you'd have to sell more of the holdings. As a result, you'd have less to use as a margin line of credit. Another asset we could possibly tap into to offset this value is the retirement accounts. However, that may create a disproportionate amount of retirement assets on Natalie's side of the balance sheet, resulting in possible adverse tax consequences for her."

"Am I supposed to be concerned about her tax consequences? You do realize how much money I'm losing in this process," Jim said.

"It seems like the difference between the rental property and our house is close," Natalie said. "Maybe we could keep the amount I have for my separate interest in the house. Meanwhile, Jim could keep the rental with the $550,000 original estimated value. Courtney, can we agree to these amounts even if the home's appraised value is different from the value we're actually using?"

"As long as you're not violating the law, you can go with whatever amount you want. Are you considering a compromise on the real estate?" Courtney asked.

Jim said he would accept Natalie's non-marital amount of $325,000, if Natalie would agree to the $550,000 original estimate.

Although the plan seemed like a good idea, Natalie said she wanted to review the scenario with her team before accepting the offer.

"I want to run it by Al too. If we settle on those values and I keep all the stock options, then it looks as if we're close to agreeing on the property division. What do you think, Courtney?" Jim asked.

Courtney concurred. With that said, she would use the $550,000 rental property value and the $350,000 of separate interest in the residence to keep the amount equal on the spreadsheet.

On the flip chart, Courtney noted the tentative decision they had made regarding the division of assets and how they would be divided. She would prepare a summary for both scenarios and send it out the next day to Natalie, Jim, and their attorneys.

IDENTIFICATION AND CLARIFICATION:
Child Custody and Support

"I see both of you agreed Natalie will have sole physical custody of Rachel and you're sharing parenting responsibility. I'm glad you were able to resolve child custody so quickly. Otherwise, it can be a real problem if not done early in the process," said Courtney.

"According to my lawyer, we can't accurately determine child support until we know the spousal support amount," said Natalie.

"Yes, first you have to come to a final decision regarding the division of property. This will give us the preliminary framework for the memorandum of understanding (MOU)—a summary of what you have agreed to as a result of the mediation process. The MOU often forms the basis of the property settlement agreement (PSA). As you know, the PSA is a legally binding document. Once the division of property is out of the way, you can determine spousal support. And after agreeing upon spousal support, you can figure out child support," said Courtney.

With Courtney's mention of spousal support, Natalie decided to seize the opportunity to state her position.

"In regards to spousal support, my lawyer has made her preliminary calculation," Natalie said. Prior to today's meeting, Natalie had rehearsed the following in front of her bathroom mirror until she had memorized it—she didn't want to miss a word or succumb to a last-minute urge to back down: "Kathleen based her spousal support amount on our incomes, my living expenses, and the twenty-five years we've been married. I'm a teacher, so I'll never earn as much as Jim. In fact, because he makes eight times more than I do, he'll easily recover from the divorce. She proposed $9,000 per month of spousal support until I reach age seventy."

Jim leapt from his seat. "Nine thousand dollars a month! Where the hell did you come up with that? You're not the only one who crunched numbers with an attorney. Al's alimony calculation is nowhere near that high. This is *bullshit!*" Jim said.

"Jim, please take a seat," Courtney said.

He glared at Natalie.

"And before you slap me on the wrist—yes. I know I'm not supposed to swear, but I can't help it. Do you see what she's doing to me?" he asked.

He continued to glare at Natalie. "You act all nice, talk about compromise and fairness. Then you drop bomb after bomb. Now you want me to support you for the rest of your life, even after I agreed to give up custody of Rachel. I swear to God, you won't get any of this!" Jim said.

"Let's step back and reflect on how far we've come and how much we've accomplished," Courtney said. "Support is always an emotional issue, which is why it's always wise to have a lawyer involved. Your attorneys will help you with the support issues, and maybe we can come close enough to compromise."

"Screw compromise! Hasn't done squat for me so far—other than make me hate my soon-to-be ex-wife. I'm outta here," Jim said.

He gathered his belongings as quickly as he could and stormed out of the conference room.

Natalie and Courtney sat in silence.

Her husband's words both stung and empowered. In all their years of marriage, Jim had never once used the word *hate* toward her. So she knew he was as hurt and angry as she'd ever seen him. At the same time, she realized that just a few months ago, she would have caved and immediately tried to diffuse his temper tantrum, but not anymore.

"What now?" Natalie asked.

Courtney recommended she meet with her lawyer as soon as possible. She hoped Kathleen and Al would discuss the spousal support issue and figure out a way to overcome the negotiations impasse and come to an agreement regarding the amount.

The two concluded their meeting.

On her way home, Natalie phoned her sister.

"Barrett, you'd be proud of me. I was terrified to do it, but I stood my ground and told Jim how much alimony I wanted. He blew up and ran out of the meeting," Natalie said.

"Good for you, sis. He's on the defense and retreating in defeat! You should have demanded even more from that bastard. But it's time to put all that behind you because we're going to have a great weekend. Are you ready?" Barrett asked.

The two had made reservations to stay at a nearby resort. Natalie needed the mental break, and Barrett was happy to support her sister.

As much as Natalie felt satisfied about bringing up support

figures during the mediation, part of her was afraid if she pushed Jim too hard, he might decide to call mediation quits and go straight to court. After her conversation with Barrett, Natalie contacted Patrick and Kathleen. She scheduled a meeting at Patrick's office for Monday afternoon at 4:00 p.m.

That evening after the third mediation, Courtney began preparing a draft MOU describing what the couple had agreed on concerning the property division. In it, she also identified the unresolved issues surrounding the support. She emailed an updated summary of the mediation to Al and Kathleen:

The third mediation went well, and the property division is mostly done. You will need to make a few adjustments concerning the actual amounts of the E*Trade and the retirement accounts; they need to be divided in such a way as to bring an overall balance to the division.

From my perspective, they're very close to having the final property division agreement. They need to focus on the support as the final step. Jim had a strong and negative reaction to Natalie's proposal concerning the support amount. I am hopeful that both of you will be able to negotiate an agreement on support in a timely manner so that we can generate a final MOU that can be used to draft the PSA.

The next mediation may be the last if the support issues are resolved. In that session, my goal would be to review the MOU and tie up any loose ends.

CHAPTER 20

NATALIE'S FINANCIAL PLANNING

Friday morning, Natalie and Barrett took off for their weekend adventure. During their four-hour drive to The Greenbrier, a mountain retreat in West Virginia, the two talked about Jim's budding romance with Claudia.

"If it were up to me, I'd throw that lowlife to the wolves," Barrett said. "You only get one shot at this, and there are no second chances."

"I understand your point. But I've got a favor. . . . I *really* need a mental break from all this. Could we avoid divorce discussions for just this weekend? I'd really appreciate it," Natalie said.

"Honey, I only want what's best for you. Won't say one more word about the bastard or your divorce," Barrett responded.

For the first time since Jim had announced he wanted a divorce, Natalie was able to relax that weekend. She and her sister indulged in spa treatments, enjoyed the resort's famous cuisine, and went hiking.

On Saturday night, they took a cab to a local pub.

"You won't need this anymore," Barrett said as she slipped her sister's wedding ring off.

"What are you doing?" Natalie asked.

"Making sure you have a blast tonight." She slid the band into Natalie's purse.

The driver pulled into the pub's parking lot. It was country western night, and they could hear the live band's two-step from their seat in the taxi.

The sisters stood at the bar and ordered drinks. As they sipped Coronas, two men walked up to them and offered to buy the women another round. Rob and Allen were best friends. Barrett could tell her sister was reluctant to accept their offer.

"You're a single woman, so it's about time you get used to the new you," Barrett shouted in her ear over the band's music.

Being away from home made Natalie feel less constrained by the rules she'd faithfully stuck by: loyal wife and devoted mother. Natalie took her sister's advice.

For the next three hours, Natalie felt free, sexy, the object of another man's attraction, and as if singlehood might be a role she could actually embrace. She and her sister danced with Rob and Allen, chatted with them at the bar, and drank more than was their wont.

Still, the deeply embedded habits that had dictated her entire adult life prevented her from spending the rest of the night with Rob—even though she knew Barrett would have been thrilled if her straight-laced sister broke the rules for once.

Last call and Natalie and Barrett decided to bring their evening to a close. They kissed their new friends good-bye and returned to the hotel hours later than they had expected. Natalie collapsed in bed and slept better than she had in months.

After she returned home Sunday evening, she experienced a surge of optimism regarding life after divorce. She found herself wanting to reach an agreement as soon as possible so she could move on.

PATRICK AND NATALIE MEET

Natalie sat with Patrick in his conference room and reviewed the third mediation. It started smoothly. Jim and Natalie had reaffirmed what they had previously agreed to. Jim seemed receptive to using the margin line of credit for the E*Trade account, which would allow him to keep it intact.

"He thinks he knows how to pick the right stocks," she said.

"He's not alone. So many are convinced they have a knack for buying stocks until they pick the wrong ones and get burned. Too many wind up buying high and selling low," he said.

Natalie described how tensions rose on the valuation and decision phase of the home equity using the Brandenburg formula and the rental property. When it came to spousal support, they hit a wall that abruptly ended the mediation.

"Jim needs a cooling-off phase. This whole process has rattled his nerves because it has turned out completely different from what he'd planned. Once Jim meets with Al, his lawyer will talk some sense into him. My hope is he'll come back to the table willing to work out the final details," Patrick said.

He added that he had prepared new versions of the property division spreadsheets. These were based on the outcomes of the previous mediations. They were a complete summary report that included the following three parts:

1. A spreadsheet identifying all the assets.

2. A spreadsheet clarifying the marital and non-marital assets.

3. A spreadsheet combining the marital and non-marital assets in one property statement. This included valuations, the final division of assets, and liabilities.

This summary report was the information Patrick would use to develop Natalie's financial planning analysis. He would use different support amounts to see their impact on her long-term financial wellness so she would be prepared for whatever ended up being the final amount.

SUPPORT AND NATALIE'S FINANCIAL FUTURE

Patrick presented a plan that would address Natalie's concerns regarding retirement. Specifically, it would answer one of the essential divorce questions:

Will the settlement allow me to be financially secure now and in the future?

He provided long-term projections using **probability analysis** and scenario testing based on different levels of support over different periods of time. The alternative strategies also indicated how long she could keep the house before downsizing was necessary.

"What is probability analysis?" Natalie asked.

Patrick explained it was a computer-generated mathematical calculation that considered multiple variables, such as market returns, interest rates, and inflation as well as the likelihood, or probability, that clients would have enough assets to provide for their financial needs over their lifetimes. The probability analysis software creates thousands of different scenarios and then develops results based on what is most likely to occur under various circumstances.

He provided her the following example:

Imagine you retired at the end of 2007. If you had most of your investment in the stock market, the aftermath of the 2008 stock crash would have most likely wiped out 35 percent of your investment's value over the next year. This would have a significant impact on your long-term retirement income—that is, unless you had taken steps to reduce risk before the market plunged.

If, on the other hand, you retired at the end of 2009 and continued to invest mostly in stocks, for the next six years, you would have ridden a wave of prosperity, which would have had a positive impact on your retirement portfolio.

As these two examples demonstrate, variables outside your control can dramatically impact your retirement portfolio and income.

Probability calculations give you a sense of how these variables might impact your long-term financial well-being. In other words, probability analysis considers a variety of future changes that might influence the performance of your investment assets. It provides a likely path of your financial well-being moving forward.

Another type of formula that projects future financial success is called **linear analysis**. This uses static assumptions. Examples of static assumptions are fixed rates of return, interest rates, and inflation. This method is primarily used to show cash flow during a certain period. Because the calculations are based on static assumptions, they aren't an accurate assessment of the likeliness of your long-term financial well-being. Rather, they indicate the direction your finances may be headed in the short term.

"So let me see if I grasp the idea. Probability analysis considers changes to variables, such as rates of return, interest rates, and inflation, in order to reach different conclusions based on those variables. And linear methodology runs a calculation using numbers with static rates of return, interest rates, and inflation. By using variables that don't change, the different calculations are easy to project but they aren't necessarily realistic," Natalie responded.

"Couldn't have summed it up better myself. Next, let's see how you do when you see it wrapped up into one report, which includes the probability *and* linear analysis. This will give you a better understanding of your future financial well-being," said Patrick.

"In regards to support, how sure are you about the amount I'll be receiving?" asked Natalie.

"Kathleen and I have discussed this at length. We're confident our support numbers will be close to the amount we're showing. The real issue will be the length of time you'll receive it," Patrick said.

Patrick based his calculations on the conservative premise that Natalie would be eligible to receive support until at least age sixty. Meanwhile, Kathleen thought Natalie would most likely qualify to receive support until she reached full Social Security retirement age, which was sixty-seven years old.

In either case, Patrick believed Natalie would be able to maintain the standard of living she sought. He had also made several adjustments to spending projections that took into account alternative support amounts. He wanted to prepare Natalie, as soon as possible, to see how lower support amounts would affect results in case the final figures were less than what she had otherwise anticipated.

"In order for you to fully understand the probability analysis results, we need to start with the four areas people can control when it comes to their financial lives: **spending and saving**, **timing and choices**, **risk**, and **legacy**. I'll explain each," said Patrick.

SPENDING AND SAVING

Patrick described how spending included month-to-month core living expenses, such as the mortgage, utilities, food, health insurance, transportation, and credit card debt. Spending also included non-recurring items, such as entertainment, clothing, vacations, home and auto repairs, dinning out, and emergencies like the kids needing help unexpectedly.

"What's the difference between core living and non-recurring expenses?" Natalie asked.

Patrick responded that core living expenses were those paid each month. Meanwhile, non-recurring expenses were mostly elective, in other words, ones in which Natalie determined what and when she made a purchase and how much to spend.

"Think of non-recurring expenses this way," he said. "Do you buy clothing every week or seasonally? How often do you go away for the weekend or to special events or buy a car?

"I also include saving for retirement as part of the non-recurring although it should be something that is done systematically—but this isn't a requirement. My recommendation is putting away 20 percent of gross income every year. So if you received $8,000 of support every month, it would add up to $96,000 per year. Add your teacher's salary, and the total would be about $143,500. Twenty percent of $143,500 is $28,700," said Patrick.

"So $28,700 toward retirement savings every year? That's a ton of money," Natalie said.

"Remember, you're already contributing about $3,000 to Social Security from your salary. This amounts to 2 percent of your total income. So you only need to contribute another 18 percent, or $25,700, to reach your 20 percent target. In addition, your employer matches your contributions to your retirement plan, so you're more than halfway there," Patrick said.

Patrick suggested Natalie allocate a portion of her monthly income to her personal investment portfolio using a systematic investment plan. Much like having her retirement plan contribution deducted from her salary, she could set up a plan where a predetermined amount would be automatically deducted from her bank account each month and invested in her portfolio. He added that contributions to her employer's retirement plan were based on pretax income, which would reduce her income tax withholdings. Meanwhile, the contributions to her personal investment plan were *after tax,* which meant they would not affect her income taxes.

"The most important part is to get started. So pick an amount you're comfortable with—it doesn't have to be 20 percent in the beginning—and then increase it over time in order to reach your target," Patrick said.

TIMING AND CHOICES

Patrick explained that timing and choices addressed when to make significant purchases or expenditures, such as a vacation, large gifts, or a car. When deciding upon what to buy and when to buy a particular item or service, he recommended Natalie think about the risks and rewards for each of her purchases and consider the costs and benefits of the following:

- Buying at full price versus waiting for a sale
- Traveling during peak versus off season
- Purchasing a new car versus a pre-owned vehicle
- Needing the latest fashions versus waiting for seasonal sales

"Remember, all your decisions will impact your financial well-being over time," he said.

"Do you mean I need to start clipping coupons?" asked Natalie.

"That's not a bad idea. But timing and choices have more to do with a mindset," Patrick said.

He provided the following example:

Imagine two people wanted to buy a car. Sam had a particular make, model, and color in mind. The car had to come with specific options that were difficult to find. He also insisted on buying his car right away. In his search, he found only one car for sale that met all his criteria.

Meanwhile, Tracy wanted a four-door sedan that had great gas mileage and a standard set of amenities. She didn't particularly care about the car's color, and she was willing to wait until she felt comfortable with her final decision. In her search, she found twenty cars for sale that fit her criteria.

Which person do you think would be able to negotiate a better deal on his or her car?

"I think Tracy would," said Natalie.

"I agree. So be more like Tracy!" Patrick said.

He encouraged Natalie to remain flexible and open-minded regarding her purchases and expenditures and to maintain reasonable timelines when it came to her decisions. This could wind up saving her lots of money.

RISK

Patrick explained that risk applies both to investment and personal decisions. Too often risk was associated only with investments. This was largely because investment risk was frequently the subject of TV and Internet chatter.

Conventional wisdom says the younger we are, the more investment risk we are able to take, which allows us to focus on growth. This is because younger people have more time to recover from poor performance or market declines.

"Keep in mind," Patrick said, "the eighth wonder of the world is compound return."

Meanwhile, when we are older, we may still seek growth, but we must temper this aspiration with a realization we may not have the opportunity to recover from a major downturn—one that could significantly decrease our portfolio's value and our future financial well-being. This scenario is what millions of retirees experienced after the 2008 stock market crash.

Once we retire and are not contributing to our portfolios, risk takes on a new meaning: We must not only address stock market risk; we must also consider the following:

- **Interest rate risk**—changes that affect borrowing, earnings, and savings.

- **Inflation risk**—the loss of purchasing power over time. If you have a fixed income, you are actually earning less as time goes on due to the increase in the costs of goods and services.

- **Liquidity risk**—the ability to maintain access to your money. An example of an illiquid investment is if you own rental property and the housing market takes a tumble. As a result, you'll be unable to pull your money out of the investment because you won't be able to sell the property easily.

◘ **Health risk**—a change in health. Especially a dramatic one can easily impact your ability to save due to increased expenses.

◘ **Tax risk**—changes in the tax code. New tax laws can change how an investment is taxed or the rate at which it is taxed.

◘ **Personal risks**—how you spend your discretionary money. Hobbies, travel, and gifting to family, friends, and charities can be done to excess. Think of lottery winners who are broke a few years later.

LEGACY

Patrick defined legacy as how you want to be remembered, what values you want to leave for the next generation, or whom you wish to benefit from your estate.

Legacy issues play a role in working on your estate planning and understanding what your intentions are for the disposition of your estate.

If financial legacy were a continuum, on one end you'd have people who plan to leave their nest egg to the next generation. On the opposite end, you'd have those who hope that the check written out to the undertaker will bounce.

Sometimes finances play a subordinate role in one's legacy. For instance, a parent's priority may be to pass down to the kids a specific set of characteristics and ethics—not just an investment account.

Whether your motivation is financial or otherwise, a legacy plays an important role in your overall financial planning.

"Spending and saving, timing and choices, risk, and legacy—I've never thought of finances this way," Natalie said.

She reflected on how she'd relied on Jim to manage their money. Throughout their marriage, his sole focus was to achieve investment returns that would allow them to fulfill their current needs and wants.

At one point, she had wanted Jim to think beyond their current investments, and she had asked him to obtain a will. But because he was concerned only about increasing his wealth in the present, planning for life events wasn't a priority for him. As a result, it took him ten years finally to agree to have wills written.

NATALIE'S DRAFT FINANCIAL PLANNING REPORT

Patrick projected Natalie's report on the large monitor in the conference room. He first addressed the amount she could spend in order to maintain her standard of living. The amount was based on the income and expense spreadsheet he created using the expense worksheet Natalie provided, along with adjustments he made that were used to determine spousal support. In regards to spousal support, Kathleen and Al were still negotiating this and would probably have an agreed-upon amount before the next mediation session.

For the time being, he was using $8,500 per month for spousal support and $1,100 per month for child support in his planning analysis. He also indicated that he had tried a number of alternative amounts within the range they had discussed earlier.

Patrick determined Natalie would need $8,000 per month of spendable income to meet her core living expenses.

"If we start with that basic premise and then add for health care, vacation, and contributing to your children's college expenses, you end up with a good overall picture of your actual total spending needs," Patrick said.

His calculations also included paying off her credit card debt and selling the house after Rachel left for college. While paying off credit card debt appealed to Natalie, she didn't want to sell the house so quickly.

"What if I wait for Rachel to finish college before deciding to sell the house?" she asked.

"I thought you might ask that question. That's why I've prepared alternative projections based on retaining the house for longer periods of time. We'll be able to see the effect this would have on your long-term financial stability," Patrick said.

He added that although the results showed a reduction in the probability number, she would still be able to maintain her long-term goals. The downside of paying a monthly mortgage and regular maintenance costs for four more years meant her ability to save on a monthly basis would be limited. In his opinion, as long as she sold the house within the next ten years, she would be in financially solid shape.

"That at least gives me more time to think about the pluses and minuses of keeping the house. It also alleviates the pressure of feeling that my only option is to sell right after Rachel graduates from high school," she said.

"Yes, and over the next couple of years, you'll have time to assess the actual cost of ownership, which will help you make your final decision," Patrick said.

Next, Patrick recommended she increase contributions to her employer's retirement plan and set up a systematic investment plan to invest regularly in her already existing Schwab portfolio.

The two continued to address the items in the financial report. After they completed their review, Natalie requested a copy of the new planning analysis with the options they had discussed.

"What's the next step?" Natalie asked.

"We'll have one more three-way meeting between you, Kathleen, and me, so we can all be on the same page *and* so we can coach you through the next and maybe last mediation, where you'll resolve the final numbers on support and we can address any last-minute adjustments to the other numbers involved in the division of the assets," Patrick said.

Experience told him the couple might need only two more mediations: one to finalize the support numbers and another to review the draft MOU with Courtney. Al and Kathleen would then review the MOU before Jim and Natalie signed it.

"The gap between Jim and me regarding support seems so wide at this point. Do you really think we'll be able to come to an agreement soon, or will he call mediation quits and want to fight this out in court? He did storm out of the last meeting, after all," Natalie said.

"I think Al will help him recognize how much mediation has accomplished, which will make him see the strengths of this process. Al will also educate Jim on the reality surrounding spousal support and the child support guidelines. Jim will also realize the cost associated with changing course right now. Speaking of mediation, when's the next one?" Patrick asked.

"Jim requested a break. So we agreed to meet in two weeks. He's probably taking off on his boat with that shameless woman. Maybe his beloved boat will hit a rock, sink, and take him down with it. If that happened, at least I wouldn't have to worry about another tense meeting with him," she said.

Patrick smiled. He knew she didn't really mean what she said, but her resentment was a familiar emotion he had seen in many of his divorcing clients—particularly among those with unfaithful spouses. He then told Natalie he would make a few adjustments to the report based on their discussion. Once he prepared an updated financial planning report, he would send it to her via overnight mail.

They also discussed having a team meeting next week because, by then, Kathleen would have the final numbers from the division of assets to determine the amount of spousal support to propose. Al would also be doing the same thing with Jim. It might be possible for Kathleen and Al to come to terms with the amount of spousal and child support that would avoid conflict in the next mediation.

CHAPTER 21

NATALIE'S PREPARATION FOR THE FOURTH MEDIATION

Natalie and Jim had experienced many tense moments throughout the mediation process, but only one had pushed Jim to abruptly leave the meeting. The thought of paying Natalie $9,000 per month both enraged and shocked him. Because the subject remained unresolved, the focus of Natalie, Kathleen, and Patrick's meeting was support.

Natalie dreaded broaching the topic with Jim again. At the same time, she was willing to spend the financial and emotional currency necessary to protect her interests.

"Today, we'll cover the various support calculations we've made," said Patrick. "And we'll guide you through the nuances of each. We'll also go over two support plans we've prepared for you to present in the next mediation."

"This mediation is going to be the toughest of all," said Natalie.

"I won't deny it will probably be tense. As we've discussed, support is the hardest part of the divorce process for most couples. The good news is when it's done, it signals you're ready for the MOU," said Kathleen.

She added that many disagreements stemmed from the opposing goals between the providers and receivers of support.

"Unfortunately, too many women understate their needs. So after their divorces, they receive lower support amounts, which reduces their ability to reach financial independence," Patrick said.

The plan Kathleen and Patrick developed focused on allowing both parties to maintain their current quality of life and be financially secure for the long term. As much as Natalie might want to punish Jim for his transgressions, it was not in her best interest to have a combative relationship with Jim once the divorce was settled. To the contrary, the goal was to allow each to move on and maintain a respectful relationship and continue to have an active participation in their children's lives.

"We hope the plan we've developed encourages a brainstorming session between you and Jim during your next mediation. As you work through the issues, you'll be able to present the calculations we've developed as possible alternatives. Ideally, you'd be able to steer the conversation in a direction that would motivate Jim to bring up ideas on his own. From there, you'd fill in the numbers," Kathleen said.

SPOUSAL SUPPORT *WITH* CHILD SUPPORT

"As you recall," Patrick said, "in a previous meeting we presented a *preliminary support summary*. Now that we have better data, we've been able to make more accurate calculations."

According to her team, Natalie might receive $8,000 to $8,500 per month of spousal support and about $1,100 per month of child support, which they determined by adhering to the statutory child support guidelines.

Kathleen reminded Natalie that because Rachel would turn eighteen years old in December, which would be *after* her high school graduation, child support would terminate upon Rachel's eighteenth birthday and *not* upon her high school graduation.

Patrick then developed a new calculation that increased the spousal support amount after Rachel turned eighteen years old. He pointed out, however, a risk associated with requesting a spousal support recalculation after child support terminates.

If Jim's income increased after child support ended, Natalie could be entitled to more spousal support. If, on the other hand, his income decreased, she might receive less spousal support.

He reminded Natalie that spousal support was tax deductible. So in Jim's case, if he was to pay $8,500 per month in spousal support, his net after-tax cost would be about $5,000.

"The good news is, $5,000 is about what Jim initially proposed as a gross support amount," said Kathleen.

"Wait! I thought we estimated $9,000 per month of spousal support. Why did I tell Jim $9,000 during the last mediation if the new figures are lower?" Natalie asked.

"I made my preliminary estimate before we had the data necessary to make an accurate assessment. Keep in mind it's our intention to ask for $9,000 during negotiations because the higher amount would match well with the income and expense spreadsheet you and Patrick developed," Kathleen said.

She added that the spousal support terms were negotiated. In her case, the length of time she would receive support could last up to her seventieth birthday because they'd been married for over twenty-five years.

Patrick planned to run alternative illustrations showing the spousal support lasting until she reached sixty, sixty-seven, and seventy years old. In general, the longer spousal support lasted, the more likely Natalie would be able to build up savings for her retirement.

SPOUSAL SUPPORT AND SOCIAL SECURITY

Although at age sixty Natalie would be eligible to withdraw from her retirement accounts without penalty, Patrick recommended she defer withdrawing until spousal support ended. Ideally, he suggested she defer to age seventy in order to maximize the time for her retirement accounts to grow before tapping into them. After age seventy, Natalie would need to make required minimum distributions (RMDs) from her retirement accounts.

Furthermore, according to Social Security rules, age sixty-seven would mark when she reached **full retirement age** (FRA), which is the age at which the government declares men and women eligible to receive Social Security benefits *without* a reduction that's a result of drawing benefits before reaching FRA. Also, under Social Security rules, if she waited until age seventy to receive benefits, she would be eligible for as much as a 24 percent increased benefit compared to beginning to receive benefits at age sixty-seven.

Patrick pointed out the Social Security benefits *were not* part of the division of assets because they were categorized as **government entitlement programs**, which meant they came under the federal law. In Natalie's case, being married for more than ten years entitled her to receive Social Security benefits based upon her own earnings record or based upon being a spousal beneficiary under Jim's Social Security retirement benefits record. Any amount she would receive under either method would not affect in any way Jim's benefits.

In her situation, she might be able to take advantage of a special opportunity that would allow her to request Social Security retirement spousal benefits when she turned age sixty-seven allowing her own Social Security benefits to grow until she reached seventy years old. That way she would have income at age sixty-seven from Social Security while at the same time delaying receiving her own benefits.

If at age seventy her own retirement benefit was higher than the spousal benefit she would otherwise receive, she could decide to take her own benefit rather than the spousal one. If at age seventy her own retirement benefit was lower, then she would be better off continuing the spousal benefit that started when she turned sixty-seven years old. In the end, she was only allowed to receive one benefit. It was in her best interest to select the one that paid her the most.

If she remarried, she would be eligible to choose between her own Social Security benefit and that of her new spouse. In this instance too, she should select the benefit that paid her the most.

SPOUSAL SUPPORT *WITHOUT* CHILD SUPPORT

Patrick recalculated support based on the year *after* the termination of child support. By this point, he estimated spousal support would need to be at least $8,000 per month. This amount would depend on Natalie's ability to demonstrate her need for support and Jim's income being high enough to make the proposed spousal support payments.

Her team emphasized their calculation was a placeholder. Thus it *did not* indicate the final amount of spousal support she would receive. Rather, it would give her an idea of what support might look like.

NATALIE'S NEW SUPPORT PROPOSALS

Kathleen used Patrick's updated income calculations and income and expense spreadsheets to develop two support proposals. Her goal was to negotiate for higher support amounts that would be payable until Natalie retired.

Under the *one-step support plan,* Natalie would request a higher amount of spousal support early on. This amount *would not* be recalculated after their youngest daughter, Rachel, was emancipated.

The *two-step support plan* was similar to what her team told Natalie during their prior meeting. Natalie would receive an initial support amount that would *increase* after child support ended. But the number would be an agreed-upon amount and *not* a recalculated amount. Kathleen also planned the support to be non-modifiable until at least Natalie reached age sixty. Kathleen would add the standard exceptions that accounted for either party's death or Natalie's remarriage.

In either the one-step or two-step plan, her team determined Natalie, in the least, should receive spousal support until she reached FRA under Social Security guidelines.

Her team provided the following breakdown of each of the steps:

MONTHLY ONE-STEP SUPPORT PLAN

- Spousal support would continue till Natalie reached sixty-seven years old: $9,000.

- Child support would continue until Rachel reached age eighteen: $1,100.

MONTHLY TWO-STEP SUPPORT PLAN

Step 1

- Initial spousal support amount: $8,500

- Child support until Rachel reached age eighteen: $1,150

Step 2

- Spousal support from when child support ended and until Natalie reached age seventy: $9,000

"As you can see, there's little difference between the one-step and two-step plans' child support amounts; it is just the amount of spousal support that changes. The two-step plan saves Jim about $16,200 in the first three years. But he'll have to pay an extra

$324,000 for the balance of the term, which would be from your age sixty-seven to seventy. That's why we think Jim will most likely prefer the one-step plan," Patrick said.

"I have a feeling Jim doesn't want to pay long-term support, so he won't be happy about either plan. At first, he proposed around $5,000 of spousal support and $1,000 of child support. He planned to end child support once Rachel graduated from high school and spousal support after ten years. Clearly, he's not going to get what he wanted based on what you've calculated. How much pushback should I expect from Jim and his attorney?" Natalie asked.

"Thankfully, now that Al's in the picture, he'll point out to Jim that his initial amounts weren't feasible," said Kathleen.

EXPENSES RELATED TO CHILDREN

In addition to support, the couple needed to address other items that would appear in their PSA, including expenses related to the children, health care, college costs, cars, insurance, and more. Unfortunately, these were often overlooked in the heat of the divorce battle.

Patrick's plan was to base the costs of college, medical, extracurricular activity, and all other expenses associated with their kids on Natalie's and Jim's respective incomes. He projected the following chart on the conference room wall:

NATALIE'S ANNUAL INCOME	Amount
Salary	$47,000
Spousal Support	$102,000
Child Support	$13,200
Investment Income	$6,000
Net Income	$168,200

JIM'S ANNUAL INCOME	Amount
Gross	$407,800
Spousal Support	($102,000)
Child Support	($13,200)
Investment Income	$5,000
Net Income	$297,600

According to Patrick's calculation, Natalie's income would be about 35 percent of the couple's total income, and Jim's would be about 65 percent. Thus they would share costs following a 35 percent to 65 percent ratio. If the final spousal support would change, so too would the ratio.

"I was hoping he'd have to cover all college costs and I would just take care of the living expenses, such as clothes, food, and entertainment," said Natalie

"Then let's go in that direction. If Jim agrees, then you wouldn't have to worry about splitting every expense 35/65—besides, that ratio has the potential of creating friction, so you may be better off avoiding it. I'll prepare a brief summary addressing those issues that we can ask Courtney to include in the proposed MOU," said Kathleen.

"Do you have any other questions? Do you think you're ready for the next mediation?" asked Patrick.

Natalie told her team that she would review her notes that evening. During the mediation itself, she would focus on steering Jim in the direction of proposing alternative support approaches. From there, she would provide the numbers to make the support plan work.

CHAPTER 22

FOURTH MEDIATION

Natalie sat in Courtney's conference room. She glanced beneath the table where she was seated and noticed her right knee bobbing up and down. *Nervous leg* was what her mom used to call the habit Natalie had since she was little. "Honey, please stop. It's unladylike," was her mom's typical response when she noticed the tick.

"Will this be the last mediation?" Natalie asked herself. "This *will be* the last mediation," she insisted. "Yes, this must be the last mediation."

The pressure to wrap up her divorce by meeting's end fueled her nervous leg.

On the other side of the table in Courtney's conference room sat Jim. He had been thoroughly coached by Al during their previous meeting.

"I hate to admit it, but she's got me scared," Jim had told his lawyer during their last appointment. "One more bombshell and I may drop dead from a stroke—right there at the mediation."

Al had reassured Jim that he and his wife had identified all major issues. Yes, the mediation would be tough, and Jim would disagree with Natalie. But, at this point in the process, as long as Jim had disclosed all financial information to Al, the likelihood of surprises was nearly nonexistent. Al was certain he and his client had reviewed worst-case scenarios and prepared the evidence and counterarguments to effectively defend his case.

Courtney entered the conference room. Years of experience had taught her the art of observing body language, and the nerves and tension she saw between the two were undeniable. She greeted the couple.

"I'm sure you're anxious about today's meeting," she said. "No doubt, we may encounter some difficult moments. But I'd like to take a moment to reflect on how much you've accomplished over the past few months. You've resolved *all* property issues, no small feat considering the complexity of your estate. From this point on, all we need to agree upon is the income needs for each of you and how this will allow both of you to maintain a good standard of living for yourselves and your children," Courtney said.

She asked if the two had worked through the support issues with their respective lawyers.

"Yes, I've met with Al," Jim said. "Overall, my position hasn't changed. I'm still opposed to what Natalie has proposed. It's as if she wants to hang an anchor around my neck for the rest of my life."

"I'm sorry if you think of our family—our kids—as anchors around your neck. Let me remind you support is simply providing for the family you created and promised to take care of," Natalie said.

Courtney could see the conversation could easily head to an impasse that could blow up just as it had during the last mediation. Rather than focus on emotionally loaded topics, she steered the conversation in the direction of financial facts, which she hoped would be a less contentious discussion. She asked about the specific support amounts Jim and Natalie had discussed with their lawyers.

"My biggest problem is I can't be 100 percent positive my income will continue to be what it is right now. By stating a support number, I feel as if I'm backing myself into a corner forever and gambling with my future," Jim said.

"You never brought up income concerns when we were together, so why this issue now?" Natalie asked.

"If you didn't realize it, having two households is twice as expensive. . . . All right, we can argue about this all day. I for one am not interested in wasting billable hours to bicker. So let's throw some numbers out and see where they take us," Jim said.

Natalie was about to state her support amounts. But she recalled her team had recommended she let Jim take the lead. From there, she would present the amounts they had developed.

"My lawyer and I came up with a spousal support of $7,500 per month until I reach sixty-five, which is when I plan to retire. The child support would then be based on statutory guidelines. I think it's fair and will give Natalie what she needs," Jim said.

Natalie resisted the urge to call him crazy. She now knew how Jim felt when she asked for $9,000 during the previous mediation.

"Can you tell us how you arrived at that amount?" Courtney asked.

Jim explained he had assessed their living expenses. He factored in Natalie's work income and how her inheritance would build up her assets over the next seventeen years, which she could use to provide for her retirement needs. Meanwhile, Jim's reduced income, as a result of paying support, would still be enough to cover his current cost of living and stay on course with his retirement savings plan, which was to retire at sixty-five.

Natalie decided it was time to speak up. "I disagree with your assumptions. Your calculations totally minimize my living needs!" she said.

She provided the following information based on the spreadsheet she and Patrick had worked on:

- ◘ The net spendable, after-tax income Natalie would require would be about $8,750 per month.

- ◘ Her teaching salary provided a net spendable income of about $2,500 per month.

- ◘ $8,750 - $2,500 = $6,250.

- ◘ $6,250 represented the additional amount of net income she would need to maintain her current standard of living.

With her current income tax rate of 30 percent, it would mean Jim's proposed $7,500 spousal support amount would actually only generate about $5,250 of net income to her.

Therefore, she required an additional $1,000 per month of net income to meet her projected spending needs. This would require Jim's support amount to increase by $1,500 in order to provide the net amount she needed—the additional $500 would account for Natalie's income taxes.

"I'm also requesting spousal support last until I'm seventy, which will at least give me a shot at having enough saved to meet my long-term retirement needs," Natalie said.

"First off," Jim said, "the seventy-years-old part is ridiculous. And you can *definitely* live on less than $8,750."

"If it's so easy, then you try. If I'm not mistaken, your expense spreadsheet indicated you need $15,000 per month of spendable income," Natalie said.

Each had previously provided an "income and expense" spreadsheet using a form from their attorneys that they had shared with each other to help make the support calculations.

Courtney interceded and recommended they brainstorm alternatives. Based on what they offered, she pointed out their proposed support amounts were $1,500 apart and the total years of support differed by only six years. She asked them for additional ideas and reminded them that whatever amount of spousal support they agreed upon would dictate the child support amounts.

"Can spousal support be adjusted once child support ends? If so, maybe we could have one spousal support amount during the child support period and then increase the spousal amount once child support stops," Natalie said.

"Are you suggesting a two-step approach? I thought of that too. But it would depend on the amounts and for the length of time I'd have to pay you," Jim said.

Natalie said that in order to reach the net income she calculated, spousal support needed to be $8,000 per month during the period she received child support. It would then increase to $9,000 per month after child support ended.

Jim exclaimed the jump from $8,000 to $9,000 was too high. In his eyes, it was reasonable to pay $7,500 in spousal support per month initially and $8,000 per month after child support ended.

"With those numbers," Natalie said, "I'd barely eke by. Even worse, I'd have to sell the house—and how would that affect the kids? And where would I move? And how would I save for retirement? How is any of what you're coming up with fair?"

"Natalie, you're talking as though they're infants. Ben and Ryann are grown, and Rachel will be going to college in just three years. So don't make this about them. Admit it, you're just terrified to downsize. You're right. Maybe you'll have to rent a place as I am. Do you see me telling you the sky's falling?" Jim asked.

Jim's words struck a nerve with Natalie. Part of what he said was true—downsizing did scare the daylights out of her, and she feared what that would look like: just another divorced woman living in a shrunken townhouse. She thought of the complex locals nicknamed Queen's Manor because of the high number of divorced women living there.

The *old* Natalie, the faithful wife who knew nearly nothing about the family's finances and blamed herself for Jim's infidelity, would have taken his half-truth and allowed it to topple her stance. But bolstered by her financial awareness and her team's support, she knew he could afford the amount she was asking for and that what she sought was fair *and* reasonable.

"You're right, Jim. The kids aren't three years old anymore. But I'm not saying I want to stay in the house forever. I realize I'll probably have to move once Rachel graduates from college, if not before. So as much as you think I'm just thinking of me, you're dead wrong. As far as our daughter's concerned, being a teenage girl is hard enough as it is, let alone when your parents are divorcing," Natalie said.

"Aren't we being a little dramatic? I can guarantee half, if not more, of Rachel's friends' parents are divorced. And I'm sure those kids have managed just fine," said Jim.

"What about the girl at Natalie's high school that killed herself last year? It turns out her parents had divorced a year earlier," said Natalie.

"I understand both of your concerns," Courtney said. "There are countless stories—good and bad—of how divorce impacts kids, especially considering how common it is these days."

"Not common in my family. I'm going to be the first. And I'm not proud of that," said Natalie.

"In the interest of moving forward, how about we continue our focus on support? We'll definitely go over Rachel's future when we discuss the parenting plan," said Courtney.

Courtney then reviewed the options they had submitted so far:

- ◘ Natalie requested a spousal support amount that would allow her to remain in the house at least until Rachel graduated from high school. But she preferred to wait until Rachel finished college first, even if it would cost her more to do so. She also sought to receive support until she was seventy years old.

◘ Jim thought spousal support should last only until he reached sixty-five years old. In addition, Natalie should sell the house sooner rather than later. He also did not think that Natalie needed such a high amount of support to maintain her lifestyle.

"Did I get the facts right?" Courtney asked.

Both Natalie and Jim agreed with Courtney's overview.

She recorded her summary on the flip chart. Courtney then projected on the wall a copy of the income and expense spreadsheets they had each created and had sent to her in advance of the meeting. She asked if either of them found areas that could be adjusted.

"The biggest issue for Natalie is the house. I just don't see any reason I should have to pay for her to live there when she has so many other options," Jim said.

"I think you'll be happy only if I wind up living under a bridge. Let me remind you, your expenses include *living in a house*. If that's not a double standard, I don't know what is," Natalie said.

"Who said anything about a bridge? I'm offering to pay you thousands of dollars a month, and you act as if you'll be doomed for life. Look, if we were to use a more reasonable amount for your housing expense, we could come to an agreement quickly and put this behind us," Jim said.

"So if I agreed to downsize after Rachel's eighteenth birthday, then are you saying you'd pay a support amount that would allow me to maintain my standard of living?" Natalie asked.

"As long as it's an amount within reason, of course," said Jim.

"So, Natalie, if you downsized the year after Rachel's eighteenth birthday, what amount would you show as your housing cost?" Courtney asked.

"I'd need to look at the specifics of the plan. For now, I'd be willing to reduce the amount allocated to housing by a third—tops," Natalie said.

"In that case, your housing cost will drop from $3,000 to $2,000 per month. If we plug that into the plan, I think the numbers would then work," Jim said.

Natalie suggested an alternative amount that would stay the same for the entire support period. It would be a compromise between both parts of the two-step support plan.

"So instead of a two-step plan, you're suggesting a one-step plan with a fixed amount that would average the difference between the two steps?" Jim asked.

"I think so . . . as long as I can understand how this impacts my long-term financial well-being," Natalie said.

Courtney brought up the missing element of their support discussion: How long would support last? They needed to agree upon the support length in order to calculate the new combined monthly amount. After all, the number of years Natalie would receive support was one of her biggest concerns.

Jim wanted the termination of support to coincide with his retirement age, which he anticipated would be sixty-five years old.

"But under Social Security, that would be before I reached FRA, which is age sixty-seven. So that would mean I'd lose support and not have any income except working until I reached age sixty-seven, three years later. I don't think that's fair," Natalie said.

"For argument's sake, let's say I was to agree to pay until you were sixty-seven years old. What would that mean as far as the amount of support I'd pay?" Jim asked.

Courtney scanned Natalie's income and expense spreadsheet, which indicated she would need about $9,000 per month in spousal support. If they reduced the amount by $1,000 after her move, the amount would be $8,000 per month.

"I realize this amount doesn't reflect any offsets for other related expenses, but let's keep it as simple as possible for now," said Courtney.

"It may take a while to get the house ready for sale and to move, so I'll need the first period to last for four years. I'll be fifty-two years old by then. So that would leave fifteen years until I reached age sixty-seven," Natalie said.

Jim launched his smartphone's calculator app. He then input the following:

$9,000 per month for 4 years, which is 48 months:

$$\$9,000 \times 48 \text{ months} = \textbf{\$432,000}$$

$8,000 per month for 15 years, which is 180 months:

$$\$8,000 \times 180 \text{ months} = \textbf{\$1,440,000}$$

$$\$432,000 + \$1,440,000 = \textbf{\$1,872,000}$$

He then divided $1,872,000 by 19 years, which is 228 months. This equaled $8,210 per month in spousal support. Jim then presented his calculation to Natalie and Courtney.

"What do you think of the amount Natalie?" asked Courtney.

"I'll have to review this with Patrick to see how that amount would fit into my overall financial plan. I'm very worried about running out of money and becoming dependent on the kids in my old age," said Natalie.

"I want to talk this over with Al too. I'm not thrilled with the amount, and I'll probably never be. But overall, I feel we're at least close to making this work. I don't know about you, but I'm exhausted," he said.

"I'm tired too. But I'm not going to rush into anything for the sake of saving time. The future of the kids and me is at stake," said Natalie.

"If you're looking for sympathy, you're never going to get any from me considering I'm paying you nearly two million dollars in support. So let's get this over with. I'm ready to address this final piece of the puzzle. If I receive the green light from Al, I think I'm willing to pay $8,210 per month until you're sixty-seven. With that much money, I guarantee you won't become a bag lady," said Jim.

"That $8,210 doesn't take into account inflation. So I'd agree to $8,500 per month until I reach age sixty-seven," said Natalie.

"How about we meet in the middle? My offer is $8,350. If you'll agree to that amount right now, we can call it a day," said Jim.

"Okay . . . well . . . maybe. I just need to confirm with Patrick. But it sounds about right," Natalie said.

"What's there to talk to him about? You *really* don't think you can survive on $8,350 per month until you reach sixty-seven? That's a ton of money. I guarantee you'll be just fine," said Jim.

Natalie continued to express hesitation; it helped her resist the urge to grin. While it wasn't $9,000, the monthly figure of $8,350 provided her relief regarding her fears about her future.

She was thankful Patrick had prepared a financial plan, which allowed her to negotiate a support amount that would align with her long-term financial objectives. In addition, her team's recommendation that Natalie allow Jim to think he was in control had worked.

Courtney witnessed a shift from the start of today's mediation to the present moment. Armed with their well-rehearsed counterarguments, the two had begun the meeting ready to defend their positions. By this point, however, they had softened toward one another. Based on the conciliatory stance they had assumed and the agreements they had reached so far, Courtney believed the timing was right to conclude their mediation. While her goal was to end every meeting on a positive note, it was impossible at times—as the previous mediation had proved.

She recommended Natalie and Jim consult with their respective teams in order to develop a final agreement on the spousal support and resulting child support. After today's mediation, she would provide Natalie, Jim, and their lawyers a summary of what took place so their teams would be able to tackle the final stages without delay.

"Before we call it a day, I want to summarize your positions," Courtney said. She stated the following:

- ◘ Jim had proposed paying $8,350 per month as a flat amount that would continue until Natalie reached sixty-seven years old.

- ◘ Natalie agreed to the amount Jim put forth. At the same time, she expressed concerns about the shortened support period under Jim's plan. She would prefer the support to continue until she reached age seventy, but she'd accept age sixty-seven as long as Patrick could show the monthly amount would support her long-term financial well-being.

- ◘ Child support would be determined using the statutory guidelines and would be payable until Rachel reached age eighteen.

They both agreed with Courtney's summary. Once she received the child support amounts from their attorneys, she told the two she would prepare the final version of the MOU and send it to them and their attorneys for review.

Courtney would also arrange another meeting with the couple. During their final three-way session, they would review the MOU with any agreed-upon modifications from their attorneys, and Natalie and Jim would sign it. Afterwards, she would send the MOU back to their respective attorneys, who would then draft the property settlement agreement (PSA), which would be based on the signed MOU.

"I know this has been a very difficult time in your lives. Considering the tough issues you've had to resolve, you've done a remarkable job coming to this agreement," Courtney said.

Shortly after, the three concluded their meeting, and Jim and Natalie went their separate ways. Courtney then went to work drafting the MOU. As the couple's mediator, she set aside her role as family law attorney and was a scrivener when drafting the document. She finished the draft late that afternoon and emailed it to the couple and their attorneys.

Kathleen and Al then quickly went to work reviewing the MOU. They sent minor revisions to one another. Once they agreed upon the changes, they scheduled appointments with their respective clients.

Patrick reviewed the calculations and produced a full **planning report,**[1] which was a summary of Natalie's financial plan. It would provide her a guideline to work from as she made future financial decisions.

---

1. An excerpt of the planning report appears in the appendix.

CHAPTER 23

THE LAST DANCE: FINAL MOU

As Natalie drove to her three-way meeting with Kathleen and Patrick, she reflected on her divorce. She could hardly believe the process had begun only eight months ago. Now, she was close to signing the MOU. The significance of her marriage's end weighed heavily on her: Twenty-five years together took only eight months to tear apart.

"Don't over-think it," she reminded herself. It was a sincere but unsuccessful attempt to stop dwelling on an uncertain and scary future as a divorcee.

The three met in Kathleen's office to review the revised MOU.

"It's pretty remarkable to think how much you've learned and the series of good decisions you've made since we started working together," said Kathleen.

"I couldn't have done this without both of you. And Dr. Michaels kept me from succumbing to Jim's bullying me into doing things his way. How could Jim possibly have thought a do-it-yourself divorce was even remotely a good idea?" Natalie asked.

"I'm just really glad Jim eventually saw the light and decided to hire an attorney. I think because of Al, we were able to make it this far. We're on the homestretch. Patrick and I think that barring a few minor changes to your MOU, you'll be ready to go," Kathleen said.

Kathleen then projected the latest MOU draft on the conference-room wall.

Memorandum of Understanding
For James Smith and Natalie Smith
By Courtney Fitzgerald, JD

The following outline is the proposed division of marital assets as a result of the mediation that took place over the past five months and is agreed to between parties. This is to be reviewed by legal counsel who will make any necessary adjustments before parties sign the final MOU. The MOU will then be used as the basis for drafting the Property Settlement Agreement (PSA). In addition to the division of assets, this MOU contains information on the proposed spousal and child support as provided by their respective counsel, as well as the division of expenses associated with the children's education, health care, and maintenance.

Division of Marital Property

		JIM'S AMOUNT	NATALIE'S AMOUNT	TOTAL AMOUNT
NON-RETIREMENT ASSETS				
REAL ESTATE EQUITY				
Residence		$0	$350,000	$350,000
Total Value	$950,000			
1st Mortgage	$275,000			
Sep. Property	$325,000			
Marital Equity	$350,000			

	JIM'S AMOUNT	NATALIE'S AMOUNT	TOTAL AMOUNT
Rental Property	$200,000	$0	$200,000
Total Value $550,000			
1st Mortgage $350,000			
Marital Equity $200,000			
TOTAL REAL EST. EQUITY	**$200,000**	**$350,000**	**$550,000**

CASH & INVESTMENTS			
Joint WFB	$0	$25,000	$25,000
Jim's WFB	$10,000	$0	$10,000
Jim's E*Trade	$74,250	$150,750	$225,000
SSI Vested Stock Options	$224,000	$0	$224,000
Natalie's Schwab	$0	$0	$0
Loss Carryforward	$50,000	$50,000	$100,000
TOTAL CASH & INVESTMENTS	**$358,250**	**$225,750**	**$584,000**

PERSONAL EFFECTS			
Personal Property	$0	$0	$0
Sailboat	$30,000	$0	$30,000
BMW	$35,000	$0	$35,000
Subaru	$0	$15,000	$15,000
TOTAL PERSONAL EFFECTS	**$65,000**	**$15,000**	**$80,000**

TOTAL NON-RETIREMENT ASSETS	**$623,250**	**$590,750**	**$1,214,000**

	JIM'S AMOUNT	NATALIE'S AMOUNT	TOTAL AMOUNT
RETIREMENT ASSETS			
IRA/401(k)s			
Jim's IRA	$30,000	$120,000	$150,000
Jim's 401(k)	$187,500	$187,500	$375,000
Natalie's 403(b)	$0	$85,000	$85,000
Jim's Deferred Comp.	$150,000	$0	$150,000
Jim's Roth IRA	$15,000	$0	$15,000
Natalie's Roth IRA	$0	$25,000	$25,000
TOTAL RETIREMENT ASSETS	**$382,500**	**$417,500**	**$800,000**

TOTAL MARITAL ASSETS	**$1,005,750**	**$1,008,250**	**$2,014,000**

DEBTS			
Credit Card	($12,500)	($12,500)	($25,000)
BMW	($15,000)	$0	($15,000)
TOTAL DEBTS	**($27,500)**	**($12,500)**	**($40,000)**

TOTAL DEBTS	**($27,500)**	**($12,500)**	**($40,000)**

TOTAL ASSETS	**$1,005,750**	**$1,008,250**	**$2,014,000**
TOTAL DEBTS	**($27,500)**	**($12,500)**	**($40,000)**
TOTAL MARITAL PROPERTY	**$978,250**	**$995,750**	**$1,974,000**

Other considerations, acknowledgements and agreements:

1. **Custody:** Wife to have primary physical custody with both sharing parenting time with daughter under a liberal schedule due to their daughter's age and ability to transport herself. Concerning the decisions affecting the care and control of the child, they agree to "joint legal custody."

2. **Health Insurance:** As long as the child or children are eligible dependents, the health insurance will be provided by father through his group health insurance plan or equivalent in event of his changing jobs or terminating employment. Uncovered expenses, co-payments, co-insurance, deductibles, and prescriptions are to be shared between the parties with wife responsible for 35% and husband responsible for 65% of any related medical expenses that exceed $100. The custodial parent at the time of the service is responsible for the cost of $100 or less for any medical expenses of the dependent child.

3. **Spousal Support:** Husband to pay wife $8,350 per month starting the first of the month following the signing of this MOU and ending the first of the month following the month wife turns age 67. The support is non-modifiable for a period of 12 years from date of first payment except in the event of death of either party. After 12 years, spousal support is modifiable due to a substantial change in circumstances (except a voluntary reduction of income by husband), death of either party, or remarriage of wife (with a co-habitation clause analogous to marriage).

4. **Child Support:** Using the current child support guidelines, including all income of both parties and after adjusting for spousal support, the amount of child support to be paid

by husband to wife is $1,130 per month until daughter reaches age 18.

5. **College Expenses:** Presently, one child is a freshman in college and one child is a sophomore in high school. It is agreed that the cost of college (room, board, tuition, books, computers, software, fees, and travel expenses) will be shared between the parties with wife's share at 35% and husband's share at 65%. If one party incurs the expense and submits a receipt documenting the expense, the other party agrees to pay his or her respective share within 30 days of the notice for amount due. Alternative arrangements for payment may be made upon agreement of both parties.

6. **Pension:** They have agreed to use the QDRO formula and that Jim's attorney will draft the QDRO for submission to the respective plan custodian. The calculation indicates Natalie will receive 31.5% of Jim's pension from prior employer defined benefit plan.

7. **Parenting Plan:** the parties have agreed to a parenting plan that has been drafted by Dr. Fredericks and will be included in this MOU as an attachment.

"I'll also go over any revisions with you to make sure they align with your intentions," Kathleen said.

Kathleen then drew attention to three items under the **other considerations section**, which provides additional explanation of select items in the MOU.

1. **Health insurance**
   Natalie's personal health insurance policy wasn't addressed in the MOU because she would obtain coverage

from her group plan. As far as her kids were concerned, Jim would be required to provide health coverage for them as long as they were eligible. If she stopped working for any reason, Natalie could not obtain coverage under Jim's plan through COBRA.

2. **Non-modifiable spousal support**
   Kathleen added a provision that made spousal support non-modifiable for the first twelve years (Natalie would be sixty years old by then). This provision would protect her if Jim decided to quit his job or experienced any circumstances where his income would decrease. It would also provide her support to age sixty, which would then allow her to make withdrawals from her retirement accounts without penalty, if necessary, under the retirement distributions rules.

3. **Failure-to-pay protection**
   The provision would protect Natalie in the event Jim failed to pay for costs related to children, such as medical or educational expenses.

In Kathleen's experience, if spouses failed to pay their share of expenses, recovering money was difficult. Generally speaking, Kathleen advised that Natalie avoid making issues of any minor amounts. Rather, she should focus on major expenses Jim was responsible for covering or contributing to. Ideally, his failure to pay could be grounds for taking him to court. Without specific language in the PSA, however, it would be difficult for Natalie to prove her case. As a result, Kathleen would be sure that the proper language was included in the final PSA.

"So I'll be in charge of my own health insurance. But I'll be protected if Jim decides to head out to sea for the next twelve years, and I'll have recourse if he's a deadbeat. As far as the MOU is concerned, is it enforceable?" Natalie asked.

"In its present form it could be, but it doesn't address many of the legal items that are included in a PSA," Kathleen said.

She added the MOU was the basis for the financial issues. Having it included in the PSA wouldn't change any of the specifics of the MOU. Rather, the PSA was more a document that addressed the financial and legal matters to facilitate obtaining a judge's approval for a final divorce decree.

"I can't believe it. I feel I can see the finish line from here. Is it premature to say that?" Natalie said.

"For the most part, you're right. The end is near," Kathleen said.

Patrick added they made minor adjustments to the MOU. For example, they included the pension as either a PV or QDRO. With those changes he felt the deal was done.

According to Virginia law, because Rachel was a minor child, the final divorce decree couldn't take place until one year from the date of the separation. Because they separated in January of this year, the couple couldn't finalize their divorce until January of the coming year. This also meant that they would likely be filing a joint tax return for this year.

Kathleen said she would draft the PSA within the next few weeks and then send it to Al for his review and comments. Because of the work everyone had done so far, she was confident the attorneys would quickly reach an agreement on the PSA. They would then send a copy to both Natalie and Jim so they could also review it and verify it reflected their wishes. Preparing the final PSA would require about a month. Once it was finalized and signed by Natalie and Jim, Kathleen would submit it to the court for the judge's review and signature. The divorce would be declared final once the judge signed the document and one year had passed since date of separation.

"Of course, I can review the PSA with you, so we can be sure you fully understand its financial implications," Patrick said. "I'll also be working with Kathleen on the financial aspects of the PSA to make sure the legal interpretation aligns with what appears in the MOU.

"It's been such a pleasure working with you, Natalie. I'd be happy to assist you or refer you to someone else who could help you with your future financial planning."

"Now that I've come this far, I realize how much financial guidance I still need, so I'd really like to continue working together," Natalie said.

Natalie then signed the MOU, and the three concluded their meeting.

On her way home from the appointment, she phoned Barrett. "Homestretch!" she said.

"What a relief! You know we're celebrating tonight, right? I already asked Jen to drop everything and come over. And I told Rachel we're coming over too. So I won't take no for an answer. I'll bring the food and champagne; you won't need to lift a finger," said Barrett.

"Wow, and it's not even my birthday," said Natalie.

"It *is* your birthday—and I'm bringing the cake. Your first day as a single woman!"

"Sounds great. I'll just need a couple of hours to decompress, maybe take a nap—I'm beat," said Natalie.

She arrived home and collapsed on her bed.

Rachel's friend dropped her off from school shortly after. She passed by her mom's room and saw her asleep. Rachel drew the bedroom curtains closed and gently covered her with a blanket.

At 6:00 p.m., Barrett and Jen arrived at Natalie's house. The two brought takeout from Natalie's favorite Chinese restaurant, a bottle of champagne, and a cake. Rachel greeted them at the front door.

"Mom's still asleep," Rachel said.

"While we get dinner ready, why don't you let her know we're here," said Barrett.

A few minutes later, Natalie walked downstairs and saw her sister and Jen.

"Congratulations!" said Jen.

She handed Natalie a flute of champagne, and Barrett raised her glass.

"A toast to a milestone!" said Barrett.

They clinked their glasses of bubbly.

After dinner, Rachel went upstairs to finish her homework. With her daughter in another part of the house, Natalie could shed her maternal role. She shared her current emotional state. "Twenty-five years of holy matrimony over in just a few months. What now?" Natalie asked.

Barrett raised her glass again.

"Freedom from that creep, that's what!" said Barrett.

The three toasted.

"Speaking of that creep, I have some juicy Jim gossip. But I'll only share if you want to hear it," said Jen.

"I don't know if I'm ready to hear anything about him," Natalie said.

"Well I'm sure as hell ready, so spit it out, honey!" Barrett said.

Jen described how one of her friends saw Jim and Claudia at the marina last weekend. From a distance, she witnessed the two standing on the deck of Jim's boat. Claudia's arms were crossed, and she was turned away from him. When Jim reached to put his arm on her shoulder, she abruptly left the boat.

"Do you know what they were arguing about?" Barrett asked Jen.

"How should I know? Besides, I've never even met the home wrecker. What I can say for sure is that her boyfriend's the world's biggest jackass," said Jen.

Barrett raised her glass once again. "The jackass is gone!" she said.

Natalie took a moment to thank Barrett and Jen for the love and support they extended her during one of the most stressful times of her life. She also expressed relief and gratitude for Kathleen and Patrick, who provided the expertise and advice she needed to make decisions that safeguarded her long-term well-being.

Now that the mediations were behind her, Natalie couldn't have imagined a better outcome, and she knew the success she experienced was largely a result of the team approach comprising foremost legal, financial, and mental health experts.

In the end, she and Jim dissolved their marriage more amicably than was otherwise possible and made their children a top priority. And last but certainly not least, her team had ensured she would not live her post-divorce years as a bag lady.

Natalie, Barrett, and Jen toasted and popped open another bottle of champagne, which signaled the party had just begun.

JIM SIGNS THE MOU AND BEGINS A NEW LIFE

Jim met Al at his office. During their meeting, his lawyer reviewed the MOU with him and explained the minor revision he and Kathleen had made. Al suggested that Jim would be better served using a QDRO rather than a PV calculation. He said he would ask Kathleen to draft the necessary document. Jim had no objections with the latest draft. He signed the document, the meeting ended, and he headed to Claudia's house. Jim was elated that because he had signed the MOU, it signaled he could stop adding funds to the joint checking account. The two planned to celebrate finally reaching this milestone.

Jim made reservations at Café con Leche—the restaurant where they first had lunch together after their business trip. He arrived at Claudia's house, they shared a light kiss, and he plopped down on the couch—*finally the marriage was over!* As always, she poured him a glass of his favorite rum.

"Aren't you going to take a seat?" Jim asked as he looked down at the vacant spot next to him on the couch.

"I've been sitting at a desk all day. If it's okay, I'll stand for now," Claudia said.

Between sips, he told her how the MOU meeting with Al went. He expressed his relief the divorce was nearly complete and how he looked forward to spending time with Claudia as a single man. He glanced at his watch.

"I think we should head out. Ready to celebrate?" Jim asked.

"Before we go, I want to talk to you about something," Claudia said.

"Of course. What is it?" Jim asked. He took one more swill and finished off his drink.

"Remember the argument we had on the boat last weekend?" asked Claudia.

Jim nodded his head yes.

"Well, you know we haven't talked about it since. If you remember, I expressed a couple of major concerns. You didn't give me any feedback at the time. Meanwhile, I've been waiting," said Claudia.

Jim remembered Claudia's concerns: his lack of emotion when it came to making decisions about Natalie and the kids, his refusal to see Claudia's viewpoint and accusing her of being confrontational, and his dismissive attitude when it came to her opinions he disagreed with.

"I thought you brought those things up in the heat of the moment. Afterwards, things seemed to go back to normal, so I assumed you'd let the whole thing go," Jim said.

"We've been through this before, Jim. You make assumptions about how I feel without bothering to ask. I think we'd both agree I was pretty upset on the boat. It's not as if we argue like that every day. Did you *really think* you could sweep my frustrations under the rug?" Claudia asked.

"No, no, honey. I'm really sorry. Can you forgive me? I've been so preoccupied lately. With the mediation so close to ending, I was worried Natalie would throw in some last-minute demand and ruin the whole process. Look, why don't we table this conversation for after dinner?—I'm starving. I promise we can talk about it later," Jim said.

"You mean table it *again?* Just so you can hope I'll forget about *my needs?* I'm tired of working around *your* timeline: your divorce, your kids, your work travel, your *everything!* What about me? When were you planning to start working around *my life?* No, Jim. No waiting. You're going to hear me out," Claudia said.

She expressed how, for nearly a year, she'd patiently listened to him complain about his wife. As time progressed, she grew upset that he never came clean to Natalie about his previous affair and he didn't think he needed to. She began disagreeing with his objections regarding expenses related to college for the kids and spousal support.

In her eyes, his actions didn't show genuine concern for Natalie or their children. And lately Claudia found his history of infidelity and indifference to his wife's and children's needs disconcerting.

"I hear you. But to be frank, nothing you've shared has anything to do with you or you and me. So what is this *really* about?" asked Jim.

"This is *really* about what I just told you—are you *listening to me?* For all the anger you have toward Natalie, she couldn't have been that bad. After all, you stuck it out for twenty-five years and raised three kids you're proud of—not exactly the sign of an evil wife out to get you. And then there's the cheating. How can I be sure you're not going to do the same thing to me as you did to her?" Claudia asked.

"Sweetie," he said as got up from the couch and stood next to her, "you've been a saint. I know it's been tough on you. But I promise everything's going to be different from now on. And you're *nothing* like Natalie, so you can't compare what we have with what I had with her," said Jim.

"I may be *nothing like Natalie,* but you're the same Jim, aren't you?" Claudia asked.

Her words were an indictment. Jim felt both judged and that his relationship with Claudia was unraveling. Part of him wanted to become an attack dog and tell Claudia to stay out his business and get a grip. But he also knew that doing so could end their romance.

"I thought you wanted to build a life together," said Jim.

"You had plenty of time to follow up with our last argument, not to mention other discussions we've had in the past. The reality is you don't know how to deal with conflict, so you just hope problems will go away. And then I'm left having no idea what you're thinking. Jim, this is fundamentally a trust issue. And without trust, how do I know your past won't repeat itself?" Claudia asked.

She had been his confidante throughout his divorce. During the mediation process, when negotiations had come to a standstill, he thought about life with Claudia, which motivated him to end his marriage as quickly as possible. Now, Claudia was pulling away, and he was terrified of being alone.

"I love you. We can work this out. It doesn't have to be this way," he said.

"Jim, I've been thinking about this for a while. . . . Maybe you're not the only one who can hide feelings. I'm sorry, but this just isn't going to work," said Claudia.

Tears welled in Jim's eyes. During their time together, she had seen Jim express a range of emotions: from the bliss of a budding romance to the rage of a husband who felt his wife was taking all his money. But she had never seen him cry.

Claudia felt terrible, but she stood strong. She dreaded being hurt again in a relationship and wanted to end things as quickly as possible. "No room for indecision," she reminded herself. "Jim, it's over," Claudia said.

As much as he wanted to deny the breakup unfolding before his eyes, he couldn't see any affection toward him in her face. "Listen, we're both under a lot of stress. How about we have a cooling-off period and circle back when we're both in the right mindset?" Jim asked.

Claudia stood silent. She felt her pulse in the back of her ear. She then walked to the front door and held it open.

"Are you asking me to go?" Jim hoped he had misinterpreted her actions.

Claudia stared at the ground without saying a word.

Jim reached for his jacket and grabbed his car keys off the coffee table. "Good bye, Claudia," Jim said as he headed toward the front door.

Claudia stood frozen—her arms crossed and her gaze cast downward.

He left her house for what he feared was the last time. Jim reached his car, slumped in the driver's seat, and tears trickled down his face. The emotion was foreign, which left him completely unprepared. Unlike Natalie, who, throughout the divorce always had a supply of tissues nearby to absorb a flood of sadness that would strike without notice, Jim had been immune to such random bursts of melancholy. He wiped his face on the sleeve of his jacket.

From Claudia's house, he decided to drive to the marina and spend the night on his boat—a place that had always provided him safe harbor during difficult times.

On Saturday morning, he woke up and prepared the vessel for a quick weekend trip.

For months, he had dreamt of this day. In his reverie, he had fantasized having Claudia's hot body next to him as he navigated the high seas on his inaugural day of freedom. Instead, reality meant he would set sail alone.

As Jim headed into the bay, he thought back to his sailing days in his early twenties. Back then, he spent countless hours at sea and in sailor bars with his buddies. His friends admired his ability to court women, and when they went ashore, he went by an alias, Mac Brown. This gave him the freedom to go incognito and lose his inhibitions when he focused on a new conquest. With his marriage behind him, part of him wasn't sure if Mac Brown existed anymore, and he was curious to find out. He knew one thing for certain—after his divorce, life would never be the same, and he didn't want to live it alone. "There are always more fish in the sea," he said to himself.

APPENDIX

TWO ESSENTIAL DIVORCE QUESTIONS

1. How much financial and emotional currency am I willing to spend?

2. Will the settlement allow me—both with my children and independent of them—to be financially secure now and in the future?

DIVORCE PLANNING CHECKLIST

◘ **Family Information:** date of birth, Social Security numbers, marital status, and addresses of family members (including children).

◘ **Professional Information:** Attorney, CPA, stockbroker, and insurance agent contact information including names, physical and electronic addresses, and phone numbers.

◘ **Benefit Plans:** Group and personally owned insurance, including life, health, disability, liability, and long-term care insurance. Also, identify beneficiaries of each.

◘ **Retirement Plans:** 401(k)s, IRAs, pensions, and deferred compensation plans, along with their most recent statements. Also, identify beneficiaries of each.

◘ **Non-qualified Investments:** Individual, joint, or trust-held investments with most recent statements including stock options.

◘ **Bank Accounts:** Statements of all accounts and the safe deposit box location, if applicable.

◘ **Income Tax Returns:** Last year's complete federal and state returns, including copies of W-2s.

◘ **List of All Liabilities:** Present debt, payments, and interest rates charged.

◘ **List of All Annual Expenditures:** Food, clothing, utilities, medical, education, loan repayment, insurance premiums, entertainment, vacation, charity, retirement plans (such as pension, Keogh, and IRA), auto payments (such as repairs and operation), savings and investments, support of others, and any other miscellaneous costs.

- **List of All Assets:** Include how they are owned (for example joint, individually, or in a trust), current market value, when they were acquired, cost basis, and income generated.

- **Marital Residence:** HUD-1 settlement documents from time of purchase and any refinance documents, current mortgage statement, and a copy of the homeowners' policy. Identify source of down payment. If a second home is owned, provide the same information.

- **Investment Real Estate:** Acquisition data, ownership interest, and income and expense statement.

- **Business Interest:** Ownership structure, assets and liabilities, agreements, profit and loss statement (P & L) for past two years, and current balance sheet.

- **Latest Pay Stubs:** Gross pay and deductions for taxes and benefits.

- **Estate Documents:** Current wills, trusts, and any other relevant documents.

- **Dates:** Marriage and separation.

PATRICK'S THREE-PART SUMMARY REPORT
Property Statement

NON-RETIREMENT ASSETS		TOTAL AMOUNT
REAL ESTATE EQUITY		
Residence		$675,000
Total Value	$950,000	
1st Mortgage	$275,000	
Equity	$675,000	
Rental Property		$200,000
Total Value	$550,000	
1st Mortgage	$350,000	
Marital Equity	$200,000	
TOTAL REAL ESTATE EQUITY		**$875,000**
CASH & INVESTMENTS		
Joint WFB		$25,000
Jim's WFB		$10,000
Jim's E*Trade		$225,000
SSI Vested Stock Options		$224,000
Natalie's Schwab		$125,000
Loss Carryforward		$100,000
TOTAL CASH & INVESTMENTS		**$709,000**
PERSONAL EFFECTS		
Natalie's Personal Property		$0
Jim's Personal Property		$0
Sailboat		$30,000
BMW		$35,000
Subaru		$15,000
TOTAL PERSONAL EFFECTS		**$80,000**
TOTAL NON-RETIREMENT ASSETS		**$1,664,000**

RETIREMENT ASSETS	TOTAL AMOUNT
IRA/401(k)s	
IRA	$150,000
401(k)	$375,000
403(b)	$85,000
Non-qualified Deferred Compensation	$150,000
Pension PV	$133,500
Non-marital PV Pension	$80,100
Jim's Roth IRA	$15,000
Natalie's Roth IRA	$25,000
TOTAL RETIREMENT ASSETS	**$1,013,600**

TOTAL ASSETS	**$2,677,600**

DEBTS	
Credit Card	($25,000)
BMW	($15,000)
TOTAL DEBTS	**($40,000)**

TOTAL DEBTS	**($40,000)**

TOTAL ASSETS	**$2,677,600**
TOTAL DEBTS	**($40,000)**
TOTAL PROPERTY	**$2,637,600**

Division of Marital Property

	JIM'S AMOUNT	NATALIE'S AMOUNT	TOTAL AMOUNT
NON-RETIREMENT ASSETS			
REAL ESTATE EQUITY			
Residence	$0	$350,000	$350,000
Total Value $950,000			
1st Mortgage $275,000			
Sep. Property $325,000			
Marital Equity $350,000			
Rental Property	$200,000	$0	$200,000
Total Value $550,000			
1st Mortgage $350,000			
Marital Equity $200,000			
TOTAL REAL EST. EQUITY	**$200,000**	**$350,000**	**$550,000**
CASH & INVESTMENTS			
Joint WFB	$0	$25,000	$25,000
Jim's WFB	$10,000	$0	$10,000
Jim's E*Trade	$74,250	$150,750	$225,000
SSI Vested Stock Options	$224,000	$0	$224,000
Natalie's Schwab	$0	$0	$0
Loss Carryforward	$50,000	$50,000	$100,000
TOTAL CASH & INVESTMENTS	**$358,250**	**$225,750**	**$584,000**
PERSONAL EFFECTS			
Natalie's Personal Property	$0	$0	$0
Jim's Personal Property	$0	$0	$0
Sailboat	$30,000	$0	$30,000
BMW	$35,000	$0	$35,000
Subaru	$0	$15,000	$15,000
TOTAL PERSONAL EFFECTS	**$65,000**	**$15,000**	**$80,000**

	JIM'S AMOUNT	NATALIE'S AMOUNT	TOTAL AMOUNT
TOTAL NON-RETIREMENT ASSETS	**$623,250**	**$590,750**	**$1,214,000**

RETIREMENT ASSETS			
IRA/401(k)s			
IRA	$30,000	$120,000	$150,000
401(k)	$187,500	$187,500	$375,000
403(b)	$0	$85,000	$85,000
Non-qualified Deferred Comp.	$150,000	$0	$150,000
Pension PV	$66,750	$66,750	$133,500
Non-marital PV Pension	$0	$0	$0
Jim's Roth IRA	$15,000	$0	$15,000
Natalie's Roth IRA	$0	$25,000	$25,000
TOTAL RETIREMENT ASSETS	**$449,250**	**$484,250**	**$933,500**

TOTAL ASSETS	**$1,072,500**	**$1,075,000**	**$2,147,500**

DEBTS			
Credit Card	($12,500)	($12,500)	($25,000)
BMW	($15,000)	$0	($15,000)
TOTAL DEBTS	**($27,500)**	**($12,500)**	**($40,000)**

TOTAL DEBTS	**($27,500)**	**($12,500)**	**($40,000)**

TOTAL ASSETS	**$1,072,500**	**$1,075,000**	**$2,147,500**
TOTAL DEBTS	**($27,500)**	**($12,500)**	**($40,000)**
TOTAL PROPERTY	**$1,045,000**	**$1,062,500**	**$2,107,500**

Total Property Division (Marital plus Separate)

	JIM'S AMOUNT	NATALIE'S AMOUNT	TOTAL AMOUNT
NON-RETIREMENT ASSETS			
REAL ESTATE EQUITY			
Residence	$0	$675,000	$675,000
Total Value $950,000			
1st Mortgage $275,000			
Sep. Property $325,000			
Marital Equity $350,000			
Rental Property	$200,000	$0	$200,000
Total Value $550,000			
1st Mortgage $350,000			
Marital Equity $200,000			
TOTAL REAL EST. EQUITY	**$200,000**	**$675,000**	**$875,000**
CASH & INVESTMENTS			
Joint WFB	$0	$25,000	$25,000
Jim's WFB	$10,000	$0	$10,000
Jim's E*Trade	$74,250	$150,750	$225,000
SSI Vested Stock Options	$224,000	$0	$224,000
Natalie's Schwab	$0	$125,000	$125,000
Loss Carryforward	$50,000	$50,000	$100,000
TOTAL CASH & INVESTMENTS	**$358,250**	**$350,750**	**$709,000**
PERSONAL EFFECTS			
Natalie's Personal Property	$0	$0	$0
Jim's Personal Property	$0	$0	$0
Sailboat	$30,000	$0	$30,000
BMW	$35,000	$0	$35,000
Subaru	$0	$15,000	$15,000
TOTAL PERSONAL EFFECTS	**$65,000**	**$15,000**	**$80,000**

	JIM'S AMOUNT	NATALIE'S AMOUNT	TOTAL AMOUNT
TOTAL NON-RETIREMENT ASSETS	$623,250	$1,040,750	$1,664,000

RETIREMENT ASSETS			
IRA/401(k)s			
IRA	$30,000	$120,000	$150,000
401(k)	$187,500	$187,500	$375,000
403(b)	$0	$85,000	$85,000
Non-qualified Deferred Comp.	$150,000	$0	$150,000
Pension PV	$66,750	$66,750	$133,500
Non-marital PV Pension	$80,100	$0	$80,100
Jim's Roth IRA	$15,000	$0	$15,000
Natalie's Roth IRA	$0	$25,000	$25,000
TOTAL RETIREMENT ASSETS	$529,350	$484,250	$1,013,600

TOTAL ASSETS	$1,152,600	$1,525,000	$2,677,600

DEBTS			
Credit Card	($12,500)	($12,500)	($25,000)
BMW	($15,000)	$0	($15,000)
TOTAL DEBTS	($27,500)	($12,500)	($40,000)

TOTAL DEBTS	($27,500)	($12,500)	($40,000)

TOTAL ASSETS	$1,152,600	$1,525,000	$2,677,600
TOTAL DEBTS	($27,500)	($12,500)	($40,000)
TOTAL PROPERTY	$1,125,100	$1,512,500	$2,637,600

INCOME AND EXPENSE WORKSHEET

Monthly Income & Expenses of _____   **Date** _____

Chancery No. _____

Employed By	
City & State	
Occupation	
Pay Period	
Next Payday	
Salary/Wage	
# Exemptions	

Children in Household

Name	Age

Avg Gross Pay per Month

LESS: Federal Taxes	
State Taxes	
FICA	
Health Insurance	
Life Insurance	
Required Retirement	
Avg Monthly Net Pay	
Other Income	
MONTHLY NET INCOME	

Household

Mortgage (PITI) or Rent	
Real Estate Prop. Taxes	
Homeowner's Insurance	
Repairs/Maintenance	
Furniture/Furnishings	
Personal Property Tax	

Utilities

Electricity	
Gas/Heating Oil	
Water/Sewer	
Telephone	
Trash	
Cable TV	

Food

Groceries	
Lunches	

Automobile

Payment/Depreciation	
Gasoline	
Repair/Tags/Inspect, Etc.	
Auto Insurance	
Parking/Other Transport.	

Childcare Expenses

Childcare	
School Tuition	
Lunch Money	
School Supplies	
Lessons/Sports	
New Clothing	

Clothing

New (Excluding Children)	
Cleaning/Laundry	
Uniforms	

Health Expenses

Doctor	
Dentist	
Therapist	
Eyeglasses	
Hospital	
Medicines	
Other	

Dues

Professional Associations	
Social Associations	
Homeowner's Association	

Miscellaneous

Gifts (Birthday, Christmas)	
Church/Charity	
Entertainment	
Vacations	
Hobbies	
Personal Grooming	
Newpapers/Magazines	
Disability Insurance	
Life Insurance	
Legal Expenses	
Other	

Other

_____	
_____	
_____	

Fixed Debts with Payments

	Balance	Monthly Payment
_____		
_____		
_____		

Charge Acct Debt

_____		
_____		
_____		
_____		
_____		

Totals per Month

Subtotal Expenses	
Subtotal Debt Payments	
TOTAL EXPENSES	
TOTAL NET INCOME	
BALANCE (+)	
BALANCE (-)	

Liquid Assets on Hand

Cash/Checking/Savings	
Other Liquid Assets	
TOTAL LIQUID ASSETS	

ABOUT THE AUTHOR

Stan Corey is a Certified Financial Planner (CFP), Chartered Financial Consultant (ChFC), and Certified Private Wealth Advisor (CPWA). His career in financial services spans over thirty-five years. Stan was born in New York City and grew up in Stony Brook on Long Island. After graduating from American International College in Springfield, Massachusetts, in 1971, he served in the US Navy. Since childhood, Stan has been an avid sailor, and navigating the seas has been his lifelong passion. He has sailed most of the East Coast, as well as Bermuda. For over twenty years, he competed in numerous sailing club and international regattas as skipper, helmsman, and tactician on a variety of boats from fifteen feet to sixty feet.

Stan is a sought-after expert who regularly provides financial commentary at national conferences, in print and online publications, and on TV. He has appeared in *USA Today, Working Women* magazine, *MONEY, Good Housekeeping,* and *Northern Virginia* magazine. Stan has been a featured speaker at the Women's Center in Virginia on the financial aspects of divorce. For twenty years, he published the *News and Views,* a quarterly newsletter covering financial topics; in the *Rappahannock Record,* he penned a weekly column, "Stan's Financial Corner"; and he co-wrote and taught the Economic Issues in Divorce curriculum, which is a required course for mediator certification at Northern Virginia Mediation Service (NVMS). Stan works closely with foremost family law firms throughout the Mid-Atlantic providing financial expertise, and he regularly serves as an expert witness and financial coach in divorce cases.

Stan currently lives in Great Falls, Virginia, with his wife, Jayme. When they're not spending time with their adult children and grandchildren, the couple enjoys traveling and golfing. On occasion, Stan still takes to the seas and visits some of his old haunts in the Chesapeake Bay.

The Divorce Dance
Continues

Order Books and Have Stan Speak at Your Next Event

Now that you've read *The Divorce Dance*, visit TheDivorceDance.com to find additional resources to support you on your journey.

On the website, you can order copies of *The Divorce Dance* for friends and family. Stan's book is also available at your favorite online booksellers.

Lastly, to benefit from Stan's over thirty-five years of financial expertise, schedule him to speak at your next event. Stan engages and educates audiences across the country. Go to "Speaking/Contact" at TheDivorceDance.com.

You can always get in touch with Stan:

- ◘ **Twitter:** Twitter.com/TheDivorceDance

- ◘ **Web:** TheDivorceDance.com

- ◘ **Email:** TheDivorceDance@gmail.com

INDEX

S

W

CPSIA information can be obtained
at www.ICGtesting.com
Printed in the USA
BVHW080811051118
532194BV00002B/59/P